..., q'usure, avarice, larcin, iuremets estranges, voire tels ... y seroient attrapez and trompez :car il n'y a que faussete ...s souvent.

Jean Moquet,
Voyages en Afrique, Asie, Indes Orientales & Occidentales, Paris, 1617.

...o be found amongst them but lying, treachery, avarice, usury, ..., strife, envy, jealousy, pride, arrogance, murder, homicide, ...runkenness, voluptuousness, sodomy, lechery, fornication, ...lasphemy, cursing, swearing, breaking of oaths and all other ... measure. Merely to witness this makes one's hair stand on end, ...annot cease to wonder at God's patience with such wicked men.

Jean Mocquet, as "translated" by J.G. Schochen, 1688, and quoted by Justus Strandes, 1899.

...BOUT THE AUTHOR

...orn at St. Louis Missouri, U.S.A. in 1928, has a B.A. degree from Bowdoin College ...nd the M.A. and Ph.D. from Columbia University. Has been Professor (1965-76) at ...he University of Florida, Gainesville and Netherland, where he edits with ltinerario, Robert Ross? His previous publications include The Fatel History of Portuguese Ceylon (1971) and Foundation of the Portuguese Empire 1415-1580 (written with the late Bailey W. Diffie). He is married and has three children.

THE BLACK LEG

Ce n'est entr'eu
que les plus fins
mensonge le pl

Nothing is
hate, anger
gluttony,
adultery,
sins in full
and one c

A

XCHR Studies Series No. 3

THE BLACK LEGEND OF PORTUGUESE INDIA

Diogo do Couto, His Contemporaries and the *Soldádo Pratico*

A Contribution to the Study of Political Corruption in the Empires of Early Modern Europe

GEORGE DAVISON WINIUS

CONCEPT PUBLISHING COMPANY PVT. LTD.
NEW DELHI-110059

ISBN: 978-81-7022-075-6

First Published 1985

Published and Printed by

Since 1974 **Concept Publishing Company Pvt. Ltd.**
A/15-16, Commercial Block, Mohan Garden,
New Delhi-110059 (India)
T: 91-11-41101460
E: publishing@conceptpub.com, *W*: www.conceptpub.com

For Lewis and Kate Hanke,
who are well acquainted with Black Legends.

Editor's Preface

Unwittingly the XCHR Studies Series has been proceeding chronologically. This third monograph, Prof. G.D. Winius' *The Black Legend of Portuguese India* : *Diogo do Couto,* His Contemporaries and the *Soldado Prático* — A Contribution to the Study of Political Corruption in the Empires of Early Modern Europe — picks up the threads where our earlier contributors, Prof. C. R. Boxer and Prof. M. N. Pearson had left them.

The author of the *Fatal History of Portuguese Ceylon* (1971) does not seem to have lost his predilection for fatal themes, but he also retains all his charm of presentation. The present analysis has more of Juvenalian touch of quasi-contemporary Jesuit author of *Arte de Furtar* than Diogo do Couto's much too bitter sarcasm. Unfortunately Padre Manuel da Costa remains 'anonymous' to Prof. Winius and *Arte de Furtar* failed to draw more than just a passing reference. However, this and other limitations that one may notice does not seriously reduce the value of the contribution the co-author of the *Foundations of the Portuguese Empire* (1977) makes to the understanding of its decline.

TEOTONIO R. DE SOUZA
Director

Xavier Centre of Historical Research
Alto de Porvorim, Goa

12 September 1984

Preface

Much has been written in recent years about the "Black Legend" of Spanish cruelty to the Indians during their conquest of Middle and South America. It is a legend grounded in a certain amount of truth and in the exaggerations of Frey Bartolomé de las Casas, especially in his polemic tract, the *Brevíssima Relación*, which was seized upon with glee by Spain's English, Dutch and French enemies. Now, four centuries later, everybody "knows" how cruel the Spaniards were, without even knowing how and why he holds the opinion.

The Portuguese empire is considerably less familiar to the gerneral public than the Spanish one, but the Portuguese have their own "Black Legend,"too, which is in some ways a counterpart to that of the Spanish—namely of political corruption. It is based almost solely on another single tract, the *Diálogo do Soldado Prático*, by Diogo do Couto, the official chronicler of Portuguese Asia, who lived between 1542 and 1616 and is thus roughly contemporary with Las Casas (1484-1566). Like the *Brevíssima Relación*, the Soldado Prático is far better known than the corpus of either writer's more extensive writings, and in fact has eclipsed them until recently. And in both cases, the allegations contained in the two works have become so widespread that relatively few persons familiar with them can say whence they came.

On the other hand, there are dissimilarities, too. The *Brevíssima Relación*, first published in 1552, appeared during its author's lifetime and immediately preceding an era of European religious wars and colonial rivalry, wherein its revelations became useful propaganda material when translated into (principally) Dutch and English. The *Soldado Prático*, though also written at a time when Spain's and Portugal's enemies (the two countries were then under the same crown) might have been happy to use it as similar anti-Iberian publicity, did not find its way into print until 1790, 174 years after Couto's death, and far beyond the time when the Northern European powers could draw any political advantage from embarrassing the now independent and rather insignificant Portuguese empire. Instead, the *Soldado Prático* took a different route to achieve the status of a black legend : it was disseminated through the moralistic writings of the 19th and early 20th century historians, who were easily convinced by Couto's interpretations, but usually neglected to mention his authorship. And in even greater degree, the *Soldado Prático* was taken over by the literati as a piece of Portugal's literary heritage, where its message was broadcast without regard to its historical setting.

In retrospect, it is easy enough to see why this occurred. In the 19th century and up to World War I, study of the classics and classical history was much more prominent than it is now, and everyone was familiar with Gibbon's *Decline and Fall of the Roman Empire,* which attributed Rome's eclipse to moral decline. Although Gibbon and Couto shared little else in common, Couto predicted the demise of his own Portuguese empire on the same grounds, even though the old chronicler's cause-and-effect was mostly (though not wholly) based on sin-plus-divine punishment, rather than the more mundane working of political rot and a weakening will to command, as in Gibbon. Since Gibbon's interpretation was long considered as the last word on imperial decline, readers of Couto must have accepted his account as equally true, and without much further reflection.

Historians of empire writing since World War II have not been so willing to accept the connection between corruption and decline so easily—and in fact almost unanimously have uncoupled the two concepts. To them, the fact that such a small nation could have created such an empire as it did despite all the odds seems the remarkable thing and the decline more like the probabilities reasserting themselves.

In still more recent years, an even greater shifting in viewpoint has occurred : historians have now tried to reason away the corruption entirely —that is, whitewash Couto's "Black Legend" itself—essentially by showing just how normal and almost honest dishonesty was in the past. (At the same time.

I notice that few can resist retailing the delicious stories of thievery they come across in documents about Portuguese India).

In my own previous writings, I admit that I have at various times reflected all the viewpoints just described, and I discovered that in discussing the problem of Portuguese Asian corruption with my colleagues in the field, nobody was really much more certain where he stood than I. So I undertook to write this little book to examine the legend and the whole problem of the Portuguese Asian *decadência* itself, a term for the phenomenon applied by Couto's 18th century editor, António Caetano do Amaral. Needless to say, the quest is not simple, and this work's real value might just well lie in the complexity and historical uniqueness that any *ad hoc* study uncovers when it undertakes to attach moral judgement to activities in the past. But I do think I can establish that the corruption was a real problem wherein the incentive to steal from the king in India was not counterbalanced by a desire to serve him, and that the Goan bureaucracy was stronger than he was.

Regarding methodology. After first discussing what is known about Couto's life, I have given over two chapters to describtion of what Couto reveals in his *Soldado Prático*. Then I have compared this to what some contemporary visitors have said about the same problems. I did not mean by this to test Couto's personal veracity—nobody doubts this—but rather to ascertain whether the literary form of the work, written as a dialogue and full of classical allusion, much influenced its factual content. In short, that one was dealing with the essentially historical.

It might be advisable to say at this juncture that, as an historian, I am not concerned with the literary aspects of the *Soldado Prático*, even though, thanks to the studies of Dr António Coimbra Martins, I think I can avoid the worst pitfalls that might otherwise entrap an unwary user of Couto's book. Moreover, he points out that there are various manuscript copies of the *Soldado Prático* in existence, which vary slightly from one another, and then there are two separate dialogues which resemble one another only in that they are both in dialogue form and treat abuses and malfunctions of the state. Of these, I have drawn most of my quotations from the second, more famous version, if only because it was this one which created the "legend" and that is what this book is all about.

Having completed this examination of the *Soldado Prático*, I then devoted my attention to an almost unknown contemporary Portuguese writer, Francisco Rodrigues de Silveira, who memorialized the crown with his tract, *Reformação da Milícia e Governo do Estado da India Oriental*, only excerpts of which have ever been printed. It was then that I received my biggest surprise : it struck me repeatedly that Couto not only had not gone too far, but that he had not gone far enough ! He had neglected his own best arguments when he failed to mention, as Rodrigues de Silveira does, that royal officials regularly stole moneys from the military and thereby weakened Portuguese India's ability to defend itself. All in all, Rodrigues de Silveira turns out to parallel and substantiate Couto even more fully than do the foreign visitors because he, like Couto and unlike them, was a Portuguese with a patriotic interest in improving the system.

At this point I was tempted to adduce other evidence, that of the contemporary correspondence between viceroys and crown, but I decided that, while suggestive, it was also fragmentary and rather hard to weave into a narrative. The main problem is that it is based on unsubstantiated whispers to Lisbon of wrongdoings in India, which were then duly reported back to the viceroy, with either a request to investigate or an order to arrest someone. Sometimes, if his reply has been preserved, the viceroy will admit that an allegation is substantially true. But on the whole, the evidence makes better material for an appendix than for the main corpus of a monograph, and that is where I finally placed it.

Having established the contemporaries' case for governmental corruption in Portuguese India, I then turned to what present-day writers say about historical corruption in general and about imperial corruption in particular. This is necessary, if only because it illustrates the hazards involving judgment of the past by our own standards and suggests how abuses in other imperial systems did not really resemble in kind that of Portuguese Asia. Finally, I discuss two aspects of the problem brought to attention by two of my colleages at Leiden University, namely that all of the witnesses were either wholly or partly extrinsic to the system—in a word, outsiders—and that the system itself may be more Indian in nature than European. These observation only serve to emphasize the fact that the corruption is of a special nature, both in regard to the class structure and the location. In short, I found that the *Soldado Prático* may have created the "Black Legend" virtually by itself, but that in order to evaluate the historical phenomena which underlay that work, one must search considerably farther afield. In doing so, I tried to confine myself to the years around which Couto lived in Goa, but as will be seen, I could not resist dipping a bit further into the Portuguese Indian past, if only to make one important point.

Incidentally, I decided to include short chapters on what remedial measures Couto and Silveira had proposed, immediately following ones on their allegations of corruption. Even though none of their suggestions were ever taken seriously, I decided that they formed an integral part of the two men's analyses which, besides being interesting, go far toward helping us understand the writers' viewpoints.

Thanks are due to my colleagues, Teotonio de Souza, Michael N. Pearson, Robert Ross, Leo Blussé for helping me clarify my thinking at various junctures, as well as to Jan Heesterman, who was a continual source of inspiration and ideas. As thanks in no less measure to Astrid van Ekelenburg and Jennegien Nieuwstraten of the Faculty of Letters of Leiden University for their endless patience when confronted with my squiggly handwriting and numerous textual "improvements".

And finally, I should like to express my appreciation to WOTRO (the Netherlands Foundation for the Advancement of Tropical Research), The Hague, for the grant which enabled me to visit Goa and to perceive for myself that the context in which the Portuguese operated was always an Indian one.

May, 1984 GEORGE D. WINIUS

Contents

Introduction

Goa had been a Portuguese city for nearly 44 years when Diogo do Couto arrived there in 1559, and its function as the capital of a far-flung thalassic empire was already well established. But unless one knows a great deal of early modern history—and even Portuguese history—no image which that word "empire" conjures up, will quite suggest its nature. It was not, for example, at all comparable with the contemporary Spanish empire in the New World. It possessed only bits of land, of which Goa, to ether with Bardes and Salcete and perhaps Bassein, was then the largest, but, as the names of the principal ones suggest, they were important for their strategic nature, not their size—Moçambique, Sofala, Hormuz, Diu, Colombo, Malacca, Macau, Ternate, and, in a certain sense, Nagasaki. In addition, there were about a score of less strategic fortresses, mostly along the western coast of India—such as Bassein, Daman, Chaul, Honawar and Barcelor, and a protectorate over Cochin, with an important fort there. Of these holdings, some had been conquered, some acquired by treaty and some acquired through testaments of rulers who had been converted by Christian missionaries. It was the oceans, not the land that this necklace of strong places around the Asian littoral was designed to control, though even the word "control" may be as unsuggestive as the word "empire" just was.

For the seas of Asia were too vast and too populous for any power to master, much less a small power like Portugal in the 16th century, when ships, sails and guns were crude, even in comparison to the 18th. But Portugal's presence there did allow it to make a living of sorts by exploiting its peculiar opportunities. For however frail its vessels and equipment might have been, no Asian power possessed anything like them, nor the system of strategic bastions.

When People think of Portuguese Asia in the early modern period, they usually assume that the spice trade supported the whole of it. Actually, this was mostly an affair of the king, while the expenses of maintaining the Goan viceroyalty, the *Estado do India Oriental*, were derived locally, in essence from tribute moneys levied on native vessels sailing up and down the west coast of India between Portuguese fortresses and, secondarily, on vessels passing through the Straits of Malacca.[1] This was augmented somewhat by rents and levies derived from Portuguese—held lands principally in and around Goa and in Ceylon, by the proceeds from concession voyages to Malacca, the Far East, the Moluccas and other places, and by the sale in India of horses imported from the Persian Gulf. In short, Portuguese Asia was intended to be self-supporting, while the king's private circuit, that of providing European silver and buying with it spices on contract for resale in Europe, was supposed to yield pure profit for him.

This might seem like an odd financial organization, but it was little different from that of the Spanish empire in America, whose internally-produced revenue was absorbed by its own administration(s), while the crown's profit lay in the royal one-fifth on silver mined in the New World and in its monopoly on trade between Seville and the Indies, wherein lay considerable customs levies on all imports and exports.[2] I think such arrangements can best be understood in terms of the much smaller bureaucracies available to the early modern monarchies; one always sees the tendency to simplify and to devote specific revenues to specific purposes.

In their organization, both empires bore a decided resemblance, one which was hardly coincidental. The two mother countries shared the same peninsula, the same traditions and many of the same home institutions. On top of this, Portugal's fifteenth century African experience had resulted in the creation of the *Casa de Guiné e Mina* (later called the *Casa da Índia* after this name was added and the others dropped), a combined customs, warehousing and outfitting organization for colonial voyages which the Spanish adopted and called the *Casa-de Contratación*. Then both nations seem to have looked to the medieval Mediterranean empires of the Italians, Venice, and particularly, Genoa, for other features of their administrations, most notably the office of viceroy. Moreover, both organizations settled on the three-year norm for all offices.

But there were great differences, too, some administrative and some caused by the logistics and scale of the two operations. I think these are worth considering because many more people have some acquaintance with Spanish America than with Portuguese Asia, and probably the moment someone points out the overall similarities in structure, the tendency is to assume that the two organizations were roughly comparable. This is true only to a limited extent, and I have the feeling that the sum of the differences is greater than that of the concordances.

First of all, the scale and the logistics, Spanish America was, in terms of nautical miles and sailing time, about four times as close to the Iberian Peninsula as Goa in Portuguese Asia. An average sailing time from Cádiz to Vera Cruz or the Isthmus of Panama was seven weeks; to Goa it was five or six months. The total area of lands under Spanish control in America was something like 5,000.000 square miles, while that of Portuguese Asia was around 600—roughly 8,000 times smaller. Something like three million indigenes lived in Spanish America, all of them administered by Peninsular Spaniards, against only a couple of hundred thousand in Portuguese Asia, including Southwest coastal Ceylon, and it must be considered that most of the native peoples in Portuguese Asia were only indirectly ruled by Europeans—the Portuguese used native headman instead, who effected justice according to native patterns and passed on revenues after retaining their cuts.[3] Probably all of the European born Portuguese, living in the whole *Estado da India* were no greater than the European population of Mexico City, which according to Antonio Vázquez de Espinosa, was around 15,000 in 1620[4]

Moreover, consider the fact that Portuguese Asia was surrounded by enemies, being never more than a few miles from potentially hostile powers on its land frontiers, while its fortresses were usually directly at water's edge. By contrast, Mexico City and Lima were far too for inland for even the most ambitious English, Dutch or French flotilla to attack. And of the major seaside fortresses protecting Spain-to-Spanish American communications, only Havana was ever captured—and that only during the seven years war, in 1762.[5]

In administrative terms, I think these contrasting circumstances far outweighed the similarities in approach and led to fundamentally divergent lifestyles. I will develop this theme in two latter chapters, but for the time being it is perhaps enough to say this : that the comparative safety of Spanish America allowed the Spanish crown to counterbalance fundamentally military character of the viceroy, captains—general and provincial governors (*corregidores*) with a predominantly civilian system of *audiencias.* These were administrative-judicial bodies, technically subordinate to the viceroy. They acted as viceregal councils in the capital cities, but sometimes existed alone as in Quito, Charcas and New Galicia. What set them apart from the Portuguese viceregal council, the Goan *Conselho do Estado* is that they had the privilege of corresponding directly with the crown, and this gave them a *de facto* checking power over the viceroy. Furthermore, the *oidores,* or judges, of the Spanish *audiencias* of the capital cities not only served as the viceregal administrative councils, but, unlike the Goan viceregal *conselho,* they also constituted the viceroyalty's highest court.[6] Their nominations came not from the viceroy, as in Goa, but from the metropolis. In Goa, on the other hand, the viceroy remained undisputed boss, at least for decisions which could not be referred to Lisbon. In a region where, as Couto remarked, it was most necessary to go about with weapons in hand, the *audiencia* never evolved and it was not later instituted by the Hapsburgs, as was another Spanish institution, the *residencia,* or judicial review of conduct.

Although the *Estado da Índia* was virtually independent in its sources of income, what bound it to the mother country was its dependent administrative structure and need for European manpower. The viceroy was the king's appointee and factotum, in theory anyway, and so were all the other officers of the state. Certainly, if one reads the correspondence between Lisbon and and Goa, one gets the impression that the crown was the control center and the Goan officers the chessmen (or perhaps more appropriately for India, the pachesi stones). Nobody who reads beyond the official correspondence, however, believes this to be so—and in fact a between-the-lines reading of the official correspondence itself reveals that, although at all times respectfully subordinate, the viceroy complied with orders in ways more apparent than real. And judging from the number of times a command had to be repeated—often throughout whole decades and longer—the kings had to inure themselves to that reality.

The constant need for European manpower in the *Estado da Índia* should have made it responsive to the king's control, but in fact the opposite seems to have been true. Nearly all offices were held, just as in the Spanish empire, on three-year terms. But Spain was a more populous country and the Spanish Indies were easier and safer to reach; in the Portuguese Asian empire, the few eligible and available people had to be recycled among the middling and lower administative and military posts.[7] While the king made the actual appointments for them, the viceroy made the nominations, which was tantamount to holding the real power. Nominees thus had to look to the viceroy and the bureaucracy surrounding him for their jobs; in the end, neither the supply of manpower from Portugal nor the formal power of appointment gave the king real influence over the activities of his distant officeholders; nor could he effectively punish them, for by the time he could identify a malefactor and order his arrest, it was more than three years later when the order arrived, and by then often only God and the (ex-) officeholder himself knew what had become of the rascal.

Nominations for all jobs were made on the basis of the *certidão*, or certificate. Every man carried the basic one with him on the outward voyage from Portugal and this really amounted to his birth certificate, passport and family tree all rolled into one document. Without a sufficient pedigree reflecting at least a minimum degree of gentility, no man arriving in India could expect to hold one of the attractive offices or probably a command post above what would be called today that of a non-commissioned or petty officer. Exactly what the *certidão* system's origins were, is far from certain. It is apparent, however, that those *fidalgos* without relatives or friends at court or already in India were at a disadvantage from the very beginning, as was Couto, who apparently sailed there out of loneliness and desperation. It is significant, I think, that he spent some years as a soldier (though at what level we do not know) before he returned home in 1569. Probably, in this case his credentials as a (lower ranking) nobleman did not do him any automatic good. But then it is fairly obvious thereafter that once he returned with some seniority and knew his way around, they did; as we will see, no amount of experience seems to have done much *per se* for another man in similar circumstances, Francisco Rodrigues de Silveira, who seems to have remained a soldier or not very much more than a scribe during all his service years. So probably, the division line between commoners and the lower sort of *fidalguia*, or nobility, was real enough, but not so marked that an unconnected *moço fidalgo, fidalgo cavaleiro*, or *fidalgo escudeiro*, a second or third son of some seedy Alentejan or Beiran gentleman, could simply wave his *certidão* under the noses of Goan officialdom and expect a sinecure.[8]

On the other hand, the *fidalgos de costado*, the older nobility, or the *fidalgos* of the king's household, sailed to India not as Couto did, but only upon royal appointment; kinsmen, bribes or connections could assure them of preferential treatment. Or, of course, they went when the viceroy took them along in his entourage—in which case they were also sure to be of his family or those of his retainers.

Once on the scene, however, everyone collected *certidoẽs*. for they amounted to a personnel file retained by the individual concerned rather than deposited (as would be the case today) in a central bureau. Each time any *soldado* or any officer or office-holder had served the crown in any capacity—whether on a single campaign or in a particular three-year charge, he obtained a *certidão* from his superiors duly registering the fact. Certificates had two functions, although, for that matter, so do all personnel files : to show the individual's level of experience and to record his years of service for an eventual pension or other reward.[9]

In the *soldado's* case, the careful keeping of his *certidões* was of vital importance. Because the monsoons limited sailing activity to a few months per year, soldierly services were normally required only during the summer season, that is, beginning in September and ending before Christmas. Upon the beating of drum—the traditional call to enlistment throughout the Christian world—soldiers would enlist, receive their yearly pay in a lump sum and have the fact of their enlistment certified. Then, after a campaign, normally spent protecting vessels co-operating in the revenue-producing convoy-and-fee system or in carrying out pre-emptive strikes against pirates, most notably the Kunjali pirates harbored by the Samorin of Calicut, the soldiers would have this certified, too. Seven or eight years of such service entitled the *soldado* to a pension, to a minor office or a special status, though rarely a feat of conspicuous bravery might turn the trick for him earlier.

Some *soldados*, incidentally, did not persist until they had gained a minor post or a pension, but instead dropped out of *state service; many left* Portuguese territory entirely and took up soldiering elsewhere in India, and some, apparently, blended into the Indian peasantry. But others married (hence their name, *casados*) and went into shopkeeping or the "country" or inter-Asian trading of various commodities, using Goa or another fortresss as a base. Some even operated from lands and ports not under Portuguese control. Since the crown had no competing interest in this interport commerce, many *casados* appeared to have prospered and some are known to have built considerable fortunes.

It is not known whether *fidalgos* of the humbler varieties entered personally into trading, probably military service provided a surer road to honor and fortune. Rising to command one of the summer galley fleets put one on the way to nomination to the captaincy of a fortress, a small one at first, but with luck, one might end up with a major one, though probably not Sofala, Malacca or Hormuz, since one of the richer or higher-ranking *fidalgos* usually got his hands on there through influence with court or king—or by paying more. Of course nothing prevented *fidalgos* of all levels from investing in trading enterprises—except perhaps that it was against the law for crown officers to do so.

The chief administrative and judicial positions in Goa were clearly out of a climber's reach. That of *vedor da fazenda* (comptroller of finances), the *feitor* of the port of Goa, the man in charge of the cargoes in—and outbound to Lisbon and from the concession voyages, and the justice officials, *ouvidor geral da India*, the *desembargador da coroa*, plus the other ouvidores, desembargadores and *juizes*, were not chosen from among the ranks of those seasoned in lesser Indian posts, but were selected carefully by the crown, presumably for a candidate's demonstrated reliability, training and experience at home. So far as I can determine these posts were never within the power of viceregal patronage. The middle and upper-ranking judicial officers of the various legal departments were all Coimbra University-trained *letrados* who did not belong to the group working their way upwards through the more junior posts.[10] But once they arrived in India, they usually all remained for more than a single three-year office (providing, that is, they survived the initial onslaught of microbes which carried off the new arrivals). And no doubt viceregal support aided them in obtaining renomination.

Many modern corporations have larger payrolls than the whole company of Europeans who lived in *Asia Portuguesa*. Even contemporary Spain probably had nearly as many bureaucrats engaged in operating its empire, if one includes scribes and notaries, as Portuguese Asia had European-born people. In the very large Spanish administration, which in effect contained eight centers of power (if one counts both viceroyalties, the *audiencias* of Quito and Charcas, the *Presidencia* of Nueva Granada, the captain-generalcy of Hispaniola, the governorship of Havana and the frontier province of Nueva Galicia) there could be no imperial common denominator. In the case of the unitary Goan viceroyalty, though, the machine could either be imbued with a single purpose—as in the administrations of Nuno da Cunha or Dom João de Castro, or else it could stagnate into self-seeking, as it often did under other leadership. The reason seems obvious enough : the bureaucracy comprised only a few hundred people, and they adjusted themselves rapidly to prevailing circumstances. In a larger operation like Spain's where there were more supervisors, more channels and more chains of command, obviously the system could display no uniform character, either of zeal or of flagrant dishonesty.

Finally, the three-year term, though common to both empires, no doubt had a more stultifying effect on *Asia Portuguesa* than it did on Hispano-America. Not only did it cause the triennial musical-chairlike or ladder-like recycling of subordinate personnel who soon became more expert at pocket filling than devoted to service, but it seems to have fostered a terrible inertia among the men at the top, especially the viceroys. Nearly everyone writing about the system, from R.S. Whiteway on, has remarked that the enormous time-distance equation made it impossible for viceroys to carry on any sort of meaningful dialogue with the metropolitan government While a viceroy in Mexico might query Madrid on some course of action and expect an answer back the following year (or perhaps it sent by special packet, the same year), a viceroy at Goa, unless he served more than one term consecutively, something fairly rare in the 16th and early 17th centuries, could not query Lisbon at all and receive a reply while he was in office. Unless, of course, he did so on the returning fleet which brought him out — unlikely because he would be so new that he would not know enough to ask the right question. By his second year, he could not expect to receive any answer at all while he was still viceroy. This, of course, tended to discourage all initiative. Which seemed to be exactly what the crown wanted, to judge from the number of times viceregents were cautioned in official correspondence : "Don't innovate." — "*não innovar.*"

On the other hand, not carrying out orders from Lisbon was a simple matter. The Spanish formula *obedezco mas no cumplo* ("I obey but don't carry out for the time-being") was put even to better use in India than in Spanish America; it took not just one, but three years to receive new orders after one had explained to the metropolis that "Your orders have been received; I know what you mean, but to apply them would not only stop ——, which you intended, but also damage ——, which you did not. I will merely point this out, and await clarification." The clarification would arrive only after the viceroy who requested it had left for Portugal. All his successor had to do to avoid carrying the order out was to state he hadn't seen it, but promised to look into the matter. Then, a year later, he could write and say : "So changed are conditions that I wonder if you could amend that a bit. I will await further word."

Meanwhile, if fortresses ran down, river channel silted up,

enemies grew in strength or fortress commanders gradually usurped prerogatives which were detrimental to the state, viceroys seldom believed the trouble would come within *their* term of office. Hence the tendency to make things sound well under control until they became alarming. Then viceregal letters would suddenly reveal that everything was in a sorry state — and had been for years.

Of course the same thing was true of the Spanish system — being similar in structure — and its inertia may have even been greater because it was larger and more complex. But it probably mattered less than in *Asia Portuguesa* that its administration was cumbersome and unwilling either to carry out orders which didn't suit its interests, or to develop plans and strategies which may have resulted in better long term prospects. As already remarked, Spanish America was far better insulated than Portuguese Asia from the consequences of neglect and inertia, being all but inaccessible to enemies on land, and after adoption of the convoy system, on the seas as well; any viceroyal initiatives would properly have had as their goal economic ends or improvement of communication. The Portuguese in Asia, on the other hand, surrounded by competitors and enemies, needed viceroyal planning to maintain their security. Moves to rationalize or streamline military organization (as per the ideas of Francisco Rodrigues de Silveira in Chapter VI, below) might have paid big dividends. But after the efforts of Nuno da Cunha and Lopo Vaz de Sampaio resulted in the acquisition of Diu, in 1534, no other Goan chieftain ever pursued an intelligent military objective, such as the capture of Aden or the destruction of the Kunjali pirates. (Although many did acquire fortified places of questionable value, mostly for the sake of leaving a monument behind to their rule).

Perhaps it was not so much the colonial governments that were at fault as the metropolitan ones. Spain and Portugal were both early modern absolutisms, if one can use that term for the sixteenth century, and I believe that, as such, they were shaped as much by fear of their own nobility as they were by a specific desire to centralize. When forced to innovate an imperial administration, their negative thinking—their fear of what might happen at such a great distance — probably was stronger than their understanding that great local experience was needed, plus a free hand, if their colonial rulers were to be effective. In Asia, the three-year term was alone enough to turn Portugal's overseas realm into a perpetual 'tyroarchy," i.e., a government headed by greenhorns and tenderfeet. Viceroys were appointed *because* they lacked all local experience, while the *fidalgos* who had gained some, as, for example, a captain of Malacca, might come to rule only by an emergency nomination called the "successions" in case the original appointee died at sea on the way to take up his office. No doubt the resulting want of insight on the part of Goan chief officers kept them from contemplating any disloyalty, but it must account for much of their inconsequence, as well. It would seem that here, as elsewhere, the bureaucratic tricks were easier to acquire than solid administrative perceptions, and what mostly transpired in any three-year term was that royal orders were sidetracked while the things which really needed to be done either went unoticed, or else the viceroy convinced himself that he d d not have the competence — or the funds — or the latitude — to undertake them. Meanwhile, he depended for the running of the state on lesser officers who had long been in India and who were anything but inexperienced.

It is amusing that what the Iberian colonial governments lacked in real power (including even the right to legislate permanently), they made up in falderol and pomp. This must have been designed to dazzle the indigenes who had come to expect as much from their native rulers, but it no doubt also gratified the egos of the European nobles, as well. Goan viceroys always went abroad from their palace, in ornate sedan chairs, heralded by flutes *and trumpets* and *drums*, accompanied by a full retinue.[11] So far as I know, no *regimento* — set of standing orders — ever prescribed this; it must have been a natural outgrowth of the vanity of the nobles designated as viceroys, plus the expectations of the native populations. In nearly every case — and this includes the attire and ceremonials of the more recent British viceroys of India — the grandiosity of the viceregal establishment seems to have exceeded even that of the kingship on which it was based.[12]

In sum, the administration of *Asia Portuguesa* was very small, but too large to replace from Portugal every triennium; its access, except for the very minor jobs, was restricted to those with noble blood, the nobler the better, and it was very far from Lisbon — farther even than Quito or Charcas in South America in terms of communication. Due to the peculiar set-up, the viceroy was always the least experienced of all the personnel, and his negative powers, that is, his ability to impede royal initiatives, were greater than his own abilities and incentives to inaugurate improvements and reforms — he was in office for too short a time and could not gain permission from Lisbon swiftly enough to get anything ambitious underway before his successor arrived. Hence he was restricted to short-terms (and usually rather meaningless) activities, should indeed he even wish to accomplish anything beyond the routine. If so, this usually meant adding another fortress somewhere in his area of command, often one where the additional revenues, if any, barely offset the expenses and extended Portuguese manpower still further.[13]

But before arrival of the Dutch, the inefficiency of *Asia Portuguesa* seems not to have affected the crown very deeply. Th *feitor* of Goa was fairly careful in seeing to it that royal specie sent from Lisbon was destined for the purchase of pepper, as contracted, and that this (if not always in full measure or prime quality) was stashed aboard ships bound for Portugal. Hence the king received what he had bargained for.[14] The royal treasury at Goa was something else again. Its income was supposed to be sufficient for the defence and administration of the viceroyalty, but it was always coming up short, and long before the end of sixteenth century, it became acknowledged both in Goa and in Lisbon that extra moneys were needed.[15] That is, moneys sent to Goa from general metropolitan revenues. There is evidence to believe that kings were never terribly happy about this, and it would seem that the reforms of 1549, which created the high office of *vedor geral da fazenda*, or chief overseer of the royal treasury, were an attempt to put an official more responsible to Lisbon in command of the colonial till. But the structural changes were not great and none resulted in a surplus in the

Goan treasury which might have buttressed it against attacks by enemies or the demands of military campaigns.

For what really ailed Portuguese Asia, if one believes Couto, was not that its revenues were insufficient for its needs, which they probably were not, but that the bureaucracy systematically pillaged the state in what may have been one of history's most blatant transfers of public money into private hands. So thoroughgoing was the conspiracy, it would seem, that even the two books Couto wrote to reveal its nature were sparately stolen and not recovered and printed until 174 years after his death.[16] The following chapters will examine his allegations.

NOTES

1. See Niels Streensgaard, *Carracks, Caravans and Companies, The Structural crisis in the European-Asia trade in the early 17th century*- Scandinavian Institute of Asian Studies Monograph Series, number 17, Copenhagen (Studentlitteratur, 1972, pp. 86-90; M.N. Pearson, *Merchants and Rulers in Gujarat*; Los Angeles and Berkeley (University of California Press), 1977, pp. 30-56; Panduronga S.S. Pissulencar (ed.), *Regimentos das Fortalezas da India*, Bastorá, Goa (Tipografia Rangel), 1951, pp. 527-30. This citation shows how much money in proportion to all the other sources the *alfândegas*, or customs revenues, brought up. Notice that the crown spice revenues are not included.
2. See Helmut G. Koenigsberger, *The Practice of Empire*, Ithaca, N.Y. (The Cornell University Press), 1969, pp. 43-58, and 140-143 for a discussion of the limited benefits the Spanish crown derived from its non-Castilian possessions. Revenues were only exported from local administrations under the Spanish crown like Sicily in times of clear danger (as from a Turkish invasion) and were to be used by Castile only for the common defence.
3. See Bailey W. Diffie and George D. Winius, *Foundations of the Portuguese Empire 1415-1580*, Minneapolis (University of Minnesota Press), 1977, pp. 331-335.
4. Antonio Vazquez da Espinosa, *Description of the Indies* (tr. Charles U. Clark), Washington, D.C. (The Smithsonian Institution Press), 1968, p. 156.
5. By a large force of 12,000 under Pocok and Albemarle. Even so, the fall was far from inevitable. The garrison was understrength

and, initially taken by surprise, lost valuable ground before beginning to fight back.

6. The standard source is Clarence H. Haring, *The Spanish Empire in America*, Cambridge, Massachusetts (The Harvard University Press), 1947. For information on the *audiencias*, see Chapter VII.
7. Evidence for this rests upon the reading of the *Monçoẽs* series. It can most easily be verified through a glance at the *Archivo Portuguez Oriental*, Fasisculo 5, the phrase *já em India* is frequently repeated. One can also gather this from the *Requerimentos* (see note 9, below).
8. In fact, I suspect that no *fidalgo* sailing for India without a definite nomination from the crown could gain even a minor Indian office immediately without having a kinsman there or family connection in a position of power.
9. At the end of his service, the holder would turn his whole file over to the government together with his petition for whatever he wanted — normally a pension or an office. Until the 1950's or 1960's these records were stored separately in collection of 164 bundles, called *Requerimentos*, first in the *Biblioteca National de Lisboa*, and later in the *Arquivo Histórico Ultramarino*. But in 1965, I discovered these papers had beed integrated into chronological boxes, according to region, with each document in a folder, according to its date. This makes the papers of, say, Felipe de Albuqerque no easier to find, and in many ways a lot harder, because they are filed solely by the date when the papers were entered. In most cases, this is unknown to the researcher. One thing the service records all indicate is how most officers and officials went from one job to another while remaining in India.
10. See Fascísculo 5 of the *Archivo Portuguez Oriental*, for instance. For the training and scope of the Portuguese (colonial) judiciary, see Storat B. Schwartz, *Sovereignty and Society in Colonial Brazil; the High Court of Bahia and its Judges 1609-1751*, Berkeley, Los Angeles, London (University of California Press) 1973, pp. 3-68.
11. As described, for example, by Linschoten, see vol. 1, p. 218.
12. A Modern example is that of the 20th century imperial palace of New Delhi and its attendant staff, which far exceeded that of Buckingham Palace in size and grandiosity.
13. Intelligent observers were already aware of this problem by 1540. See Dom João de Castro's letter to the infante Dom Luis, of 29 October, 1539. In Elaine Sanceau (ed). *Cartas de D. João de Castro, Lisbon (Agência Geral do Ultramar)*, 1954, p. 44.
14. Leaving aside. of course, whether the king was able to market his spices profitably in Europe. This is a separate story, for which see Diffie and Winius, *Foundations of the Portuguese Empire*, pp. 412-418,

15. See Pissurlencar, *Regimentos das Fortalezas, pp.* 2-4 n.
16. *In writing this monograph, I did not want to give the impression that all* officials were corrupt, which obviously they were not. There were, besides Couto himself, in his own time, most notably the *provedor-mór*, Francisco Pais; Pedro Barreto Resende, at various times contador of the *Matricola Geral* and secretary of state, Antão Vaz Freire, treasury official and compiler of the *Tombo de Ceilão*. And there were doubtlessly many others. Professor M.N. Pearson has pointed out *Chapitre Premier*, of Vitorino Magalhães Godinho's *Les Finances de l'Etat Portugais des Indes Orientales* (1517-1635), Paris (Fundacão Calouste Gulbenkian), 1982, especially pp. 17-23, 29-31 and 36-38, as indicative of honest service on the king's behalf.

1

THE VICISSITUDES OF AN HONEST CHRONICLER

DIOGO do Couto, soldier, official and chronicler of Portuguese Asia, was the first to identify and describe the syndrome of official corruption in detail, and so it is proper that this book should begin with his story. It is just possible that the whole period would have missed historical notice as anything special had it not been for his *Soldado Prático*. But it was certainly that work (or works, for there were really two of them) which set others, including myself, to examine the period for its peculiar nature.

Couto views Portuguese India from much the perspective we would choose had we been present ourselves—from that of an ordinary, but well educated citizen. For he was not of the inner circle, the privileged and protected group to whom government service meant easy enrichment, but (like most of us), a man of education whose happiness depended upon a career open to talents and the successful marketing of his own skills. I think there can be no doubt that he was an extremely honest individual to begin with—but there can also be small doubt that what really aroused his wrath was the fact that birth left him vulnerable to attack and ultimately limited his opportunities. I will develop this fully in the last chapters, but I will only observe here that he likely would never have produced the *Soldado Prático* had the system worked to his favour. What little is known of his early career is personal and revealing from the outset.

In the *Discursos Vários Políticos*, published at Lisbon in 1624, there appeared a brief, rather sketchy, biography of the late

Diogo do Couto. Though its author, Manuel Severim de Faria, man of letters and canon of Évora cathedral, seems to have known him solely through correspondence, he supplies some suggestive information concerning the chronicler's early life and parentage. This is worthy of more than passing interest because it not only provides the basis for his eventual literary career, but casts light on a handicap that vexed him all his life : his humble birth.

By sixteenth century standards, his father was a selfmade man. Native of Amarante, a picturesque village inland from Oporto and married to a local girl, one Isabel Serrão de Calvos, Gaspar do Couto left his unfrequented birthplace when he entered household service of the Infante Dom Luís, son of King Manuel I. In 1535, during the military expedition to Tunis, he distinguished himself beside his master and was knighted immediately. Unfortunately for his son, this glorious moment was not to prove sufficiently ennobling.

Born seven years afterwards, the future historian seemed destined for an identical career, if one facilitated through an education befitting his father's new dignity. Sent off to the Jesuit *Collegio de Santo Antão de Cidade*, Diogo do Couto was drilled in Grammar and Rhetoric by two highly competent Latinists—Faria is at pains to state their admirable qualifications analogous to those of professors who publish.[1]

No doubt because of this excellent teaching, Faria continues, the juvenile Couto became a humanist of ability and ardour. Upon completion of basic educational training, he was singled out by the Infante Dom Luís for advanced schooling at the monastery of Bemfica, as a companion to his own son, Dom António. Both boys studied philosophy and the Liberal Arts under the humanist clergyman, Dom Bartholomeu dos Mártyres, later Archbishop of Braga and a guiding hand at the final session of the Council of Trent. Besides considerable erudition, as Faria remarks, Couto's genteel, cloistered education had nourished in him "virtues which abounded all the more for it—well he demonstrated in later years the temperance, modesty and piety he retained all his life."[2]

At this high point, the bottom dropped out of his profession as gentleman to royalty before it fairly began. No sooner had he finished his studies when he was called, as he relates, to keep vigil, "torch in hand"[3] at the death bed of his patron. In a few months, his own father followed Dom Luís. Bereft of his patronage and without money, Couto enlisted in the military and was shipped to the Orient as a soldier in the fleet of Pero Vaz de Siqueira. This was in 1559. For the next decade he served in landing parties against the Moslems. In his *Soldado Prático* he has his soldier speak of "this sword wound on my arm, others on the legs, from which both are lame, arrow scars and others on my body and burned five times" and it could be that he is speaking of his own experiences.[4] Then in 1569, he returned briefly to Lisbon. The voyage was at once memorable because it marked the last trip to Europe for him and, upon his carrack's stopover for cargo and passengers, the final homecoming for his companion, Luís de Camões. It is indicative that the two struck up warm friendship (it is probable they had known one another in Goa), so close a one that the great poet requested Couto to write a commentary on his new *Lusiadas*. If Couto actually completed this, the manuscript has been lost. No doubt Couto and Camões were especially compatible because, as Faria remarks, Couto was himself an amateur poet, not only in Portuguese, but in Italian and Latin as well.[5]

Upon his return to Goa in 1571, Couto appears to have held middling administrative positions no doubt based on his education, plus his ten years of military service. During the next twenty years events in his life are unknown except in barest outline ; Faria is hazy while Couto's own accounts of the period are directed largely toward others. It becomes apparent toward the last quarter of his life, however, that Diogo do Couto indeed possessed some most unusual virtues, ones which ran him into the trouble that embittered his declining years. Wrote de Faria : "He was not greedy—which for a man who lived so many years in the Indies ... was a miracle."[6] In fact with Couto, honesty was akin to an affliction. Made chief of the Viceroy's certifications office (whose function it was to authenticate colonials' claims to privileges and pensions), he enraged Goans through running it honestly in a colony where nearly everybody treasured false credentials.

Meanwhile, in 1595, his more memorable occupation had

begun. Apparently because of Philip II's repute as patron to literary men, Couto composed and mailed off to him a history of Far Eastern affairs, beginning with that monarch's accession to the Portuguese throne in 1580. The maneuver was successful; Philip quickly responded by appointing him to update the *Décadas* (Decades), the official chronicle of the Portuguese in Asia, a serial begun by the great João de Barros and seemingly carried only through the year 1525 at Barros' death, in 1570. Couto was further called upon to organize and head a new colonial Torre do Tombo, the official archive, at Goa. If these honours assured Couto of a certain place in the Goan bureaucracy they only aggravated his unpopularity. For as a chronicler, it was likewise Couto's policy to give to every man his due, and this due frequently caused consternation among prominent families. Manuscripts vanished from his home in Goa ; others were tampered with at press in Lisbon.

The reaction to this truthful reportage was not long in coming : by 1596, the enemies he created had contacted the Escorial. The immediate occasion may have arisen from Couto's reconstruction of a shameful brawl over the governorship that had taken place in the '50's between Pero Mascarenhas and Lopo Vaz de Sampaio.

What transpired may be inferred from a letter to the viceroy written by Philip I (II of Spain), and dated March 5, 1598. Couto's adversaries, underhandedly enough, had chosen to strike him in the Achilles tendon. It reads :

> In cognizance of the fact I am informed that the aforementioned Diogo do Couto is not so competent as I understood by my earlier information, and due to the revelation of his faulty lineage—which as I wrote last year, you should have discovered when you first arrived in India—I advise you to let the Archbishop of Goa know what you might propose. If both of you find him unsuitable—in the archives as well as in the writing of history, or at least in one of these things—hide it from him in the best way you know how until you can advise me and I send you whom I choose for my service.[7]

Fortunately for Couto, before Philip could duly have been informed of anything, he was summoned off to his eternal reward on the following September 13. Moreover, it would seem thereafter that the Goan plotters had been plotted against by those whom Couto's verdict happened to favour.

Though his job had been saved, phantoms of the historiographer's defective ancestry were not so quietly gathered to Father Abraham's bosom as was Philip's soul. Doubtless because smear tactics had once revealed him as a parvenu, Couto in later years was denied membership in the exclusive Order of Christ, the Portuguese imperium's counterpart of the Golden Fleece. He wrote in 1607 to his friend Dom Francisco da Gama, the Count of Vidigueira: "I couldn't care less of a fig whether His Majesty (now Philip III, II of Portugal) makes me a noble or a Knight of Christ, or not. The world is so full of their ilk that I would rather be known as a man lacking the honour."[8]

Actually, Couto obviously coveted this reward for his faithful service. Only the next year he alludes to having written that his majesty's Indian histories might gain in credit if they had been composed by a man with the appropriate honorific.[9] If he did, he makes it perfectly clear to his friend da Gama, that he scarcely expected an answer.

Though lack of recognition may have damaged the old man's self-esteem, a concern which only reinforced it was lack of money. Upon appointment as chronicler of the Indies and head of the Torre do Tombo, he petitioned for an additional 80,000 *réis* annually—a modest figure, considering that it added up to less than double his salary as chief of the certification office alone. He received but 30,000—something "they wouldn t offer a clerk."[10] It is obvious enough even today that when an employee is given two additional duties, each comparable to or exceeding the first in importance, he deserves more than a one-third raise in pay. Out of this, Couto was even expected to support publications costs. "It is not the worst portent of what is going on here to see the neglect of the man with the pen," he commented. "I only console myself with the thought that while India suffers so many shipwrecks and tribulations, it is fitting for her chronicler to share the same fortune."[11]

As it turned out, printing and sale of his *Decades* proved a ruinous enterprise. Of some 300 volumes sent him for marketing in the Indies by his unpaid Lisbon agent (his brother-in-law), he was able to dispose of only thirty. He gave forty more away to prominent people, among them the Archbishop of Goa. The prelate did not so much as send him a jar of preserves! In a final attempt to make ends meet, he then gained permission to sell remaining volumes to soldiers on a kind of payroll deduction basis. The plan as one might imagine, had few takers.

If Carlyle's bad humor was aggravated by loss of his manuscript *French Revolution*, Diogo do Couto should by all rights have become paranoidal. Probably no historian before or since has seen more writing stolen, misplaced or destroyed. When countrymen failed him, Englishmen and even the elements conspired to destroy his output. The story is almost incredible.

In all, Couto composed eight official *Decades* following the pattern set by João de Barros. Barros had composed four down to the year 1538—but the final one was temporarily misplaced in Couto's time; as a consequence he began at the year 1525 and duplicated thirteen years of Barros' chronicle in his own *Fourth Decade*. Ironically, this one had smooth sailing to Lisbon, was given swift royal approval and found its way into print almost immediately. In a like manner, the Fifth was approved by 1602, but for some reason, it was not printed for ten years. When it finally did appear, the text had been seriously tampered with.[12] This was only a beginning.

No sooner had the Sixth come off the press when fire demolished the Lisbon print shop where its volumes awaited removal. Luckily for posterity, a handful of copies later turned up in the Convent of St. Augustine, delivered just prior to the blaze. The Seventh was consigned to the ship *Santiago*, Lisbon-bound in the fleet of 1601, but when the *Santiago* ran afoul of an English privateer on the way, its crew conceived Couto's manuscript as fit only for the edification of porpoises. News reached him in 1603 and he started over.[13]

The Eighth and Ninth were ready for the outgoing fleet by 1614, but when Couto fell ill that year, persons unknown broke into his study and made off with the whole effort. Undaunted, he pulled himself together, recast them into one volume and contributed two more *Decades* for good measure, the Eleventh and Twelfth. *Decade Ten* had been written years earlier, for this number was assigned to the work Couto first sent Philip I (II). It reached booksellers in 1778.

For all Couto's courage, misfortune would still not release him : *Decade Eleven* was stolen in Lisbon on arrival, as was possibly the Twelfth, whose fate today remains unknown. So far, only fragments of either have been turned up. Nonetheless, Couto in the last days of his life had made good a vow which appears in the text of his *Fourth Decade* :

> Neither out of respect nor fear will I omit anything; and should anyone do away with one volume, he will presently see another which presents the same thing.[14]

At times, the old man became despondent. Once, he threatened to order all manuscripts burned at his death so that no one else might profit by them.[15] He even considered, though not very originally, the following classical epitaph : INGRATA PATRIA, OSSA MEA NON POCEDEBIS – "Ungrateful Country, you shall not claim my bones."[16] He also wrote the *Soldado Prático*, a book expressing his conviction that Goan practice was more than a matter for personal concern. If its origin lay in his own frustrations, its import was wide as the Portuguese Far Eastern domain.

NOTES

1. In João de Barros, *Da Ásia*, Lisbon, 1778, Vol. 9, p.v.
2. Ibid., p. vii.
3. In *Da Asia*, vol. 13, p. 218.
4. Diogo do Couto, *O Soldado Prático*, ed., M. Rodrigues Lapa, Lisbon (Colecção de Clássicos Sá da Costa), 1937, p. 151. Some attributes of the soldier in the dialogue are purely fanciful ; so, it is hard to know whether this is actually true. But at least he did the right kind of duty to incur such wounds.

5. In *Da Ásia*, p. ix.
6. Ibid., p. xix.
7. *Revista Litteraria*, July-Dec., 1843, pp. 456-57.
8. Letter of Dec. 16, 1607, *Revista Litteraria*, p. 461,
9. Letter of 1608 (no month), *Revista Litteraria*, p. 548.
10. Letter of Dec, 16. 1607, *Revista Litteraria*, p. 461.
11. Ibid.
12. Aubrey F.G. Bell, Diogo do Couto, Oxford, 1924, p. 34.
13. Ibid., p. 35.
14. In *Da Ásia*, Vol. 9, p. 330.
15. *Revista Litteraria*, p. 462.
16. Ibid., Camões, among others, also toyed with it.

2

O SOLDADO PRATICO; THE ALLEGATIONS

THE *Soldado Prático* remained in manuscript until 1790 for a very good reason. In it, Couto alleged that the whole bureaucracy of the *Estado da India Oriental* was engaged in systematic thievery of the Goan royal treasury. Had Couto written it in Lisbon, he might have hovered protectively over the book until it was printed and distributed. But he was in Goa, and his usual bad luck held.

In reality, the *Soldado Prático* is, or is commonly assumed to be, not one, but two, works, both in dialogue form, vaguely similar in scope, but differing in style, arrangement and date of composition and perhaps in intent. Faria, in his bibliographical sketch, gives the following—and rather puzzling—account of their interrelationship. He explains :

> Since there accompanied Diogo do Couto a great zeal for patriotic welfare, together with insight and experience, he turned to consider the causes of malfunction such as existed in the government of the realm, particularly in the rule of India where he lived—where through the absence of the sovereign and the excesses of his ministers there were ever-growing disorders. To remedy this evil, while King Sebastian was still alive, he composed a book which he called the *Soldado Prático*, in which he introduced through the medium of dialogue a newly elected viceroy conversing with an old soldier from India, who had come to court at his request to inform him of things necessary for his trip, and of matters concerning royal holdings and the army. He pointed out all these things with gentility and brevity, giving both fundamental reasons and examples of what to pursue and what to avoid in such a way that they provide excellent instruction for that government.

> However, before he could perfect this work, the original was stolen from him...and found its way to the realm (Portugal) without its author's name, where several copies were made and held in great esteem by those who came by them. Being told of this by a friend in the year 1610, he set to work rewriting this book or rather forming it anew, because he introduced as characters in this dialogue a governor who had once been in India, with an experienced soldier from there, both at the office of a royal official, discussing the affairs of that state, bringing things up to the present time, with such careful thought and judgement that it might not only serve as a north star for those who governed, but for all time as a clear disabuse of its affairs.[1]

King Sebastian was slain at Al-Ksar-el-Kebir in 1578, which would fix the first version, according to Faria, at least a third-century prior to the final one. "Being advised by a friend" is a somewhat tenuous connection between two events nearly half a lifetime apart. However this might have been, Faria was in a position to know when the first dialogue had in fact been written. He owned the one manuscript copy now extant.

This first version is simply written, matter-of-fact and partially captures the give-and-take of actual conversation. Its objective was to more prove instructive and to help officers govern and avoid pitfalls, in short a work of the "mirror for princes" sort. By contrast, the second version with the date 1610—and a dedicatory epistle of 1612—makes use of the governor and royal official mostly as props for soldierly soliloquies. Unlike the earlier work, it is full of classical allusion as if the author had lost faith that the bureaucrats would listen to him, but rather wanted to register a protest in such a memorable way that posterity would vindicate him instead. It is biting, pessimistic and blunt. Couto's major preoccupation this time was not to urge toward better practices, but to unmask evil ones, and perhaps to get even with those who both committed them and slighted him.[2]

In his preface, dated January 2, 1612, and addressed to "the Count of Salinas and Ribadeo, Duke of Vila-Franca, of the Supreme Council of State of His Majesty," Couto makes his outspokenness clear enough :

> Everything Your Excellency might wish to know of him (the soldier), he dares to say without importunity, adulation or passion ; and I am convinced he succeeds in this because he undertakes matters that hardly might fall from the mouth of any other soldier ; nor does he seek any satisfaction for his work other than a hearing from Your Excellency, because Your Excellency will then go out of his way to remedy the ills complained about.[3]

The experienced soldier is of course essentially Couto himself, the soldier's "very learned rusticity," as Couto terms it, his own. Incidentally, most of what I have summarized here has been taken from this latter dialogue because the earlier one could never have created a Black Legend, while this one obviously did all the damage.

To provide a setting for his dialogue, Couto prefaces it with the following description : "A *fidalgo*, who was once governor of India, happens to be in the office of an official of Portugal, when an old soldier from India enters, who has come to file his petition and certificates ; and between the three there transpires the following conversation." The time is set in the reign of King Sebastian, more than thirty years before.

"My affairs are already off to a good start," says the soldier, "for it is my luck to find Your Mercy here, who can attest my services." The *fidalgo* then expresses delight at having "a witness to the things of which we were speaking"[4] and invites him to take part in the conversation. From this point until the book's end, only an occasional sop is made to credibility through reference to the characters' coming and going ; there is little attempt to achieve realistic exchange of ideas. Perhaps only the colloquial ring of the language itself embodies something of the true-to-life.

If writers speak of works which leave out part of the information necessary for the reader's comprehension as "elliptical," one might call the *Soldado Prático* and many contemporary treatises "circular." Points in it seem to revolve past the reader, disappear in a tangle of judgments and irrelevancies, and then return for further development. In describing it, I have taken an arbitrary circuit of the Goan situation as Couto conceived it. It will remain for the following chapter to examine his view of what caused it to explore his view of what should be done as a remedy.

The soldier first establishes that the crown in Portugal has no true idea of Indian affairs because judges and captains asked to make *residencias*[5] or reports are either frightened or untrustworthy ; nearly always the result is a whitewash for all parties concerned. Viceroys scarcely look with favour on those who testify against them. Couto tells of one returning viceregent who, miraculously enough, seems to have been confronted with his acts. Later this man wrote cynically to friends in Goa : "So-and-So testified to this effect and So-and-So to that, but I got 'my hands on them."[6] As a result, Couto says, Goan subjects were guided by this motto : "Never offend your king/ never swear to anything." The worst that could conceivably befall an ex-viceroy for any crime committed in office was banishment from court upon his return.[7] The knowledge could scarcely encourage witnesses to risk their lives on behalf of justice nor a viceroy in office to ponder possible consequences.

While kings might thus be kept in the dark, Couto lays much of the blame squarely at their feet, "because they have come to prefer flatterers to wise counsellors."[8] Occupied with the chase and pleasant company, aloof from their subjects, he feels they had in fact vacated their high calling by ceasing to concern themselves with what went on around them. Had they interviewed personally a few pension applicants, he says, they might have gained some troubling insights.

If kings at home had isolated themselves from their citizenry, so had the viceroys in India—for somewhat different reasons. Fifty years before, the crown had loaned money to subjects as a means of promoting trade and welfare; viceroys of Couto's time concerned with creating but one aspect of prosperity : their own. To this end, they had gradually complicated judicial machinery. Until Jorge Cabral's time (in office 1549-1550) there had been only a *Provedor Mór, an Ouvidor Geral* and a *Procurador de coroa* ; in João de Castro's (1545-1548) but an *Ouvidor Geral.* Yet, Couto says, justice was swift, often dispensed personally, "from the knee."[9] Viceroys no longer had any inclination. Instead, they had vastly augmented their legal staffs, causing all contacts to be made in writing through the *Mesa de Relação*. "Plato has said that where there are many doctors, there are many sick people, and one can now add that where there are many ministers of justice, there is too much injustice," Couto observes.[10]

The *Mesa de Relação*, the High Court of Appeals, was an august body that displayed a remarkable capacity for making cases seem tenuous and doubtful until the appropriate lubrication was administered to its machinery. Payments placed with one near the viceroy, it seems, swept away doubts, clarified legal tangles, made laws plain and judgments certain. Meanwhile, Couto continues, "If a judge is asked to arbitrate verbally some trifle, like the complaint of some Indian, they try to make it into a libel suit ; scribes are not satisfied until they can draw up official documents, call witnesses and rob the wretches blind, without proving anything at all."[11] When Indians died intestate, the same magistrates confiscated property in the king's name, then divided it equitably among themselves.

Though justice might be at a standstill in other departments, those who owed money to the crown were not only clapped into jail with utmost dispatch, but contrary to royal guarantees for civil offenders, might be chained and tortured.[12] Couto quotes a friend as saying : "If you don't owe money to the crown, kill as many men as you wish--and go free ! "

With his king in ignorance and insulated from his subjects' petitions, the viceroy and his followers then proceeded to turn Portuguese Asia into a panorama of baroque corruption, the veritable counterpoise to More's *Utopia*. License for most dubious innovations was taken via perversion of the clause in royal instructions that king's representatives should "above all do what appears to further my service."[13]

Outwardly, the falderol of viceregal "flutes, trumpets, velvet cushions and gilded fringe" was grand. This increasing emphasis on frippery merely concealed the shabbiness of viceregal statecraft. Where once the governors had looked to promulgation of the faith, to enrichment of the king's treasure, to bearding of Turks and squelching of Malabar kings, they had now become little more than local masters of ceremonies. On a civic level, they fribbled away their hours in such profitless enterprises as mediating the endless squabbles between Dominican and Augustinian.[14]

Goan administration had become little more than a fraternal organization for sycophants, highest bidders and viceregal relatives ; the rest went begging. Jobs were found for men rather than men for jobs.[15] While Couto says it was clearly in the royal intent to give posts to the well deserving, they fell to henchmen unless a king should expressly nominate his own candidate.[16] Even then, bolder viceroys sometimes flouted such decrees. One man sent by the sovereign to fill an office had to take refuge in a convent to preserve his life, then sail back to Lisbon empty-handed.

Soldiers and others who had earned enough certification to entitle them to civil service positions even after a roundtrip to Portugal often found themselves thwarted on Goan technical grounds. Dear to the viceregal heart was the *falência*, or "defect," a means of rendering certificates null and void on the pretext that these were improperly executed. It remained simply for legal staffers to find a minor mistake on the part of Lisbon, declare that they could not honour the holder's patent and disbar him from the office it indicated with a wave of the hand—either this, or keep him in indefinite suspense. After a 15,000-kilometre trip that likely as not had exhausted the applicant's savings, such a ruse might indeed assume tragic proportions. Couto intimates that more than one had died waiting with his patent, like a monk's habit, "hanging on his neck."[17]

So far as Couto was concerned, most Goan insiders were no more than perfume-drenched nincompoops, whose "velvet capes, doublets and pantaloons of the same, silken hose, gold buckle hat, gilded sword and dagger, cleanshaven faces and high topknots it seems to me would have made the good king (Manuel I) die of shame,"[18] especially when compared with the bearded faces and rusty swords of the conquerors. Properly connected young *fidalgos*, though they might have arrived without a *real* to their names, immediately acquired silver caparisoned horses, an expensive house with gaudy furniture and hangings in the hall and bedrooms, while other chambers were empty enough to fence or play games in. The object : to deceive married women. Higher officers simply used force.

With ordinary soldiers expected to sleep in open boats, live on rotten rice, salt fish and polluted water, Couto wonders that any might volunteer to serve in India at all.[19]

Meanwhile indeed, there was scarcely an artilleryman in all Goa who could hit the side of a mountain. Fleets had become disorganized, soldiers begged money on the streets, especially those who had just arrived from Portugal, and fencing schools had become dancing studios. "I can remember meeting more old captains and fidalgos on the streets of Goa capable of becoming viceroys of the world than I meet simple soldiers worth the name today," Couto snorted.[20]

Though lip-service to peace might be justifiably stylish in the late 20th century, devastation of Malabar strongholds was considered essential by Couto to keep Goa's enemies off balance. Once, he said, the expeditions that sailed against Moslem and infidel had fought hard and plundered nobly; under Dom Francisco Barreto (1555-1558) gains from such raids had replaced handsomely the fourteen ships lost to combat in a single season.[21] Even prostitutes had formerly partaken of this fighting spirit. Once when a soldier rapped on her door, a certain lady of negotiable virtue inquired who was without. "A man of peace," came the reply. "Well I believe that," she sneered. "Whoever runs about in Goa when the Viceroy is off to war—he is a real man of peace !"[22]

Gross Goan income might now be far greater, but there was no longer a single ship in the harbour capable of rendering account of itself in battle; for a payment to the viceroy's entourage of 200 *pardaos*, a teenager had even been given command of a galley. Initiative had long since passed to the enemy. While viceroys followed a cautious policy of appeasement, the Samorin of Calicut broke agreements insultingly whenever it suited him.[23] All this time, returning viceroys had been bringing home a paper navy that made their king believe India was safe for years to come. Couto's verdict: In our present need, we have nothing to hold onto save our own hair."[24]

"If [the neighbouring sovereigns] did not have their hands tied, Gentlemen," he told the fidalgo and the official, "I am certain this business would have been over long ago—thank God they are kept in rein by the Great Mughal, who menaces their kingdoms. We ought to say masses for his health, because if he were to die and liberate those barbarians from their fright, they would unleash all their strength upon us. Since Dom Luís de Ataíde's administration (1568-1571), the time has come to an end when we can defend ourselves against one and all."[25]

It is fortunate that such a work as the *Soldado Prático* should have been written by one finely attuned to the bureaucracy. Resumé so far has been concerned with more visible aspects of Goan misrule. Couto was able to penetrate to the core and reveal the mechanisms by which viceroys and their cohorts actually mulcted inhabitant and crown. He was able to show that these were not merely grafters on the scale of a subtropical Tammany Hall, but scoundrels on a bolder scale. One can only admire their ingenuity.

Perhaps the most open device for shaking down subjects was that of the *dividas velhas*, or old debts. It worked this way. In times of emergency, the viceroy was empowered to pre-empt from subjects any material he deemed necessary to raise an armada grain, rice, pitch, fibre, wood, etc., for which he was to issue certificates appraising just value and promising payment at some future date. Victims knew perfectly that restitution would never be offered. In order to realize any value whatever, these were obliged to sell such papers to members of the clique for one-quarter face value. The latter would cash them in full.[26] Debts outstanding at the close of a three-year tenure were dispatched even more shamefully. "Five or six days before embarcation, it is proclaimed through all churches and parts of the city that (upon presentation of their claims) all creditors will be paid; with the (viceroy's) foot in the stirrup, no one bothers; then the scribes turn out a thousand certificates (to that effect) with which to shut the eyes of the blind and to pay off the servants, leaving all India scandalized."[27]

Once they had outfitted their fleets with confiscated property, viceroys were unlikely to use them for war; instead they were wont to visit captains and governors of distant forts and territories in order to shake them down for favors rendered, such as the acquiescence in personal trade monopolies either within or outside their spheres of command.

While reaction of the royal official to such revelations was regularly one of shocked surprise—perhaps fitting for one who had seen no Indian service—the *fidalgo's* character momentarily becomes real at this turn in the dialogue. Where the official can only interject his usual *Valha-me Deus* ! (God help me !), the former governor lapses into the lame self-justification that must have prevailed among those who recovered their consciences at the Cape of Good Hope: "How else" he cries, "could you expect me to repay my friends of noble blood who have served me, except in this way and others ? Nor am I the first governor who has done so—they would have ample cause for complaint if I should deny what has been conceded so many times!"[28] In another instance, when he pleads innocent because he had no leisure for somewhat different practices, the soldier assures him: "If you had not been too busy. . . your entourage would have persuaded you."[29]

For fortress captains, one tried-and-true method of rewarding one's self was through the usage of "*soldos velhos,*" or "old salaries." It was simple. They might simply neglect to remove long-dead solidiers' names from garrison muster. Many had not served for fifty years. The resulting quarterly pay, however, took only fifty seconds to vanish into commanders' pockets. Should things become uncomfortably warm in course of enquiry, members of this phantom garrison would suddenly be annihilated by paper Moslem lances.[30] The fortress captains, Couto reports, were petty tyrants, who monopolized trade, frequently abused the inhabitants of their jurisdictions, Portuguese as well as Indian, and departed from office with three times as much money as they had produced in taxes and customs duties for the crown.[31]

Another shakedown practice was similarly directed at the king's treasury, but involved purchasing for the colony and diplomatic gifts to its allies. Its mechanics lay in the gross overpricing of goods together with a system of rebates. Couto goes into detail over procurement and inspection trips to the northern fortresses. In this case, the *vedores de fazenda,* or royal treasury overseers, might volunteer several times per year to set out on the combined errand of investigating distant captains' books and ordering ships, wood, lumber, oil, rice, wheat, cloth and the like for government use in Goa. Frequency was entirely at their discretion. The motions that ensued showed all the marvelous refinement of a mechanical clock n a Swiss town hall.

First, the *vedores* drew handsome salaries for their self-appointed errands and took with them at royal expense all of their friends, together with ample bags of gold for their transactions. Next when they arrived at Ormuz or Diu, or Ceylon, or all stations in between, they received additional compensation for a tolerant glance at local ledgers. Then they procured materials for provisioning of the state. Finally, "the king had spent ten or fifteen thousand cruzados when (the equivalent of) three or four might have sufficed ... and it would have been more profitable to buy things at this rate in Goa."[32]

Upon their return, the *vedores* made it clear that they had not exactly been laboring in the vineyard. "If you should walk into one of their houses," Couto wrote, "you would find the whole veranda full of tailors, some making mantles of silk and satin, others, rich quilts. Inside, craftsmen hammered out silver carafes, Chinese-style tankards, chains and bracelets for wives and daughters; other men trimmed caskets with tortoise shell, silver and coconut from the Islands. Below, in the courtyard, turners and carpenters were busy at orders for pleasure boats of all varieties, desks in marquetry work and wardrobes for commercial use. You might think yourself in a warehouse, rather than the home of a *vedor de fazenda*."[33]

Even viceroys were unable to resist plundering the crown's exchequer through much the same device. "When they command an ambassador to be sent to Balagate or Mogador, he by custom must bring presents, and they enter on the ledger four, six or ten horses, which the viceroy sells from his own stable at exorbitant prices: a horse worth two hundred goes for six hundred or more, and they enter the name of another on the receipt."[34]

In the *Soldado Prático* it is not discernible whether viceroys may have received percentages from that racketeering that did not directly involve their persons, aside from shakedowns of fortress captains. Seemingly they did not, though as will later be seen, two Frenchmen, François Pyrard and Jean Mocquet, believed they were able to enrich themselves during their tour of duty each to the tune of 600,000 to 1,000,000 cruzados. Surely viceroys did not stop at the overpricing of a few horses, plus an occasional trip to the forts with a new fleet. Seldom, if ever, did they work for the crown's welfare. "Show me a viceroy," Couto wrote, "who would lose a *cruzado* from his own estate for the benefit (of the king)—it is hardly the custom; before doing this, he would build his own at the royal expense, and God knows who else's."[35]

From what Couto writes, one can speculate instead that viceroys derived the real bulk of their own incomes from a number of other practices like the sale of public office, including renominations to the magistracies.[36] With office so lucrative in itself, there could have been little reason to extort modest fees. Then there would have been bribes for countersigning dubious—or even genuine—service certificates. By taking all current expenses, legitimate or dishonest, out of the royal exchequer, the viceroys and their hangers-on could have salted away virtually every *pardao* and *cruzado* gleaned from the time of their arrival. Couto also mentions debasement of currency to such an extent that Indian merchants threatened Goa's food supply.[37] When viceroys resorted to this practice during their tenures, it is hard to see who else might have profited.

Otherwise, from all grafting procedures and trickery Couto has seen fit to describe, it must be assumed that members of the coterie collectively managed to stagger off with as much or more Goan booty as the viceroy. And to reward these still more fully, viceroys frequently broke into payments labelled for Ormuz and other forts.[38]

There is some intimation in Couto that this viceregal open purse to associates was all not merely a touching instance of misplaced charity. For the fidalgo rises to defend it through the following line of argument: "I had license to do whatever seemed best to me toward deriving consent for all that governors might wish to accomplish, and with these little (fraudulent) devices that prevail in India, I was able to make my friends rich, in order that they should serve me, and by this means represent the dignity of my office."[39] Earlier, one will remember his pleading that they expected as much, together with Couto's insistence that had such henchmen actually urged him to inaugurate a new abuse, he would surely have consented.

It is unlikely that viceroys who appeared so zealous for the king's service when they arrived could have changed completely "in four days" except through the "infernal inclinations of men" in Goa who awaited their employ. In fact the machine for imperial sabotage seems not to have required viceregal initiative at all. More probably, king's regents merely took an uneasy look around—and capitulated.[40]

It is these allegations alone which have fascinated historians, readers of Portuguese literature and even schoolboys since the *Soldado Prático* was first printed in 1790. Curiously, all commentators on Couto to date have accepted his ideas uncritically, which hardly allows one to use, or understand them properly. The following chapter will first examine another, even less explored, aspect of the work—Couto's proposed remedies for the evils he describes—and then the following ones it will compare and criticize his ideas in light of what contemporaries, antecessors and modern observers have written on the same subject. The result, I think, will be that this process will permit a much better appraisal, not only of the *Soldado Prático*, but of the so-called *decadência* itself.

NOTES

1. In *Da Ásia*, p. xvii.
2. In a paper offered to the second International Seminar on Indo-Portuguese History in 1980, Dr. António Coimbra Martins has adduced much evidence to indicate that the "second" *Soldado Prático* was not at all a revision of the first version, but an entirely separate work, and that the 1612 dating of its dedicatory epistle may be misleading as to the actual date of its conception - which Coimbra Martins believes may have been contemporaneous with the first version. He prefers to call only the first dialogue *O Soldado Prático*, and gives the title *Enganos e Desenganos da India* to the second. Certainly, he is correct in observing that the two dialogues are too different for the second to be considered merely an updating of the first which it barely resembles. His case for the existence of an earlier manuscript is based upon certain

anachronisms in the text of one known manuscript of the second version have apparently been emended by Couto himself in another version. Hence the date of his writing it could well be considerably anterior to 1612. The article is entitled *Uma Questão de Método sobre O Soldado Prático* and, hopefully, it will be published among the papers of the Congress. Until this writing, publication has been delayed by the untimely death of Admiral Avelino Teixeira da Mota, in April, 1982.

3. *Soldado Prático*, p. 2.
4. Ibid.; p. 4.
5. The *residencia* was a judicial inquiry into an officeholder's conduct held immediately after its term had expired. It was not a native Portuguese institution, but was introduced into Portugal and the empire by the Hapsburgs.
6. *Soldado Prático*, p. 12.
7. Ibid., p. 112.
8. Ibid., p. 16.
9. Ibid., p. 157.
10. Ibid., p. 159.
11. Loc., cit.
12. Ibid., p. 31.
13. Ibid., p. 32.
14. Ibid., p. 116.
15. Ibid., p. 58.
16. Ibid., p. 33.
17. Ibid., p. 152.
18. Ibid., p. 144.
19. Ibid., p. 153.
20. Ibid., pp. 149-50.
21. Ibid., p. 170.
22. Ibid., p. 217.
23. Ibid., pp. 123-24.
24. Loc., cit.
25. Ibid., p. 114. This statement, incidentally, is the only contemporary expression I have found of a situation which is fairly obvious in retrospect. Dom Luís had a second term of office (1578-1581), but Couto has set the scene as during the reign of Dom Sebastião, who died in 1578.
26. Ibid., pp. 74-5. See George D. Winius, *The Fatal History of Portuguese Ceylon; Transition to Dutch Rule*, Cambridge, Mass. (Harvard University Press), 1971, p. 100, for an example which occurred thirty years after Couto wrote.
27. Ibid., pp. 36-7
28. Ibid., pp. 74-5.
29. Ibid., p. 77.
30. Ibid., pp. 87-8. This practice, however, was common among commanders in Europe of the time. It still existed in India in the 1690's.

See the reports of Francisco de Mello de Castro, *Documentos Remetidos da India*, Livro 55, fl. 135.

31. First dialogue, called the *Observações sobre as Principaes Causas da Decadência dos Portuguezes na Asia*. Lisbon 1790, pp. 29-32. For another example of their conduct, see the *Vida de laques de Coutre*, MS 2780, Biblioteca Nacional de Madrid, fls. 183-188. The captain of Rachol tried to rob Coutre, a jewel trader, and push him into a deep well in the fortress. Coutre said he had almost depopulated the area as a result of his "tyrannias".
32. Ibid., p. 82.
33. Ibid., p. 83.
34. Ibid., p. 28.
35. Ibid., p. 27. Although the Count-Viceroy of Linhares (1629-1635) and at least one other are known to have done so.
36. The *Documentos Remetidos da Índia* are full of nominations lists—the viceroys to the king, and the king's appointments back to the viceroy. In virtually all cases they are identical. Sale of office by the crown was tried for short periods, notably in 1615-1616, but was soon discarded, no doubt, because viceroys would have been obliged to pass on to the crown moneys paid to them by candidates. Any measure stubbornly resisted by the Goan administrations could not be enforced from Portugal. See Luís Augusto Rebello da Silva, *Historia de Portugal nos Séculos XVII e XVIII*, 5 vols., Lisbon, 1860-1871, vol. III, p. 283. Frei Vicente de Laguna asserted as early as 1530 that offices were indeed sold by courtiers, if not by the king. See António da Silva Rego (ed. comp.) *Documentação para a Historia das Missões do Padroado Português do Oriente*. India. 12 vols., Agência Geral das Colónias / do Ultramar, 1947-1958, II, p. 194.
37. Ibid., p. 213.
38. Ibid., p. 28.
39. Ibid., p. 29.
40. This is confirmed by what Dom Vasco de Mascarenhas, the Count-Viceroy of Óbidos, wrote some 40 years later. He recounts in a letter to a relative that he had resisted all bribes upon his arrival and even furnished his palace with goods from the second hand market. He also admits that, in doing so, he sowed the seeds for his own downfall. He was overthrown by a revolt on 22 October, 1653. See M.A. Hedwig Fitzler (ed. & comp.) *O Cêrco de Columbo; Últimos dias do domínio Português em Ceilão. Rompimento das hostilidades pelos holandeses até a rendição de Columbo* (1652-1656), Coimbra (Coimbra University Press), 1928, pp. 140-143.

3

O SOLDADO PRATICO; THE REASONS WHY

So FAR, my essay's sole objective has been to record Couto's reportage conveniently in English and to indicate his possible motivation for his writing the *Soldado Prático*. It might now be interesting to consider the reasons he himself assigns for Portugal's plight and the remedies he would have seen fit to apply.

When Couto turns (in Faria's words) "to consider the causes of such malfunction as existed in the government of the realm," his appraisal of the crumbling imperial situation is compounded roughly of one part religion, two parts common sense and three parts bureaucracy. This last invisible ingredient will become fully apparent in his corrective suggestions.

God, he feels strongly, is punishing Goa because of her colonial leaders' transgressions against king, subject and Himself. Again and again he states that this multitude of injustices alone might constitute sufficient reason why Goa could not long endure.[1]

If the ramifications of this injustice reached to the heavens, its root lay in the prevailing attitude "work to make money, the rest is wind!"[2] He illustrates with the following story: "One day when I was in a convent," he has the soldier say, "I saw a fidalgo bound for [command of] one of the choice fortresses of India, who had come to say goodbye. In the conversation that followed, I overheard a monk tell him: 'Sire, remember that you are going in the responsibility laid upon you by the king, and that you wear a kind of cowl, like mine, in this respect. Be content with that which is yours, feed the poor and do justice.' To which the fidalgo replied: 'Father,

I do exactly as the other captains do; if they go to Hell, I will be their companion, because I am only going out to that fortress to get rich."[3]

Not only did Portuguese leadership ignore the clergy; it was unable to heed the voice of experienced commoners in affairs of state. "There are many who could give excellent advice in all matters," Couto declares, "because they have dealt with them longer than fidalgos called (to do so), many of whom totally lack experience. It is the Portuguese curse that a non-fidalgo is never consulted on anything."[4]

"You cannot tell me that just because they are not noble, they should not be in Council."[5] In an empire sprawled from Sofala to the Moluccas, he added neither the viceroy nor his captains could have sufficient knowledge of all things; and while the Greeks and Romans elevated great captains from humble origins, Couto said, "this is our wretched nation, where we all work to destroy one another."[6]

There was not so much wealth available, he said, as many might be led to estimate from the hoards of money in viceregal vaults. It was only there because payments were withheld from the poor, because forts were never built and necessities went begging in a realm where officials were ever imposing new taxes.[7]

Actually, Couto felt, Goa might have suffered from a relative poverty notwithstanding the corruption because it lacked a ready source of specie like that possessed by Spain, which allowed "those Catholic kings" in Flanders alone" "to spend "more than forty millions" against the rebels. "If it did not have mines in New Spain and elsewhere, how could it stop the gap at all?"[8]

In addition, Couto seems to regard all foreign elements holding property in Goa "and living in all the delights now spoken of" as injurious to the state.[9] Of this, I will presently say more, for it seems indicative of his mentality.

The medicine he prescribes for his country's colonial weakness shows him as a thoroughgoing, if hyperconscientious, bureaucrat. After more than fifty years of public service, he could envision little but a tightening of the system. Nor was he able to perceive its fundamental faults : that so long as appointees from the viceroy on down served only three years, and so long as so many opportunities for private wealth existed in trade not monopolised by the state, there could be no possibility for officers at once to gain experience of the East or, as he put it, to stop the "looking at pearls".

For the crown Couto recommends a return to Christian duty and a smaller dose of courtly pleasure. Kings, he feels, are vicars of Christ. Just as Jesus never turned away men who sought him out, sovereigns should freely allow visits from their subjects.[10] Then they could render justice and know what was going on.

As for Indian affairs, he advocates a special tribunal of overseers, "men just and zealous," to hear complaints, so that the king would not inadvertently short-circuit fair play by routing these back to the viceroy himself. "For it is certain, Gentlemen," he says to the *fidalgo* and official, "that the king has no greater enemies than some of these very viceroys".[11] He does not explain, however, where these men are to be found, or how they are to be expected to maintain their independence when once in Asia.

Rather than on the present basis of family alone, Couto thinks that viceroys should be chosen for qualities of clemency, of liberality and of wisdom. Moreover, he feels that kings of Portugal might take a lesson from the "kings of China" and not appoint viceroy or governor who had relatives in territories they were given to command and besides this, he should not take them out in his personal retinue when he went to India. As it was, he lamented, "three states of India would not be enough" for viceregal nephews and fleets were scarcely large enough to carry them home. Instead, the viceroy should arrive alone and leave alone, "without majesty," that he might fear the king and be more easily held accountable for his acts.[12]

In order to avoid the *falência*, the nullification of certificates on spurious Goan technical grounds, he believes it necessary to create a unified bureau in Lisbon that would issue them all from one source and, apparently simultaneously, "so in India there could be no argument about their defects."[13] Before any might be voided, a special court (more technically, *a mesa de consciência*), presided over by none other than the Archbishop of Goa himself, would have to consent.[14]

When it came to the beaux brummel, he would joyfully have crimped their plumage. His recipe for soldierly attire: "Half-knee stockings of cotton or twill, short sword, sword belt of leather and iron—not so many fancy pants, so much gilded cutlery, gold braid and so many of the baubles and embellishments I constantly gape at."[15]

For those who promenaded all winter in Goa, but vanished temporarily when there was a seige to raise at one of the fortresses, he endorsed a knotted rope. After four such hangings, he felt, the military manpower shortage might improve dramatically.[16] The Samorin of Calicut would then be administered a richly-deserved whiff of grapeshot.

But above all, Couto would have mustered a strong military force to sweep into Africa and capture the rich silver mines at "Chicoua, from the King of Monomatapa." Unless the Portuguese had such a ready source of hard cash as their sister kingdom of Castile, he felt, it was virtually impossible for his nation to pursue an aggressive policy. "It has to have mines," he said, "because the state that lacks them is always poor."[17] He believed further conquest in the Indian perimeter to be totally unprofitable. Instead, he would merely have expelled all its natives from Portuguese possessions as undesirable foreign elements.[18]

From these suggestions, it seems obvious enough that Diogo do Couto was less successful as politico-economic consultant than as a seventeenth century prophet of imperial doom. No doubt it would have been all to the gain for his country to have effected the emendations he proposes. But they are all indicative of a certain viewpoint, a naively nonbusinesslike one at that. He would cure the system by aping Spain and conquering some mines from which to mint money. Apparently, it had never occurred to him that the nation battering at Portugal's very colonial foundations—Holland—was managing prosperity without so much as a deposit of iron pyrites. In a fit of xenophobia, he even advocates the expulsion of wealthy foreign traders. He takes no proper account of the fact that a merchants they may have held more of the keys to Goa's prosperity than did the mines of Monomatapa.

What Couto could scarcely apprehend was that government by three-year *fidalgo*, or perhaps more basically, *fidalgo* at all, was at best a faulty tool when a commercial empire was at stake. With or without Coutonian reform, the result would have been ruled by men who could only belabour a commerce they scarcely understood, a point made by Couto's contemporary, Duarte Gomes Solis.[19]

The honest chronicler's true service has been to call up the unhappy ghosts of Goa, and to rattle their chains. He did, after all, perceive that Portugal was fast approaching the end of its importance as an Asian power and he has faithfully reported how the corruption manifested itself in colonial practice. He depicted the muddy vesture of Goan decay as no other writer has. That Couto was essentially accurate in his characterization of Goan ills can be established from the accounts of foreign visitors to Goa during the years he hired those, or within a few years after his death. The following chapter will discuss what these said about the very things Couto described.

NOTES

1. *Soldado Prático*, p. 58, p. 62, p. 146, etc.
2. Ibid., First Dialogue, the *Observações*, Edition of 1790, p. 95.
3. Ibid., Edition of 1937, p. 14.
4. Ibid., p. 92.
5. Ibid, pp. 131-2.
6. Loc. cit.
7. Ibid., p. 52. It is interesting that Couto says this. By the Restauração, it was claimed that there was nothing whatsoever in the treasury. See *Documentos Remetidos da Índia*, Livros 56, fl. 470; 61, fls. 379-380, Arquivo Nacional da Torre do Tombo, Lisbon.
8. Ibid., p. 225.
9. Ibid., p. 219.
10. Ibid., p. 19.
11. Ibid, p. 110.
12. Ibid., p. 174.
13. Ibid., p. 139.
14. Loc. cit.
15. Ibid., p. 218.

16. Ibid., p. 217.
17. Ibid. They had already been tried in 1571, during the time of King Sebastian, by a special appointee, Dom Francisco Barreto. But it failed then, and on subsequent occasions. See Diffie and Winius, *Foundations of the Portuguese Empire*, p. 224.
18. Ibid., p. 219.
19. For instance, see his *Mémoires Inédits* (ed. Léon Bourdon), Lisbon, 1955, pp. 13-14; also Solis' *Alegación en Favor de la Compãnia de la India Oriental* (ed. Moses Bensabat Amazalak), Lisbon, 1955, pp. 13, 25, 52, 58, 65, 67. Solis wonders on this last page, why the king doesn't confer viceregal honours and office on a rich merchant!

4

WHAT VISITORS OBSERVED DURING COUTO'S TIME

In the previous chapter, Couto's *Soldado Prático* has been examined in the context of his career as Goan civil servant. It might now be useful to see what visitors to Goa during or shortly after Couto's time wrote about the same problems, in order to check its essential validity against them.

Of the dozen non-Portuguese authors who paid visits there during the years that Couto actually lived in Goa,[1] perhaps only two, Jan Huyghen van Linschoten and François Pyrard de Laval are of prime value as corroborators of Couto's allegations. A third, the Parisian Jean Mocquet, former custodian of Henry IV's museum in the Tuileries, is less important because he became so biliously anti-Portuguese after having been chained by his throat to the deck of an eastbound ship that he crowded his Goan pages with every tale of petty cruelty and perversity that came to his ears. He was so busy in the pursuit of gossip and domestic scandal that only once or twice does he pause to say something pertinent. And finally, there was the aristocratic Roman, Pietro della Valle, who travelled on the West Coast of India in 1623 and wrote a number of letters home to relatives. In them these are a few suggestive passages.

Linschoten, an Amsterdammer who had long lived in Portugal, travelled to Goa in the 1580's in the retinue of Dom Vicente da Fonseca, the Archbishop of Goa; Pyrard, a French sailor, was shipwrecked after taking part in a dismal French trade venture to the Indies, whereupon he eventually found his way to the Malabar coast. Both were keen observers who shared no such bias as Mocquet's and it is safe to assume their accounts were independent as possibly could be. Neither knew or writes of the other, and while Pyrard might conceivably have read Linschoten's *Itinerario* (French edition, 1598) before he left home in 1601, it seems unlikely that he was so intellectual, or could have remembered much of its detail when he arrived in Goa six eventful years later—more than a decade after Linschoten had sailed away.

I do not claim that these four foreigners had a monopoly on Goan reportage, but I have chosen them only because they wrote even while Couto lived in Goa. (It is for this reason for example, that I have not employed the account of Jean Baptiste Tavernier, whose writings were based on visits which took place thirty years after Couto's death.) What these men write, however, fully corroborate Couto's claims. (For further contemporary substantiation, please see the Appendix.)

Of viceregal policy, Linschoten and Pyrard are, if anything, blunter than the old chronicler. Pyrard reports :

> So it is for the three years the viceroy and the other captains and governors are in the Indies, they take more pains to enrich themselves than to protect and to preserve the state; and in so short a time, they are unable to effect great results in war. For in the first year, it is all they can do to learn the details and forms of government, know the various peoples and dispatch fleets and armies. The second year, they fill their purses. For they give nothing of their own, and if aught has to be given to the (native) kings, ambassadors, etc., it is at the expense of the king. The Portuguese captains and lords receive no other [personal] presents than licenses to make voyages and trade, or privileges and office.
>
> The third year, the viceroy in some cases employs in visiting all the fortresses of the Indian coast, with a large force, i.e., between Coilan and Ormuz. But he draws large profits from this voyage, as well as from the captains and governors, as from the other officers, and from the countries visited, although the king is debited with the whole expense. So it is no wonder that the viceroys enrich themselves so much, nor that their officers and servants, who to the

number of fifty or sixty live at the palace sumptuously, do the same.[2]

Based upon the same popular image, Linschoten's three stages of government are even more graphic :

> When the viceroys have continued out their time, which is as soon as another viceroy arriveth. . . [they] prepare the palace, so that there stayeth not a stool or bench within the house, nor one penny in the treasure, but they leave the house as bare and naked as possible. . . so that the new viceroy must make provision to furnish it, and gather a new treasure. . . For they say, and it is found to be most true, that the first year of the viceroy's time, he hath enough to do to repair and furnish his house, and to know the manners and customs of the countries without any further troubling of himself. The second year, to gather treasure and look unto his particular profits, for the which he came to India. The third and last year, to prepare himself and set all things in order, that he may not be overtaken and surprised by the new viceroy when he cometh, but that he might return into Portugal with the goods which he had scraped together. The same is to be understood of all the captains in the forts and all of the officers in India, whereof it is to be considered how they use themselves in their places and the king's service, whereof the inhabitants and married Portuguese do continually speak, but they are far from the king's hearing, who knoweth not, but that the officers do him good service, whereby there is small amendment and remedy to be hoped for.[3]

He continues :

> There is not one of them that esteemeth the profit of the commonwealth, or the furtherance of the king's service, but rather their own particular commodities, as you very well may think, so that the common speech is, that [people] will never look for any furtherance of the commonwealth by any viceroy, as long as the government of three years is not altered [4]

Regarding the practice of highjacking fortresses, Linschoten has this to say :

> The viceroys in the last year of their government do use to visit the forts lying round about the country...on the north and south side of Goa, to see how they are governed. They look well into them, but commonly another (note : doubtless the *vedores de fazenda*) supplieth their place, and if they do it themselves, it is to fill their purses and to get presents, (rather) than further the commonwealth.[5]

"As for salary and fixed pay of the viceroy," Pyrard takes up again, "it is but a small matter compared with the great profits he can make during the three years of his office ; these amount sometimes to a million of gold. His fixed pay is thirty thousand cruzados, each worth two *pardaos* or thereabout. This, however, would not be sufficient for his maintenance, were it not for the presents, the profits and the perquisites, which amount to a large sum. As soon as he arrives, all the captains, governors and king's officers come promptly to meet him, and to obtain some favor of him, either an expedition, a dignity, or other such thing ; and with this in view they give him grand presents, and even without such intent, according to the value and revenue of their fortresses, whereof the least is worth from twelve to fifteen thousand cruzados, for they cannot well plunder and make their fortunes without his favor. All of them have their offices for three years only, during which they must amass enough for the rest of their lives."[6]

Says Linschoten : " . . . they have great presents and gifts bestowed upon them from all sides. For it is the custom in those countries, when any viceroy cometh newly over, that all the kings bordering about Goa, and all that have peace and friendship with the Portuguese, do then send their ambassadors unto him, to confirm their (alliances) with great and rich present, therewith likewise to bid the viceroy welcome, which amounteth to a great mass of treasure : these presents...the Jesuits...had (customarily) obtained of the king, ... until a long time since, a viceroy named Dom Luís de Ataíde (1568-1571) ... refused to let them have them, saying the king, being in

Portugal, know not what was being given him (in India), and that those presents were being given to the viceroy and not unto the king, and said the king had no power to give them unto the Jesuits: so that he kept them for himself...; from this time ... since viceroys have used to keep them for themselves ..."[7]

Pyrard continues: "He (the viceroy) has many offices in his gift. Those who have been in the king's service must have their certificates from him, and then only is it valued; it must also be signed by the captains. But the mischief is that the viceroy takes money of all those gifts and offices, and makes out to the king that he has given them in full."

"In this way he answers numbers of petitions for gifts and presents, and the *Vedor de fazenda* and the treasurers are in league with him, none of whom like parting with money. For all that, they charge the king in account, and so they do with the pay of the soldiers, officers and mariners."[8] Pyrard adds that the *vedor* also cost the crown vast amounts in the (non-) payment of customs duties; Portuguese remitting goods to Lisbon regularly arranged matters with him in advance and then the shipments would be assessed at a trifling amount by customs officials. Observed Pyrard: the vedor could "play the thief" in the royal treasury more effectively than anyone else save the viceroy himself.[9]

From such a withering enfilade of testimonial, several things may be judged about the *Soldado Prático*. In the first place, Couto seems vindicated from any suspicion that his frustrations had caused him to magnify a normal amount of seventeenth century chicanery into a vast schema of corruption. Pyrard and Linschoten, whose interests ranged in so many directions that their Goan writings form but an episode in a panorama of description, could not have felt so intensely as Couto about its plight. Yet in outline, they tell much the same story.

In addition, one can see immediately that with a few exceptions Couto had far more insight than the less experienced men into actual mechanisms of Goan distemper. Where they speak in general terms of certificates with price tags, raids on the king's treasury and lucrative trips to the fortresses, Couto shows how the abuses were actually developed. On the other hand, it is apparent that their very disinterestedness allowed them to perceive a simple fact that never seems to have occurred to Couto, if only because he was himself a part of the mechanism : that the three-year term was entirely too short a time for officials to govern effectively. They saw clearly it only promoted a frantic stuffing of pockets.

To the voices of Linschoten and Pyrard de Laval, it is perhaps now appropriate to add briefly that of the embittered Jean Mocquet, a man who could see nothing good in all India including the Indians themselves, or at least their Hindu religion. He arrived there, just as Pyrard was about to leave, that is about 1606. He supports Couto's social judgments that men no longer had use for fighting, but instead had taken on airs and he verifies the pitiful state of soldiers just arrived from Portugal.[10] Only the scoundrels, he said, managed to get ahead.

"As soon as they arrive in the Indies, they make themselves gallants, calling themselves *fidalgos*, or gentlemen, though they be but peasants and tradesmen. They themselves relate that a certain one among them named Fernando, who had kept hogs in Portugal, coming to the Indies and adding three letters to his name, caused himself to be called Dom Fernando, and was in a little time so well-known and esteemed among the women mestices (half-castes, often wives of officials and merchants) that one having chosen him for her servant, she caused him to ride about with a chain of gold around his neck and a great many slaves after him; but one day it happened that his master's son, whom he had served in his own country for a swineherd, having met him in this rich equipage . . . saluted him, saying . . . 'God save ye, Fernando, how goes it ?' But the other, making shew as if he knew him not, asked who he was, to which the other made answer, was he not the same who formerly kept hogs for my father?" Whereupon Fernando lost his swagger. Mocquet's conclusion: "Manners change when they arrive. They get a boy to carry their parasol and cloak and take on majestic gravity . . . all become *fidalgos* and noblemen, changing their more obscure names to more illustrious. I know one who enrolled himself for the war, and he changed his name three or four times, as 'twas found out by the secretaries and registers of Goa."[11]

In one of his rare political observations, Mocquet writes:

> These designs (to punish allies who trafficked with Hollanders) were never effected, for not long after came another viceroy, who was more intent on filling his coffers than the war, during his three years, which is commonly worth to them above 600,000 cruzados; especially those who cruelly tyrannize over the poor people.

Of how these poor people must have felt, Pyrard leaves no doubt whatever. He reports: "They tell a parable, how that one day there lay a poor man at the door of a church, his legs full of ulcers and so covered with flies as was pitiful to behold; up came a neighbour, who thinking to do him a kindness, drove away the flies; whereas the poor patient was much vexed, saying that the flies he drove away already had their bellies full and would not bite him more, whereas those that would come would be hungry and would sting him worse. So it is, they say with the viceroys, for the gorged depart and the hungry arrive."[12]

To this, Della Valle added in 1623 that the Portuguese were "weaker and more confused in their government than ever, and all things (were) in bad order . . . for remedy of which they took no other course, but loaded themselves with new, unusual and most heavy impositions, to the manifest ruine of the state, taking no care to prevent the hourly exorbitant defraudations of the public incomes, which otherwise would be sufficient to maintain the (government) without new (taxes). But if the thefts continue, both the public incomes and the new (taxes), and as many as they can invent, will all be swallowed up."[13]

It can be observed from the foregoing testimony that Couto's allegations in the *Soldado Prático* were essentially correct.[14] One can also gather that the dishonest goings-on at Goa and the surrounding Portuguese fortress territories were virtually public knowledge. Of course, the writers did not have the familiarity with the bureaucracy's inner working that Couto possessed, and that shows in their writings, too.

But there was one other eyewitness to the corruption, a Portuguese, who even though he never served in such responsible posts as did Couto, nevertheless brought a searching intelligence to the problem and took a somewhat different—and even wider—view than did the old chronicler. For he was in many ways the real *soldado prático* : he shows how the corruption impinged on Portugal's military strength—and seriously weakened it. Moreover, the remedies he suggests sound far more sensible than Couto's, at least to twentieth century ears. Until now, he has been puzzlingly neglected by historians.

NOTES

1. They were the Italians Cesare Federici, Filippo Sassetti, and Gasparo Balbi, the Frenchmen Jean Mocquet, Sieur de Feynes, the Comte de Montfort, and François Pyrard, The Pole, Christophe Pawlowski, the Dutchman Jan Huyghen van Linschoten, the Fleming Jacques de Coutre, and the Englishmen Ralph Fitch and John Newberry, although Newberry wrote only a few letters (reproduced by Hakluyt in the *Principall Navigations*). Pietro Della Valle's visit of 1623 came only seven years after Couto's death and so I have included him, too.
2. François Pyrard, *the Voyage of François Pyrard of Laval to the East Indies* (ed. & tr. Albert Gray), 2 vols. in 3, London (Hakluyt Society), 1887-1889, II, p. 85. Another traveler, Johan Albert van Mandelslo, who visited Goa in 1638, wrote: " . . . every year he makes a visit for sixty or eighty leagues about, which is worth to him very much. But the presents which the neighbouring princes and governors make to him are not to be valued . . . ." *The Voyages and Travels of J. Albert de Mandelslo*, tr. John Davies of Kidwelly, London, 1662.
3. Jan Huyghen van Linschoten, *The Voyage of Jan Huyghen van Linschoten to the East Indies* (from the English translation of 1598; ed. A.C. Burnell and P.A. Thiele). 2 vols., London (Hakluyt Society), 1885, I, pp. 221-22. Mandelslo writes (when the new viceroy arrives): "his predecessor makes way for him upon the first news he receives of his arrival, unfurnishes the palace and leaves only the guards and the bare walls." Mandelslo, *Voyages and Travels*, p. 108. I have somewhat revised the 1598 English translation of Linschoten, which sometimes strays from the original. If one reads Dutch, it is preferable to use the edition of 1596, entitled: *Itinerario ofte Schipvaert van Jan Huyghen van Linschoten naar Oost ofte Portugaels Indien*, Amsterdam, 1596, fls. 49-50.
4. Linschoten, Ibid.

5. Ibid., pp. 219-20.
6. Pyrard, Vol. II, pp. 83-84.
7. Linschoten, Hakluyt Society translation, pp. 220-221; original version pp. 50-51.
8. Pyrard, Vol. II, pp. 83-84. Regarding the profits of the viceregal office Mandelslo writes: "the king of Spain has many lords to gratify with an employment, which enriches them sufficiently in that time (3 years)." Mandelslo, *Voyages and Travels*, p. 108.
9. Ibid., pp. 43-47.
10. Jean Mocquet, *Voyages en Afrique, Asie, Indes Orientales & Occidentales*, Paris, 1617, p, 287. The translation is by Nathaniel Pullen (1696), in the London edition, entitled *Travels and Voyages into Africa, Asia, and America, the East and West Indies; Syria, Jerusalem and the Holy Land*, pp. 246-247.
11. Ibid., pp. 303-304; London edition, p. 247.
12. Pyrard, Vol. II, p. 87.
13. Pietro Della Valle, *The travels of Pietro della Valle in India* (from the English translation of 1664 by G. Havers; ed. Edward Grey) 2 vols., London (Hakluyt Society), 1892, pp. 196-197.
14. For evidences of corruption at a later stage, see Winius, *The Fatal History*, Chapters VI and VII.

5

SILVEIRA'S REFORMAÇÃO
The "Real" Soldado Prático

WHILE Couto has made known the extent of Goan corruption during his era and visitors to Goa have corroborated his allegations fully, there still remains a considerable gap between what he proves—namely the existence of extensive official miscreance, and what he predicts—namely the consequent downfall of Portuguese India. Certainly, within forty years of his death, little of its former greatness remained, but whether the sort of corruption he reveals had anything directly to do with this decline is highly unclear. At least people of the late twentieth century no longer share his Biblical faith that the Deity would have brought about the ruination merely to punish the Children of Portugal for their sins.

Instead, we tend to reason that Portugal was too small a power to resist the entry into Asia of the hostile English and the Dutch—and that, consequently, her imperial time had passed. This may sound more modern and acceptable to our ears, and it is substantially true. But in a way, it begs the issue. For one thing, Portugal was always small, even when Almeida and Albuquerque did the original empire building, and for another, neither the English nor the Dutch were ever so overwhelmingly strong that the Portuguese were merely bowled over. Rather, time and time again, the battle accounts as cited by modern writers like C.R. Boxer, Admiral Botelho de Sousa and myself show that better Portuguese tactics and strategy—and in most encounters only a few more soldiers and ships in the right places—would have made all the difference between defeat and victory. Moreover, in many places like Macau,

Moçambique, Malacca and Ceylon, the Portuguese (temporarily) turned the tables and outfought the enemy. If one studies the terrain very closely, it would often seem that the difference between the adversaries was smaller than one might suppose—and indeed often resolved itself into a matter of efficiency and martial craft.

You will notice that we are now talking of Portuguese decline not in terms of corruption, but of battles and the military. It would seem we have left Couto far behind in our discussion of Portuguese decline. In fact we have not; it merely happens that we need a new witness to show us the connection between mere corruption and actual imperial weakness, Franciso Rodrigues de Silveira. In many ways, Silveira was the true *soldado prático*, for it is he who actually concerns himself with soldiery—while Couto really only deals with the conduct of the bureaucracy. Silveira transposes the *decadência* into a different key; he argues that corruption, the insatiable greed of the viceroy and his officials, were at the bottom of Portuguese military impotence.

Silveira's manuscript, the *Reformação da Milicia e Governo do Estado da India Oriental*, has reposed since the 19th century in the Additional Manuscripts collection of the British Museum, a highly conspicuous location which, one thinks, should have resulted in its becoming familiar to virtually all students of Portuguese imperial history. Yet it remains practically unknown to them. I would like to digress for a moment before turning to its contents and its author, to suggest why.

The British Museum Library has no omnibus manuscript catalogue of its own extensive collections but instead it uses ones prepared by scholars, usually those of the countries in which the papers originated. Copies of these exist not only at the Museum Library, but in many research libraries throughout the world, as well. In the case of Portuguese manuscripts, the original guide was compiled by one Federigo Francisco de la Figanière, then first secretary to the Portuguese Embassy, in 1853. By 1917, hundreds of new documents had come into the Museum's possession, and at this time, a young scholar, the Conde de Tovar, then working in diplomatic history, set himself to update it. Such work is always exasperating at best, and when he came to the Silveira manuscript, he either mistook it for one of the 18th century—or else a typesetter made his intended "séc. XVII" read instead "XVIII" and the mistake was not proofread out. Since few scholars are interested in the Portuguese Asian empire after 1700, this error might tend to mislead them into passing Silveira's *Reformação* over. Even if they did escape this trap, however, there lay another in wait for them.

For after the citation regarding Silveira's manuscript on pp. 189-190 of his supplement to Figanière, the compiler notes that one A. de S.S. Costa Lôbo, in 1877, published excerpts and extracts from the manuscript, under the title *Memórias de um Soldado da Índia.*[1] Since it is a practice among historians—and usually a sound one—never to consult in manuscript sources which have previously been published, it is then only natural for one to look up the printed version first, especially if one is using the catalogue at a library other than the British Museum itself. At any rate, printed words are easier to read than handwritten ones—and even an extract might give one an idea whether Silveira merited further scrutiny. In this case, though, Costa Lôbo did not provide the usual editor's function of serving as guide and honest broker. His (dis-)service to Silveira was to muddle him almost beyond recognition.

Reading between the lines, as it were, it is easy enough to perceive that despite the more than two centuries separating the two writers, they represented different social classes and espoused opposite philosophies. Paradoxically, the earlier, Silveira, is the more modern, the advocate of social mobility, while Costa Lôbo, the aristocrat represents the now vanished idea of noble pre-eminence in society. He could not stomach Silveira's egalitarianism.

Costa Lôbo explained it this way: "Sifting among the rich collections of the British Museum library, through the Portuguese manuscripts, eventually one caught my eye which I judged to be of considerable historical interest. It is number 25:419 of the collection called Additional Manuscripts . . . . The principal aim of the writer was no less than to clean up the system of government of India and establish there the rule of justice, which did not arouse the slightest breath of interest." He then went on to say, "And truthfully, neither did his reforms hold any practical value for the times in which they were proposed, much less for today when they are completely destitute of importance."[2]

"Silveira belonged to that numerous class who imagine that social perfection can be attained through a clever combination of legislative rules and prohibitions," he concluded. Like all conservatives, he supposed that hoping for a moral regeneration of the upper classes was a better road to travel than, as did Silveira himself, a change effected through new laws.[3] Maybe Costa Lôbo was correct, but I think most of the world now stands firmly on Silveira's side.

Costa Lôbo, however, relented partially on the old *arbitrista*, or memorialist, when he went on to say: "What in the manuscript of Silveira is worth recalling is his testimony, though rough and crude, about the life and the customs of his times and the narrative of events in which he took part." Hence, his solution was obvious: submerge the *arbitrista* in Silveira's manuscript and turn him into a memoir writer. To do this, Costa Lôbo embarked upon a remarkable intellectual endeavour. He reorganized the whole text of Silveira around categories of his own confection, such as *Desembarque em Goa*, *Expedição ao Mar Vermelho*, *Expedição á Costa Oriental de Africa* and *Vitorias de André Furtado do Mendonça*, and so forth. Excerpts from Silveira were cast in a different type face from Costa Lôbo's own comments; then, Costa Lôbo happily mixed the two to form a brand-new sequence of his own invention.

The effect is to have thrown Humpty Dumpty off the wall, in order to break him into a thousand fragments, and then, with scissors, the paste pot and a running commentary to put him together in a new way never thought possible by all the king's horses and men. Costa Lôbo must have copied out the whole *Reformação*—all 48,500 words of it—then literally snipped it apart, classifying, or re-classifying the whole of Silveira's thinking according to chapter headings of his own choosing. He must only have relented about excluding Silveira's reformist thinking after he ran out of narrative material, but was still left with a pile of Silveira's copied-out text. For not until page 181 of his book, in a chapter entitled *Soldados*—which is really the main theme of Silveira's whole *Reformação* - that he comes to terms with the *arbistrista.* Then his only aim, apparently, is to make Silveira inept, naive and ridiculous.

Costa Lôbo worked over a hundred years ago, and I will refrain from heaping upon him the same sort of scorn he reserved for Silveira. I need say no more than this: it is best to discard his work as an impediment to understanding the *Reformação*, which becomes hopelessly confused and lost in the reshuffling.

About the only utility of Costa Lôbo's editing of Silveira's manuscript is that he supplies some supplementary information about contemporary viceroys and cites pertinent passages from Couto and Faria e Sousa and others, which can be useful. But under no circumstances should one use Costa Lôbo's rendition unaccompanied by the original manuscript. The reason for this is simple: Costa Lôbo has excerpted all the illustrative historical narrative to the front of his *Memórias* and buried all Silveira's prefacing thoughts about it in the back. So let us turn again to Additional Ms. 25: 419.

In the very first pages of his work Silveira quickly comes to the heart of the matter when he says that the essence of the Portuguese empire in Asia was military force—"The aim of the whole discovery . . . was to impede the trade in spices . . . which via Egypt was carried into the possession of the Venetians and from thence were transferred to all the provinces of Europe, from which they all drew a great, almost inestimable profit, as well as from all sorts of other things of greatest value—things from which Portugal, a poor and limited kingdom could become rich." He goes on immediately to say "And this is the basis of being able to acquire this commerce: the domination of the shores of India against which (in spite of the long voyage the Portuguese must make) the peoples there are incapable of making adequate naval resistance. The purpose of the fortresses is to act as brakes on all navigation in those seas, in order to impede the natural commerce, to keep it from passing to Turkey."[4]

Hence it is that Silveira establishes the context for what he proposes to say: that the whole existence of the *Estado da*

India Oriental depends upon an effective military force. But, he observes, this force has been allowed to decay. The root of the problem is the *cubiça insaciavel*, the insatiable greed, of the viceroy and ruling classes who embezzled the moneys needed for preparedness. The early chapters of the Costa Lôbo version, incidentally, are no more than those historical passages which Silveira has written to illustrate the malfunctions occasioned by this thievery and by its consequences, disorganization and inadequate leadership of Portuguese military power.

Silveira's *Reformação*, in immediately tying the whole survival of the state to its military function – in fact showing that the state's wealth is an artificial creation of Portuguese naval force—sounds a much more fundamental note than does Couto's *O Soldado Prático*. As mentioned in the opening paragraph of this chapter, Couto has specifically chosen the malfunctioning of the higher officialdom as the terrain for his dialogues, but he neglects to tell why the abuses he describes are destructive, except to suggest that they are offensive to God, who is using Holland as a scourge to punish the whole Portuguese nation. Silveira, to be sure, occasionally gives voice to this purely Biblical nation, but his thesis is that whatever damages Portugal's military effectiveness in Asia erodes the underpinnings of the whole state. I suspect that Couto was more interested by the time he wrote in exposing the inter-working abuses of the higher offices than he was in dealing with the state's military foundation, per se. It is ironic that he calls his work *O Soldado Prático*—and then talks about everything but the soldiery.

Silveira does talk about it and he follows his analysis of the importance to Portugal of military power with a description of the arrival of a soldier in Goa with the yearly fleet. Unless he has friends or connections, says Silveira, he will sleep in a doorway, or a boat—and eventually perhaps simply disappear—either die of disease and malnutrition, fade into the wretched native population, or even flee Goa completely and take service with an Indian ruler, possibly even one hostile to Portugal. The only soldiers who prosper are unscrupulous riffraff in the service of the viceroys or other officers or *fidalgos*, used mostly as private armies when not serving on campaign. Because ordinary soldiers were to be paid only when they were needed for military operations in season, they might have to wait an indefinite time before collecting a salary. This was sorry enough, but in practice matters were far worse: viceroys were frequently so greedy that they were willing to pay the soldiers only in part, or even nothing at all.[5] Then, when a muster was proclaimed, soldiers would not turn out knowing that they were being asked to endanger their lives gratuitously. To which the viceregal reply would be to send out goon squads to find the soldiers and jail them, but then turn them over to the military to serve—of course without pay.[6] On one such occasion, to which he was a witness, Silveira says troops who had already embarked in the Mandovi roads opposite Goa railed, half good naturedly, at a viceroy who was seeing them off, about their want of salary. At this, the royal lieutenant flew into such a wanton rage that he had himself rowed to the vessel, stormed over its rail and made the air whistle with his gold-headed cane, all the while threatening the soldiers with beheading unless they should plead with him for mercy. Instead, the frightened men jumped into the water, followed by curses "the likes of which had never emerged from anybody's mouth, whether in command or in government, much less in such an exalted position." Then, the viceroy, "as satisfied and smug as if he had just achieved a famous victory against the Turks," returned to his barge.[7]

As they mustered in, soldiers were expected to provide their own weaponry—the nature of which was left entirely to their own choice. As Silveira shows, this was as highly capricious business—some recruits showed up with rusty, old blades, others with a musket or a pike, still others with fancy weapons really made only for show—and some with modish clothing, but no arms at all.[8] Commanders cared little, anyway. When the time came to fight, there was no strategy, no planning and not much of anything else. For example, the annual campaign against the Kunjali pirates in that part of the Malabar Coast dominated by the Samorin of Calicut was only a mindless *pro forma* exercise: everybody knew that the soldiers dropped off each year to blockade the river inlet to the pirate stronghold did no good at all. The pirates had already received their season's rice supply before the operation began. Moreover, many of the armadas sent out to intimidate the enemy had no idea of how to go about it. The commanders were mostly timeserving, waiting for better commands, and merely sailed aimlessly about. On one of the few occasions they did carry out a landing operation to attack the Malabar pirates, their operation was so badly officered that the men all ran off in search of booty and ended up dead in a counter attack. Even many of the survivors drowned when their very ships did not wait for them. In general, the only tactics employed were these: everybody simply charged the enemy, street-gang style, and if that failed, everybody fled.[8]

Silveira reckoned that there were over two thousand Portuguese soldiers who had left Goa and taken up residence in Bengal alone, men who should form the basis of a formidable Portuguese army in Asia.[9] Yet the army in Goa was only about 1500 men strong, and it had continually to be replenished from Portugal because of the viceroys' regular mulcting of the military payroll. He says that these sent out urgent requests to the king each year for more soldiers to be sent out in the fleets, as if they themselves were not the cause of the scarcity of suitable manpower. At the same time, because Silveira had returned to Portugal in 1598, he could observe and report accordingly that the local officials, when told by the king to find men for India service, used only the most despicable methods, in essence, taking bribes from the poor not to select one of their family members to meet their quotas – then doing so, anyway, chosing the poorest and least able to resist. Hence, India was provided with the unfittest type of recruit.[10]

Naturally, with such poor, unpaid or underpaid recruits and such sloppy officering, the soldiers had little respect for their commanders, and the officers little regard for them. Hence the resulting confusion was inevitable. Even an experienced observer sent out from Portugal was unable to find answers to the dilemma because he had no real authority and because he was not prepared to be radical enough.[11]

Discipline in the fortresses was as lax as it was in the field. Silveira confesses that he believes garrison duty breeds lazy or vicious soldiers; living in town amid concubines and children scarcely made for tautness of mind or body. In Ormuz, where he served for a time, he says that the Moslems—potential enemies—came and went within the citadel without any hindrance, and that there were frequently three times as many of them milling about inside as there were Portuguese soldiers on guard. An attack by stealth could have brought Portuguese rule there to a sudden end. Sometimes men on guard even leaned their pikes against an outside wall or gate and then went off to play ball around a corner. Silveira says he finally got one captain's ear who promised to do something about it; unfortunately, the man soon fell sick and died.[12]

Having made these observations about indiscipline, Silveira then proceeds to illustrate them with stories from his own military experiences. Far from being *rude e chão* as Costa Lôbo believes, they are savage and bitter vignettes which reveal a penetrating mind and a mastery of language. Please note that nearly all of the events described, that is from 1586 to 1598, fall within the period of Couto's lost *Década Undécima.* They do not constitute a full-scale chronicle of Portuguese activities such as Couto's missing eleventh volume would have provided, but they were written with no less vigorous a dedication to the truth and no less intelligence. Silveira was a participant in most of the important campaigns during his term of duty, and so he should be consulted by anybody studying the period and area. I will cite only two examples. His first vignette concerning the naval expedition into the Red Sea in 1586 not only scores its point, but is also bitingly funny: a rich prize, a large pilgrimage ship full of treasure and Moslem damsels was captured, then allowed to escape when chaplains accompanying the naval forces vetoed the sending of a prize crew to man it because the Christians, once aboard, might commit carnal sins with the damsels. Instead, the ship was merely commanded to follow the Portuguese squadron, but slipped away in the night. For the rest, the expedition accomplished nothing. Silveira's question: why did the chaplains have such influence in the first place over the naval commanders?[13]

In another vein entirely, Silveira convincingly explains why Jayawira Bandara, commander of Sinhalese troops under Pero

Lopes de Sousa in 1594, was murdered by Sousa and his captains. Versions dating from many years later have it that the enemy leader fooled Sousa into thinking Jayawira was a traitor. Not so, says Silveira: the Portuguese wanted the enormous wealth Jayawira was thought to possess. In short, though he does not pretend to be an historian, Silveira indeed is prime authority for about a dozen years worth of campaigns in which he was a participant.[14]

Just as a recitation of the few known facts about Diogo do Couto's career helps one understand why he wrote his *Soldado Prático,* a similar review of the even scantier biographical information about Silveira is more than adequate to establish his reasons for writing the *Reformação.* But while there is a sprinkling of letters and documents pertaining to Couto and even a short biographical sketch of him by Manuel Severim de Faria, all that can be gathered about Silveira's life barring some future discovery (perhaps from a notarial archive in North Portugal) is to be found in his own writings. Fortunately, the nature, if not the intent, of his books are partly autobiographical. (The second, incidentally, is called the *Discursos sobre a reformacam da iustiça da Beira e Antre Douro e Minho,* is bound with the *Reformação* in the British Museum copy, but exists as a separate manuscript in the Ajuda Palace Library, as Codex 49-XI-19.)

He was born in or about 1558 because he tells us he was 27 when he embarked for India in 1585, whence he returned in 1598. He must; like so many of his countrymen, have fallen on the hard times that followed King Sebastian's death if he sailed for India as a common soldier at such a relatively advanced age. The fact that he seems to have remained a soldier, at best a petty official or non-commissioned officer, during his entire service would indicate by itself that he was of rather humble origins. But the fact that he knew Latin and could allude to both Biblical and classical history—and indeed write eloquently—would either point to his being of the agricultural middle classes or else that he was an intelligent peasant boy who had been educated for holy orders. The date of his death is totally unknown, but he may well have lived to see the Restauração. It is entirely certain that he was alive after 1635, because the British Museum manuscript is directed to the Duchess of Mantua and he has written the dedication in his own hand. (She came to rule only in December, 1634). The work in part dates from much earlier, perhaps almost forty years before, to judge from its context. Moreover, he writes in Book Four, which post-dates the first three, that he began trying to find someone who would listen to his ideas immediately upon his return from India in 1598.[15]

Besides this he tells us that he had a ferocious and protracted dispute with a *tabelião*—a notary—and that this landed him in prison for 18 months, where he composed the last book of his *Reformação* in 1619. He must have had a wide circle of literary friends, both Castillian and Portuguese, to judge from the fact that there are no less than three poems in the British Museum codex, one in Spanish by a certain Don Francisco de Vargas and two by Portuguese writers. There is no statement in his book as to how he earned his living after his return from India (or even before he went, for that matter). But he did own land near Lamego, which he must either have inherited or purchased with income from a pension, since the twelve years of his India service far exceeds the term necessary for retirement at the end of the 16th century. So he must have ended his life as a (small) gentleman farmer.

His career in India is almost as circumstantial. He certainly served in the armadas based out of Goa and he was resident for a time in Ormuz, where he was close enough to one of its commanders to give him advice. In Goa, he describes how one viceroy tricked a *vedor de fazenda* by switching documents with him through the complicity of a crooked *tabelião*.[16] This would at least indicate that he was employed close enough to the viceregal palace to pick up information from somebody—or, conceivably, he might even have become a petty official in his last triennium. His literacy and his apparent ability to remain near the seats of power would probably explain why he was able to obtain an office if indeed he did so. For as Diogo do Couto remarks, many *soldados* were not this fortunate, but allowed themselves to be tricked out of what they earned. Silveira would have been too wise for that.[17]

What made him turn *arbitrista* on his return to Portugal he does not spell out, either, though I think what he says about the wrongness of giving administrative posts only to *fidalgos* and not to capable and experienced commoners easily explains it: he was like Couto, only more so—of even humbler birth and entirely unable to rise beyond petty rank. I also suspect that he may have been even abler than the famous chronicler; certainly, he was more descriptive in his narrative and more imaginative in his suggestions for improving the polity of the *Estado da India Oriental*. Great ability so ill-rewarded must have eaten at his vitals all his life.

There is absolutely no indication that he ever used his writings to solicit a reward, even in the form of a governmental post. If he ever had that particular idea, he would have soon been disabused of it; immediately after his return from India to Lisbon, he set out to make the rounds of the governing establishment—and it is no wonder he reports he got nowhere, for people in power are notoriously unwilling to take unsolicited advice (even good advice) from bystanders, in this case, a commoner to boot. "I do not know whether it did any good at all," he tells us. "I only know that I was born under a star to care, sweat and die all my life to set straight the crimes of those who got rich committing them."[18]

The following chapter contains some extraordinary ideas, the same "silly" ones which so offended Costa Lôbo. But they do not sound so to our ears because Silveira only illustrates a favourite theme of mine—that we reserve the term "modernity" for things in the past which we might have applied or invented ourselves. In this case, his thought processes indeed conform to those of the mid-twentieth century, while those of his "mediator," Costa Lôbo, are closer to the thinking of someone like Metternich.

NOTES

1. The Conde de Tovar's work is called *Catálogo dos Manuscritos Portugueses ou Relativos á Portugal Existentes no Museu Británico*, Lisboa (Academia das Ciências), 1932.

2. A. de S.S. Costa Lóbo (ed & comp.) *Memórias de um Soldado da India, compiladas de um Manuscripto Portuguez do Museu Británnico,* Lisboa (Imprensa Nacional), 1877, pp. 3-5.
3. Ibid., pp. 5-6.
4. *Reformação da Milicia e Governo do Estado da India Oriental,* hereafter cited as *Reformação*, fl. 4v.-5.
5. Ibid., fl. 7.
6. Ibid., fl. 72. v. From what the Fleming, Jacques de Coutre, writes, however, at least some *soldados* turned the tables on the government, staying around only long enough to enlist and collect their mustering-in salary before "fleeing through the palm groves" to Moslem territories in the north, where they used this pay as capital to enter into trade outside the Portuguese pale. See *La Vida de Iaques de Coutre,* fls. 262,263.
7. Ibid., fl. 74.
8. Ibid., fls. 15v.-19v.
9. Ibid., fl. 108.
10. Ibid., fl. 109v.
11. This was D. António de Leiva, a veteran of Lepanto.
12. *Reformação,* fl. 66-67 ; 104v. The captain was apparently one Rui Gomes da Gran. Silveira's allegation is substantiated by a *Carta Regia* of 15 January, 1607, printed in *Documentos Remetidos da India, ou Livros das Monções,* (ed. Raymundo António de Bulhão Pato), 9 vols. 1880-date, Lisboa (Acadêmia das Ciencias), I, p. 184.
13. Ibid., fl. 23v. ff.
14. Ibid., fl. 50.
15. Ibid., fl. 189v.
16. Ibid., fl. 123v.
17. *Soldado Prático*, pp. 152 ff.
18. *Reformação*, fl. 68v.

6

SILVEIRA'S REFORMAÇÃO
Remedial Measures

FRANCISCO Rodrigues de Silveira was above all a practical man and he must have had long weeks to ponder how the system might be improved while he was rowed about in galleys or stood garrison duty. The answers he formulated have none of the visionary about them, as Costa Lôbo would have us believe, but, as will be seen, they actually come to grips with Portuguese Asia's real problems. (In contrast, Couto's suggestions, one will remember, might only serve to convince us that contemporaries did not possess a real notion of how to remedy the abuses he describes.) Of course, the time for making any changes in the system is long past and no *arbitrista's* schemes now have practical applications—in this Costa Lôbo is quite right. Yet this is not to say that the best of them are devoid of value for historians.

The pattern of the past itself obviously represents the changes wrought by ideas and plans which were actually put into effect, that is, the actions of those in power, or else those who gained power. Hence, revolutions, reforms and variations in course. But my point is this : the unsuccessful ideas and programs of others, in effect *arbitristas* of all periods in history, insofar as they represent other thoughts and provide other blueprints, can supply us with our soundest underpinnings of all for our own historical judgments. For instance, Silveira's argument that *fidalguia* alone was a poor basis on which to run a government or military is just the kind of judgment we might make today concerning the managerial crisis of Portuguese Asia, but we might make it only hesitantly, without confidence that the sixteenth century was itself capable of thinking in our terms. Silveira is just our man—he not only makes the point in the historical period we are dealing with, but then builds a whole plan for a reformed militia which incorporates equality of opportunity. Couto, you will remember, has expressed this sentiment, too, though without constructing such a reform around it.[1] Silveira's idea that appointments, even the highest, must be made according to service and experience alone, appears to have been conceived during the sixteenth century, before the Dutch example could have been the obvious point of departure.[2] Silveira is similarly highly critical of the influence of the clergy on state policy.[3] Which is interesting, too.

Silveira's central plan is for a compact, yet practical and efficient armed force, one which might provide historians with an alternative by which to assess the historical reality. It is one which we would never dare dream up for ourselves, because it might not seem appropriate to the *Zeitgeist*.

Silveira begins by saying—and I tend to agree with him—that there would be revenues enough for what he proposes, were not all the incomes stolen by the viceroys and their henchmen. Then there would be adequate manpower if the soldiers which had been sent to India were not all driven away from Goa by neglect, lack of pay and cruel treatment.[4] What was needed, he said, was a militia totalling about 4000 men, and within this a striking force, to be active at all times, of a little over a thousand men. These he proposed to divide into sixteen companies, each with its captain, a man chosen purely on the basis of his experience, service and ability. Troops were to be strictly disciplined, but with kindness. They should be armed with high quality and rational weaponry, provided by the state, because few soldiers could afford the superior muskets and because what was most needed was a balance of different kinds of weaponry—pikes, swords, shields, and so on which random self-outfitting was hardly likely to provide. Victualling was to be provided out of soldiers' quarterly pay as administered by the captains; hence, soldiers would be regularly employed and adequately fed. You will notice how far ahead of his time

Silveira was, for he has anticipated military supply and quartermastering facilities, then more than a century in the future. Light galleys, each with 35 men, were to be used because they were fast and could best chase pirates and escort convoys; the muskets, with their longer range, would allow the Portuguese to damage the marauders without risking their counterfire. The thousand-man striking force, he says, would be divided into three sqadrons of 10 ships and 350 men each, in order to carry out different duties according to need, and keep the enemy on the defensive. It would make the Portuguese feared and respected, he said, because there would be nothing else like it in all the Orient.[5]

Of course nothing like this ever came into being, and if it had, the subsequent challenge from the Dutch would have rendered at least the light boats unsuitable for action against the European adversaries, once they arrived in force. But the significance for historians is clear: the plan for a real improvement of Portuguese martial efficiency existed at a time when it still might have done some good—indeed when it might still have given the northern Europeans a hot welcome. One must recall that Spaniards, based in the Philippines, were able to stop the Dutch temporarily with relatively scanty forces. Obviously, they made better use of what they had than did the Portuguese. Silveira's book alone, of everything written in and about Portuguese Asia, suggests that those in power could have made far more effective use of what they had at hand, and it suggests how.

Some of Silveira's other ideas are also interesting, if perhaps less seriously meant even by him. He follows consciously in the visionary tradition of Albuquerque when he suggests that what Portugal most needed in Asia was a true colony, that is one populated by Portuguese families and capable of reproduction without the constant infusion of *reinóis*—European Portuguese. But he no longer feels Goa to be a proper location for this as Albuquerque did, but rather prefers an island, either Sumatra or Ceylon. Ceylon most attracted him originally because it was legitimately inherited by the Portuguese, and because of its proximity to the Malabar Christians (the so called "St. Thomas" Christians). If a colony were founded in Colombo, he thought, then it might be arranged with the friendly Cochinese king for Christian wives to be sent to Ceylon for the Portuguese to marry. Such an island kingdom would provide a secure base from which to continue Portuguese domination of the seas; as stated earlier, Silveira did not think much of fortresses and their effect on the soldiery, or for that matter on the captains who commanded them. He would have closed down all but the most vital and strategic ones.[6]

When it comes to the government outside the military, Silveira has many suggestions, and if I am not mistaken, they are more appropriate than those of Diogo do Couto, in the *Soldado Prático*. Silveira would have made the viceregal office itself subject to the same criteria as all the other offices, namely ability, experience and good performance; in fact, he wanted all promotions made from below on the basis of merit.[7] As it was, he said, rewards were given promiscuously, and meaninglessly, in the form of future appointments to offices—which then proved worthless. No more than two certificates of appointment should be given for the same future job.[8] Then the way should be open to honest, dedicated service, regardless of station. "What good." he asked, "are *letrados* without virtue and *fidalgos* without experience?"[9]

If a good future with promotions assured lay before officers who served honestly and ably, then, he feels, there should be no need for the kind of frantic pocket stuffing which made every fortress captain feel he must earn enough in three years for the rest of his life. Instead, he must be absolutely forbidden all private trading activities as conflicts of interest, and so must the viceroys themselves.[10] Moreover, the extortion by captains must be stopped: so shamelessly did they extract money from passing merchants—sometimes up to half the value of their cargoes as at Diu—that ships would sail almost anywhere to avoid stopping at Portuguese—held ports. Silveira estimates that the state lost half its customs revenues this way.[11] In general, he feels, the fortress captains' salaries should be paid and their appointments renewed on an annual (and not triennial) recommendation of a review board. In addition, there should be brakes on the viceroy himself by other officials. Disbursements should be made only if countersigned by the chief treasury officer and the Archbishop of Goa, while a viceregal council should have something more like joint responsibility. I am not sure whether or not Silveira had the model of the Spanish *audiencia* in his mind, but in any case, his viceregal council would form a rough equivalent: a governing body with a measure of co-responsibility to act as a curb on viceregal unilaterality.

Whether or not the reforms Silveira proposes could have come in time to effect any real changes is not knowable—if certainly worth an evening's discussion. But one thing is certain: the existing rules and practices undoubtedly played their part in creating the evils. Silveira's ideas are certainly as plausible as any we could dream up for the circumstances today-and they bear the additional weight of being three hundred and seventy years older.

As advanced as he was in many of his suggestions, Silveira sounds very contemporary in his idea that possession of the gold mines of Monomatapa would have solved Portugal's monetary problems. But of course the idea far antedates him and was held by practically everybody, including Diogo do Couto. Of this he is entirely aware, and he develops the project more as a case study in how the application of good military discipline might help Portugal achieve a success hitherto beyond its reach.[12]

Even today, the north of Portugal seems a never-never land far from the crush of world events, and it is almost as if, ultimately, Silveira simply faded into it as befits an old soldier. He seems never to have heard of the Dutch East India Company until 1619, when his fight with the *tabelião* landed him in prison at Oporto with a Dutchman. This appears to have inspired him to add the fourth book to his old *Reformação* manuscript dating from soon after the turn of the century He had already predicted the conquest of *Asia Portuguesa* by the Dutch at the end of Book Three; now he says the Republic's East India Company "will put us in the shadows" unless action is taken immediately to create countering forces.[13] He changes his mind about Ceylon, and now chooses Sumatra as the best place for a new capital. Then he calls on the Spanish to come from the Philippines to Portugal's aid—unaware that this was even then being accomplished, and he adds some additional examples of *indisciplina militar*, as well as some material concerning André Furtado de Mendonça which he could not have witnessed himself, since it postdates his service in Asia. Then finally, in shaky hand, between 1635 and 1640, he composed a dedication to Margarida, the Duchess of Mantua. By then, he had indeed almost completely faded away. Unless I am mistaken, the whole book is in his own handwriting, and the body of it had lain around for many years when he decided to try once again. By the time he added his dedication and the prefatory sonnet (renumbering, incidentally, all the textual pages to reflect the additions at the beginning), he had entered his eighties and his handwriting had become crabbed and shaky.

But he never gave up, this lonely man with important ideas. Would it be an exaggeration to say that therein lay Portugal's true greatness—not that it did not produce enough wastrels, but that it also produced men who knew the truth and never yielded an inch of it?

Reforming Portuguese Asia according to Silveira's recipe should have been technically feasible, and he is at pains to show that the manpower and capacity for the reforms were already present. He had little luck in finding an ear however, in either Goa or Lisbon. Patently lacking was the imagination in Lisbon, while in India to enact Silveira's modest proposal would have been to eat one's own babies. In the end, his role was purely as a prophet. In fact, he was the Portuguese Amos or Hosea. For like an Old Testament figure, he painted not only a grim portrait of doom, but a brighter vision, a picture of how things could yet have been if Portugal mended its ways; he showed the way *Asia Portuguesa* might yet have triumphed over its enemies. But the self-seeking and corruption had already gone too far, and it had eroded the state's ability to defend itself. In the end, only his visions of ruin prevailed.

So far, this work has been concerned only with Couto's own writings or those of persons who wrote during or shortly after his years of residence in Goa. But there remains another question to explore. Namely, did the situation he describes come about suddenly?

NOTES

1. See Chapter V.
2. An anomymous writer, a priest, writing after the fall of Ceylon to the Dutch, drew the obvious conclusion between the Portuguese personnel policies and those of the Dutch. "Now Ceylon is governed by a sailor, son of a butcher; others of the same sort govern Malacca—it was these who won them and govern them and those (the fidalgos) who governed them and lost them. If merit were worth anything and not merely status and birth, the world itself would not be big enough to hold the Portuguese." See Fitzler, *Cêrco de Columbo*, p. 192. The Father, obviously, was inspired by the Dutch example. It is remarkable that Silveira, writing much earlier, had come to the same conclusion without its benefit.
3. *Reformação*, fl. 24, for example.
4. Ibid., fls. 76v.-77; 89v.
5. Ibid., fls. 77v. 81v.
6. Ibid., fls. 163-175. Silveira did not mind if the Portuguese mingled with non-white peoples.
7. Ibid. His program for reform of the central government begins on p. 175v.
8. Ibid., fls. 131-132. Couto does not criticize this practice in his *Soldado Prático*, but he does in *Década duodécima, Da Ásia*, Vol. 23, p. 76. "I met a man in the last armada (1686), a man granted the fortress of Mombasa, who showed me a list of the grantees ahead of him, and he had thirty-odd men ahead of him, which would have taken more than a hundred years." Such confusion obviously gave viceroys and others a chance to use the *falência* and work their own candidates into jobs.
9. Ibid., fl. 128v.
10. Ibid., fl. 139.
11. Ibid., fls. 133-135 ; 146-147.
12. Ibid., fls. 166v. ; 179; 183ff.
13. Ibid., fls. 186ff.
14. Ibid., fl. 195.

7

IN THE OLD DAYS

IT HAS now been pretty well established that everything Diogo do Couto said was true, and even that he did not go far enough. He said next to nothing about the real conditions in the military, for example, which information should have been obvious to him and which could only have strengthened his case. But there is one aspect of his dialogue which is indeed deceiving. This involves the "when" of the corruption—did it rather suddenly occur, as Couto implies, sometime after the viceroyalty of Dom Luís de Ataíde (1568-1571 and 1578-1581), or was it, or something much like it, present in earlier periods? If it in fact appears to have pre-existed, then of course one must consider that no *decadência* occurred, but that what Couto was really observing was the normal, if somewhat seamy, order of business.

Nearly all readers familiar with Portuguese Asia—and many who are more familiar with the great missionary, Saint Francis Xavier (1506-1552)—recall his biting comment (in a letter to Fr. Simão Rodrigues dated 27 January, 1545): "Allow no friend of yours to come to India with offices and nominations from the king, because of these people one can truly say: 'Let them be blotted out of the book of the living, and not be written with the righteous.'[1] Insofar as you are entrusted with anyone's virtue, if he is not as steadfast in Grace as the Apostles, you can hardly expect he will perform his duties as he ought. Because those here are all confirmed in their habits of abusing their duty—for which I see no remedy because everybody takes the path of 'I rob, you rob.' I am continually amazed how those who come from Portugal find so many moods, tenses and participles to conjugate this verb 'to rob;' and those who come with nominations for those offices are in such a hurry that they never moderate how much they take. So now you can perhaps understand what a bad sendoff those souls have from this world to the next who come provided with these nominations."[2] Portuguese Asia's first saint, however, was hardly the first to observe the propensity to steal.

Instead, if one can believe the chronicler, Gaspar Corrêa, who should have no ulterior motives, the third governor, Diogo Lopes de Sequeira (1518-1521), was the first to distinguish himself for his abuse of the royal trust. Entering into a shady business deal with a pro-Portuguese Moslem merchant who proposed taking a cargo of their pepper to the Red Sea for disposal, he pretended to be shocked when someone became suspicious and seized the entire cargo for himself.[3] Then, later, when the king's auditors smoked out a number of his other indiscretions, he agreed to give up a portion of the ill-gotten gains.[4] His successor, Dom Duarte de Menezes, was hardly better; the upright Vasco da Gama, who returned as Viceroy in 1524, had him arrested, whereupon Corrêa reports that his brother, Luís, and a crooked priest buried a chest of contraband treasure by night.[5] And it might safely be assumed that if the chief officers of the state were thus busy raking in dishonest lucre, their subordinates were hardly more zealous in the king's service.

Then a few years later, on September 25, 1530, one Frei Vicente de Laguna wrote to Dom João III : "Sire, you are being robbed by many of the officials who are here, and none of them, when they leave their office are not loaded with money. The cause of this is that all of them trade with the treasury of Your Highness, and if this treasure is lost, it is Your Highness's—while if it gains money, they say that it is their own and that Your Highness had no part in it. All of the captains of India pay attention to nothing but trade, and they only stop short of personally running through the streets hawking wine and olive oil. I say through the streets because in their houses, they all sell to passers-by."[6] In other portions of his letter, he alleges that both ecclesiastical and secular offices were sold by the king's servants, and that many of the holders did little else but "rob Your Highness and heap up money in order to return to Portugal to take new offices, until finally they go about as ones who believe that those who truly serve Your Majesty are above officeholding and all such thievery." Finally, he states that "captains and masters of ships load them with wines and olive oils and other forbidden merchandise, and to places where they should be carrying water necessary to sustain people's lives. Thus many perish of thirst and neglect."[7] Married officials who leave their wives and children at home regularly take new wives in India and beget new families, leaving those in Portugal to wonder what happened to them. Or worse, they take slaves as concubines, he wrote.[8]

Nine years later, the illustrious Dom João de Castro, who had gone to India in 1538 with the fleet of Dom Garcia de Noronha, wrote to members of the royal family in much the same spirit. In a letter to the Infante Dom Luís, dated October 29, 1539, he remarked :

> We see that the King, our Lord, sends fifty or sixty thousand cruzados to be spent here . . . but I wouldn't know what to make of past governors to whom His Highness has given such benefits, because it is almost past understanding for men to be so cruel and disloyal to a King so clement and forgiving, but I believe this is their disaster and unhappiness—or some other dark property they possess—to keep money for themselves which is meant to enable them to keep on the move and accomplish things throughout the world . . . . And if nothing else I say is true, what reason is there to send money to a land full of gold and silver and jewel mines, where the thickets are full of cinnamon and pepper trees and of every spice desired by mankind, to a land which is so subject to us that we virtually have the inhabitants for our slaves ? Certainly, the King owes little to the governors of India and they have a great obligation to pray to God for the health of his Highness.[9]

He then goes on to say :

> From the Euphrates to China there is no land with sulphur, except on an island close to Ormuz. This island

> is ours and the sulphur which we gain from it does not pass beyond it except through the hands of our officials, to the effect that by not being willing to sell to the Muslems in this region would mean that a third of the world would not have a handful of gunpowder. This being the case for us, it is a great handicap for the others. And yet, the Indians always have a great plenty of it, which is a cause for amazement! It is a great and unpardonable carelessness, if I dare not call it an evil, for sake of a private profit for one man alone who sells this sulphur, that so many should lose their lives, and that our enemies should make themselves strong at our own volition.[10]

Nor was Dom João de Castro quite through with his complaints about the way the king was served by his Indian administration. A captain and a *vedor da fazenda*, he declared," having finished their terms, each carries off a hundred thousand cruzados from his office and leaves behind countless others in debt for the king to absorb . . . "[11] Moreover, he said, the king had long paid for seventeen thousand men-at-arms, while in reality, not counting those on garrison duty, he barely had two thousand. "I took a look at the muster book," he wrote Dom João III, "and these were the lessons I derived from it: besides the many usuries, robberies, loss of shame, destruction of Your Highness's treasury . . . I found in it many cases of where men were loaned twenty and thirty thousand cruzados at fifteen and twenty per cent interest . . . and I take it almost for granted that this muster book is the headmaster which has taught the Portuguese here to lose their consciences and fear of God and desire to serve Your Highness."[12] At times, in fact, he almost felt as if the weight of all the dishonesty was beyond description.

> Oh sire," he wrote Dom Luís, "who could possibly convey to Your Highness just how many vices, how many bad habits, how little love of God, how much forgetfulness of the king's service, how much disregard for our country all the Portuguese have who go about in these parts?[13]

From what another honest man, the *vedor da fazenda* Simão Botelho, wrote ten years later, matters had not improved in the interim. Not only did he have to call in the Governor to make the captain of Malacca stop gouging merchants for exorbitant *ad valorem* duties which were driving them away from the entrepôt, but he was attacked by hoodlums hired by two men he was investigating for fraud at Bassein.[14] His letters make it amply clear that law enforcement in Goa before the arrival of Diogo do Couto in India was anything but a pleasant occupation and that no one could expect to be thanked for it.

Of all those authors just cited, however, none spoke in more extraordinary terms than the chronicler, Gaspar Corrêa. Portuguese India was at its height in 1551, when he finished his *Lendas da India*, and one might expect that he would have terminated his epic story on a note of optimism and grandeur. But he does nothing of the sort: he ends it with a remarkable tirade of reproach against his fellow countrymen. He says, among other things, in the closing passage of his chronicle:

"When I took up the writing of the deeds accomplished in these parts up to the present time, I did so with a good will because I wished to commemorate the illustrious feats done so miraculously by the hands of the Portuguese and their good captains through the will of God, as His mercy showed us; such were the foundations of this marvelous labor, which, through the working of pernicious sin, were perverted and damaged to their present evil condition, caused by the tyrannous greed, through which the initial benefits were turned into public wrongs, against which I have written vigorously, in the hopes that my works might bring things to a more appropriate end, it seeming to me that the evils, which were then growing apace, might be altered through appropriate punishment. Seeing so many murderers among them who went back to Portugal with no fears whatsoever of justice, either of heaven or earth; of great malefactors. who robbed Christians and Moslems and all people alike, whether natives or foreigners, and so many great offenses against God, almost past belief—and seeing them all pass before the King without punishment for such offenses done to his royal estate and to such destruction of his people . . . from seeing so much of this, I grow tired. But I do not wish to write maledictions and curses which will afford no pleasure . . ."[15] Hence, he does the only sensible thing and ends his narrative, begging God's pardon and invoking His mercy on himself. Eight years later, Diogo do Couto arrived in India from Lisbon.

It hardly appears necessary to add that after Couto's time, things scarcely improved; instead, the scale of evildoing, if anything, grew longer, since by then the Dutch had arrived, money was harder to make, surveillance was even less than before, and the temptation to trade with this new enemy was added to the list.[16]

The conclusion to be drawn from all of the witnesses adduced to corroborate, or modify, Couto's testimony is, I believe, quite obvious. In the *Soldado Prático* he painted a fairly accurate picture and fact understated his case through neglecting to describe the mulcting of the soldiers and the *indisciplina militar* brought out by Francisco Rodrigues de Silveira. But where he is deceiving, if not willfully, is in the impression he creates that the abuses were of his own time. Gaspar Corrêa, I think is on much firmer ground, for at least he was once Albuquerque's secretary and knew the heroic days personally—and perhaps was in a better position than Couto to judge what was decadent in comparion to what. And if one believes him, then the stealing started when Albuquerque's body was barely cold in its grave. More will be said in the following chapter, but a tentative judgment might be passed here: the *Soldado Prático* created the false impression in the 1790's and afterwards that Portuguese India rather suddenly entered into a period of decadence in the last decades of the sixteenth century.

Before leaving this section of the study, that of Portuguese official corruption as seen by contemporaries, I should remark that not only old soldiers, disillusioned chroniclers and foreign observers, plus a few comptrollers and assorted priests, were sensitive to the prevailing atmosphere of dishonesty and self-seeking : Portugal's greatest poet was, too. In one of his sonnets, written while serving in India, he penned these lines about Goa : "This Babylon, whence flows matter for every evil the world breeds . . . , where tyranny overrides honor . . . ;

this labyrinth where nobility valor and learning go begging at the portals of avarice and meanness . . . This gloomy chaos of confusion . . ."[17]

The time has now come to change course and consider an entirely different aspect : whether ideas of political corruption as we perceive them today really can be applied to the world of the sixteenth and seventeenth centuries. There is, in fact, a considerable difference of opinion on the subject. The next chapter will explore various facets of the problem.

NOTES

1. From Psalm 69 : 28 (King James version).
2. *Epistolae S. Francisci Xaverii aliaque eius scripta.* Nova editio (ed. Georg Schurhammer, S.J. and Josef Wicki, S.J.), 2 Vols., Rome (Monumenta Historica Societatis) 1944-1945, I, pp. 281-282.
3. Gaspar Corrêa, *Lendas da Índia*, 4 vols., Lisboa (Academia Real das Sciências) 1858, II, pp. 679-680.
4. Ibid., II, pp. 675-676.
5. Ibid., II, pp. 841-842.
6. Letter of Frei Vicente de Laguna to D. João III, 25 sept. 1530, in Silva Rego, *Documentação*, II, p. 195.
7. Ibid, pp. 193-194.
8. Ibid., p. 195.
9. In Sanceau, *Cartas de D. João de Castro*, pp, 44-45.
10. Ibid., p. 45.
11. Ibid., p. 30.
12. Ibid., p. 26. The musterbook, or *Matrícola Geral*, has been identified as the special target for grafters. See Arthur Teodoro de Matos, *O Estado da Índia nos Anos de 1581-1588: Estrutura Administrativa e Económica. Alguns Elementos para o seu Estudo*, Ponte Delgada (Universidade dos Açores), 1982, p. 29.
13. Ibid, p. 42.
14. *Cartas de Simão Botelho*, Carta II, pp. 11-12, in rear of *Subsidios para a Historia da India Portuguesa*, (ed. Rodrigo José de Lima Felner, Lisboa (Academia Real das Sciências), 1868.
15. Corrêa, *Lendas da Índia*, IV, pp. 729-732.
16. See Winius, *The Fatal History*, Chapters VI and VII.
17. The lines belong to Camões' sonnet which begins :

    "Cá nesta Babilónia, donde mana
    Matéria a quanto mal o mundo cría;"

    and is usually listed in modern editions as no 167. It can be found, among other places in : José Maria Rodrigues and Afonso Lopes Vieira (jt. eds.), *Lírica de Camões, Coimbra (Coimbra University Press)*, 1932, p. 168.

8

THROUGH MODERN SPECTACLES

It is probably no coincidence in our age, when traditional values are under attack, behavioural patterns are fluid and institutions are unstable, that historians have the utmost difficulty in deciding what constituted felonious activity four hundred years ago. To wit : were the men Couto, Silveira and the other witnesses wrote about really criminals ?

A few generations ago, around the turn of the century, there was not much doubt in writers' minds about the matter. The German historian, Justus Strandes, wrote in 1899: "Even when affairs are viewed in the most favourable light, it can scarcely be denied that rapacity, unscrupulousness and pretentiousness were the principal guides to conduct in Portuguese India." Goa he called a "sink of corruption."[1] The Englishman, R.S. Whiteway, writing in the same year, describes the *Soldado Prático* as "the picture of a thoroughly vicious system worked by men even more vicious than itself."[2] Moreover, the Portuguese themselves took a dismal view of the period. In past editions, the *Grande Enciclopédia Portuguesa e Brasileira* carried a heading under "D" for "*decadência*" which concluded that during this epoch, the participants were "no longer worthy of the name 'Portuguese'." "It is perhaps symptomatic that in more recent editions, the entry has disappeared entirely.

Of course history is not an exact science, or even a social science (in spite of the American and French tendency so to classify it), but it is wise for historical purposes to know what one is talking about when one uses a term or concept—in this case that of "corruption." An English writer, J. Hurstfield, has offered one of the few explanations of it as applied to the early modern period: "If we assume that the object of the state is the welfare of its members, we may define corruption as the subversion of that object for other ends." To him, the modern state and the existence of a bureaucracy are identical, but he feels there is a weak link in the system, namely the lack of state revenues to pay bureaucrats decent salaries. These then helped themselves to the substance of the commonwealth to make up the difference.[3] Another writer, M.N. Pearson, an Australian, goes further when he adds that this lack of adequate salaries was compensated by the addition to practically all offices of perquisites, i.e., the creation and retention of certain fees not specifically authorized by the crown, but more or less tolerated by it. He adds that distinctions between the "ethical" perquisites and the more nearly rapacious ones easily became mushy.[4] Finally, a Dutch writer, Jacob van Klaveren, has remarked that in feudal times, the perquisites may have been deemed proper and legitimate, but that when bureaucracies took over administrative tasks from the feudatories, the same perquisites, or ones like them, became illegal, and therefore corrupt.[5]

It is logical that amid considerations such as these, concern with the *decadência* as a special phenomenon in history has virtually disappeared. Among historians writing in the 1970's and '80's, only one, the American, Franklin C. Lane, an historian of Venice, has believed that corruption had the slightest thing to do with Portuguese Asian decline.[6] Most, including myself in a previous book, incidentally, have simply lumped Portuguese peculation together with Portuguese cruelties and then blandly declared that they are to be considered against the backdrop of a cruel age in general with standards other than ours—though I notice that few can resist the retailing of some dastardly or hair-raising story to illustrate the point. Needless to say, nobody use the term *decadência* any more

Through such an interpretation perhaps we as modern writers have actually achieved banality, a trap I believe always to lie in wait for those of us who would go to the opposite extreme from moralizings of the late Victorians and react with minimal personal involvement to what we study. I have now, I trust, come to a better understanding.

I agree, to begin with, with Pearson when he points out that it is a mistake to measure the Portuguese bureaucratic system of the 16th and early 17th centuries by 19th and 20th century standards, as the older writers do. In that antique system and those of contemporary France and Spain as well, offices were regularly sold, though covertly until 1616, and they were at all times bestowed, the higher ones by the crown and the lower by Goan authorities, without regard for administrative competence —but rather as rewards for service, bravery in battle and the like, and even for the deeds of a deceased parent or brother. When once acquired, a post was looked upon by its recipient as private property during the period of retention and he felt responsible only to the king—not to an abstract like "the public," and he was more or less expected to squeeze the most from it, especially when he had handed out a sackful of money to obtain his nomination. The crown never complained of "corruption," but merely of *descaminhos*, "deviations" and *abusos*, meaning that officials were making too much of a good thing. And Pearson is certainly right when he says that one cannot judge this system with the vehemence one would reserve for catching a more recent civil servant soliciting a bribe. This is in effect the error of the Victorians.

However this may be, I think that once Pearson has shown the way, he does not quite go far enough. I think we have every right, after acquiring the criteria, the measuring tools used by the past, to judge the era in question (in this case the *decadência*) according to them, or something like them. Hurstfield's idea of damage to the commonwealth in this case indeed provides an approximation of the crown's viewpoint, though in Portuguese India I think the king did not pose so much as the representative of the commonwealth, but regarded it more simply as his own. By any measure like this one, it is amply clear that Lisbon was anything but philosophical about the *abusos*, even if it lacked all the finer sensitivities of our age. About 10 per cent of the *cartas régias*, the royal letters to the Goan viceroys are concerned to some degree with inquiries and investigations of usurpations, irregularities and malefactions.

Moderns must also not forget that the very basis for the judgments of the late Victorians was provided by the contemporary eye-witnesses upon whose testimonies I have based my earlier chapters. It is true that all of these men were extrinsic to the system, being either foreigners or of the less than aristocratic classes, but all of them considered the *abusos* evil. They knew their Christian religion, they knew the laws, and they had consciences. No one could have fooled them with "nonsense" about mere "perks". They were not really talking about "perks" anyway. Confiscating a man's property without compensation and then paying one's own confederates its value from the treasury or issuing fraudulent draughts to a fellow crown employee, who cashed them and split the gain, were practices they knew to be wrong, not to mention forcing soldiers to serve without pay. Moderns would never have known of these practices unless contemporaries who considered them depraved had reported them. It is at precisely this point that the arguments *pro* historical relativism fly off the rails. We are not dealing with "perks", but with crooks.

If we are once again confronted with the crookedness of *Âsia Portuguesa*, we should perhaps try another route to diminish its importance: we should attempt to show that matters were no worse there than in other European colonies, not to speak of the European metropolis. If it could be demonstrated that the contemporary Spanish, Dutch and English in Asia, let alone in America, were all painted in the same colors, then one could conclude that the whole age was corrupt by our standards and Portuguese Asia was in reality nothing special.

One should say at the outset that the only contemporary empire at all comparable to the *Estado da Índia Oriental* was the Spanish, in that it was also a royal and hence governmental, as opposed to a company operation. And, save for outposts in the Philippines and after 1623 a brief one in Formosa the Spanish empire was not Asian, but American. French Canada was just then (1608) being founded as a territorial entity, while neither the English East India Company (1600) nor the Dutch V.O.C. (the United East India Company, 1602) were yet in possession of enough territory to call them colonies, though commercially managed ones. But granting all this and giving or taking a century or so, one can draw some approximate conclusions.

To begin with, one finds in the Spanish empire the official sale of offices, inaugurated during the reign of Philip II, on a scale never envisioned or approached in Portugal or Portuguese Asia. It was even possible after 1608 for the holders to "renounce" them to successors, i.e., to name the next holders pending approval by the crown. This, of course, meant private selling of the renunciation, whereupon the crown exacted as a fee to the new holder one-third of the estimated revenue. After the middle of the seventeenth century, even some of the higher salaried posts—*corregimientos*, or municipal-provincial governorships, and occasionally even an *audiencia* post, an administrative-judicial position of the top layer of colonial government were sold. At the same time, the impoverished central government kept creating new offices and new fees, just for the sake of added revenues. All of these things entailed new bureaucracy, made it more expensive and provided new incentives for officeholders to squeeze their perquisites for everything they were worth.[7]

But even so the collusive and conspiratorial activities between officials which one finds in *Ásia Portuguesa* appear to be lacking, as do the abuses which accompanied the military and the control of native shipping and trade. There are none of the viceregal "inspection" tours, the comptrollers' procurement junkets or the massive bribing of the viceroy on his arrival. There is the legend of the sack of gold under the incoming viceroy's pillow in Spanish America (which appears not to have been literally true), but it is interesting that in the story he did not add it to his own possessions but wisely slipped it under the next viceroy's bedstead in turn. The moral of the story is that administrators during the period of the *residencia*, or judicial review of performance, should go easy on one another's past actions and not that a viceregent's subordinates corrupted him, as in Goa, where the rich place trappings were his to take back to Portugal. Moreover, one of the biggest opportunities for graft was missing in Spanish America, namely the need for constant military operations and relations with foreign princes. For the most part, Spain relied on its own citizens for militia duty while there were no native princes to regale and be regaled by and few foreign traders to mulct. About the most dismal and inhumane deeds regularly committed by Spanish officials were the notorious *obrajes* of the *corregimientos de īndios*, the forced labor sweatshops in Indian districts far removed from the more settled and urbanized areas of the colonial world.[8]

A final, thoroughly dishonest, but hardly cruel, Spanish abuse was official connivance in smuggling. This was "victimless," except for the crown, and only officials could participate who were near points of entry—ports, or mountain villages between Argentina and Perú. In this case, however, probably the general public benefitted from the availability of lower priced or more plentiful goods.

On balance, most of the "corruption" in Spanish America falls within the borderline of the "perks" and therefore a part of daily living, albeit not daily living of the holy. There were certainly less of the unruly characters like the fortress captain Couto reports in the *Soldado Prático* who was ready to sell his soul in order to get rich.

Whenever historians think of colonial corruption, those more familiar with English history than that of Iberia tend to recall Lord Clive and Warren Hastings and the period of East India Company rule they represented in Bengal. How about this for a super *decadência*, they might ask, one which would make the Portuguese period of a century and a half earlier look like small change ? I do not quite think the comparison apt, or even the time brackets, but it is a reasonable assumption that it would arise in any discussion of colonial corruption. The answer to it lies, I think, in the special circumstances.

I would rather focus on the large fortunes brought home by some of the lesser figures of the Company than give great credence to the more dazzling allegations made by Clive and Hastings' known enemies; it is true here that the evil men do live on after them, and that the good is interred and forgotten. In this case, though, much of the evil they did not do lives after them because people tend to recall the allegations but forget that most were never proved and more than a fair number of them were viciously false to begin with. Neither Clive nor Hastings actually emerge as sullied as their accusers if one takes the trouble to run the accusations to ground.

Still, there is no doubt that more money dishonestly acquired has been built into English architecture of the eighteenth century than ever returned home to grace the Portuguese landscape at any or all periods. Seats in Parliament were bought with it. Even so, the comparison between eighteenth century British India and the Portuguese *decadência* will not stand up, if only because the times in which the fortunes were amassed were times of conquest. One will recall that the Company had had to arm itself for protection as the Mughal empire, its host, had begun to decline. Meanwhile, in 1664, the French had founded their own India company which played second fiddle to the British in Euro-Indian trade until around 1750. At that time an ingenious Frenchman named Dupleix learned how to use Indian client states to magnify his company's modest power through making war on others by proxy. In doing so, the power he created inevitably came into collision with the British.

As a young officer of the English company, Robert Clive found that the answer to this menace was provided by Dupleix himself: the English could use the same tactics. Clive, in fact, was the Frenchman's best pupil, while French preoccupations with Europe during the Seven Years War left the French too weakened to compete. Thereafter, the English gorged themselves on political and military spoils both before, but notably after, Clive's spectacular and decisive victory at Plassey. The East India Company, a trading enterprise, was not designed to cope with this sort of administrative role which had suddenly been thrust upon it, and for a time, its officials in London had no idea of the magnitude of their responsibility. Both Clive and his successor, Hastings, really came to grief because the freebooters upon whom they tried to impose discipline and order came home to attack them in parliament.[9]

Even the Portuguese in the flush of their conquests under Albuquerque had never achieved anything remotely so massive, lucrative or widespread, and if they had, the period of English imperial history I have just described, could scarcely be compared with the *decadência* phenomenon. For what one is really doing in comparing eighteenth century British India with late sixteenth and early seventeenth century Portuguese India is to compare a time of victory and spoils with a time of depression and stagnation, where the abuses were not brought about by extraordinary opportunities, but where the opportunities were created through a kind of administrative conspiracy.

Far more illuminating are the kind of everyday abuses which prevailed in the English East India Company, and in its Dutch counterpart, the V.O C., in the days before either became more concerned with warring and governing than with trading, that is in more normal days. Without going into a whole comparative discourse about the different structure of the companies vs. the *Estado da Índia Oriental*, it is perhaps enough to say that there was no hereditary, exclusive class who monopolized the best positions as there was even in Holland itself; on the contrary, there was good pay for those in the better jobs and plenty of opportunities for advancement. This took away most of the direct incentive to steal. What remained, though, was the temptation to trade privately and illegally, at the expense of one's employer, in the Dutch case especially on the parts of employees in stations too removed in distance from Batavia, the home base of the V.O.C. in Asia. This seems to have occurred so frequently in the English company in India that it was virtually routine while there seems to have been much less of it in and around Batavia. But, the V.O.C. *Wester Quartieren*, mostly Ceylon, Persia and India, the practice flourished, especially in the eighteenth century.[10] This kind of illegal trading was certainly both "corruption" in the modern sense and to use a contemporary Portuguese term, an *abuso*, but it hardly imparts a special character to the two companies, as does the kind of situation which Couto, Silveira and the witnesses describe. It is comparable to the filching and stealing practised by employees of most of the world's large department and chain stores, a hidden cost of doing business, no doubt passed on to the companies customers, both then and now. Then there were flagrant, if minor, instances of systematic oppression and dishonesty like those in the V.O.C. of the notorious *baas der Buitenrust*, director of the ship's carpenter shops on an island in the bay of Batavia, who pitilessly gouged native workers. These are also hardly comparable.

Finally, it only remains to remark that one almost never reads of corruption running amok in the Portuguese Atlantic possessions. Stuart Schwartz's studies on the Brazilian *Relação* at Bahia show that the normal venality existed, including some under-the-table investments in trade by judges,[11] but Brazil and the Atlantic islands never enjoyed—or suffered—a location so far removed from Europe, or one where so many miscellaneous opportunities existed for self-enrichment through contact with a native trade and its wealth, while the fact that not every Atlantic colonial Portuguese—or even one in a hundred—was connected with the government made the operation of a conspiracy to mulct the king more difficult. Then, there was no real military payroll to steal from, and no foreign potentates to bribe or present or be bribed or presented by. And, finally, there was never such a shortage of Europeans eligible for office as in Asia. All these factors worked to keep the Atlantic administrations of the Portuguese from being so spectacularly dishonest.

No doubt the governmental morality of Europe itself in that age was not high. Throughout the sixteenth and the seventeenth centuries, complaints are endemic that justice was purchased, not merited, and from what observers in Spain and Portugal have written, the situation there may have not been much better than in the Brazil or the Spanish American colonies. The anonymous author of the *Arte de Furtar*, published in Amsterdam in 1651, reveals that plenty of officials in Portugal were on the take, while historian Ruth Pike points to an official report in the Biblioteca Nacional de Madrid indicating that even judges of the *audiencia*, or high court of law at Sevilla, were disreputable characters.[12] Nor did corruption stop with the Iberian Peninsula or the judiciary; the presence in Europe of military payroll padding and the incredible cost overruns on fortifications and ships (most notably some of King Henry VIII of England) all show that the basic techniques of corruption were well understood in Europe.

And so they were. But in only one garden did all these *fleurs du mal* bloom at once: in the Goan viceroyalty. No place else, perhaps before or since in European history, colonial or otherwise, was there such an exquisitely designed and cultivated totality of administrative abuse. The spores did not develop like mushrooms in the dark. They did not have to; they sprouted in the sunshine. The whole apparatus from top to bottom was affected; moreover, like interlacing tendrils, the abuses depended upon one another for support. The fortress captain, knowing that he would be "audited"—i.e., obliged to share his illicit gains with the viceroy or the *vedor da fazenda*, or more likely both—had to steal enough for himself and all of them. Similarly, if the viceroy brought his own copper to the mint for coining his own spending money, treasury officials colluded with him. On his procurement trips, it was the *vedor da fazenda* who paid other officials several times the going price for their own merchandise. In order for such malpractices to succeed, the whole royal government had to be in collusion—something impossible in metropolitan Europe. Nor was this condition merely a result of rapid and spectacular conquests. It was the normal order of business.

The fact that the *Estado da India* largely supported itself may explain in part why the king tolerated its wickendness. At best, or rather, worst, the corruption did not affect him directly: it came out of the local circuit of revenues generated in India. As Helmut Königsberger, John Elliot, and Clarence Haring have shown, nearly all internal taxation of the Iberian crowns and crown possessions, such as Sicily or Perú, were absorbed almost wholly by their own administrations and by local defence needs.[13] Not only was this true for Goa, but in *Carracks, Caravans and Companies*, Niels Steensgaard has demonstrated that the spice revenues of the crown and the local incomes of the *Estado da Índia Oriental* were even kept in separate book-keeping systems[14] Thus the king's only normal stake in the India system was to finance each year the purchase of new spices, plus outfitting of the fleet necessary to go fetch them. This being so, then one might suppose that this royal operation above all would be honestly handled by the Cochinese and Goan *feitores* and their staff ; it certainly seems to have been under as tight security as the crown would devise. Even so, one might imagine that the crooks knew they had best keep their hands off what directly concerned the king, lest they provoke upon themselves a general crackdown. (It is similarly known that the racketeers of a city do not like spectacular crime which results in screaming headlines, lest it provoke in a general cleanup). But even here, apparently, keeping sticky fingers, even those of viceroys, out of his spice money was not easy; just as the king could not effectively do much about the rackets which prevailed in Goa, he had troubles keeping his full share of pepper *en route* to Lisbon.[15] Hence, even his only direct source of revenue from India was flawed. At any rate, he did not expect to use Indian non-spice revenues for metropolitan uses, and, providing he did not have to send India moneys from Portugal, the thievery may even have afforded him certain benefits.

One big reason why India was valuable to the crown was that it yielded important patronage. I am inclined to think that in all *ancien régime* monarchies, patronage was the single most important link between a monarch and his subjects. There was of course a good deal of theory (shading off into propaganda and finally, nonsense) about a monarch being a father to his people, but in practical terms he concerned himself infinitely less with the peasant digging turnips than with the privileged groups who looked toward him for employment. To employ them was to keep them happy, but to leave them idle was to court the danger that they might drift into someone else's network of interrelationships, may be even someone potentially dangerous. In Philippine Portugal, for example, of the Dukes of Bragança or another potential group of anti-Spanish nationalists. Hence the utility of the *Estado da Índia*, even if the beneficiaries, like caterpillars, picked it clean. Letting them do so no doubt even served as an added incentive to take up service in such a hardship area. From what Couto writes, the *fidalgos* recruited for the Indian service actually expected as much; otherwise they would not have come.[16]

It is even worth contemplating the emphasis on *fidalguia* in apportioning India jobs was a by-product of this reality of patronage—and it could even be that more blue—bloods of the poorer sort who died in the distant service, the better, i e., the more patronage there remained. Perhaps that was not quite the royal attitude consciously, but it is curious that Silveira's desire to benefit the crown by placing capable commoners in the India service met with so little enthusiasm. Perhaps that was not what India was all about. Poor Silveira, the ambitious bourgeois, seems after all to have been ahead of his time and place, as it were more Catholic than the pope ! To the king and upper classes, Asia was rather a good place to send their bastards, as Professor Charles Boxer has remarked.[17]

To speculate still further it is interesting to ponder exactly why the Portuguese crown apparently did occupy itself in India with patronizing its privileged classes rather than seeking to offset them with another group more dependent upon the king for its livelihood. Historians like Mack Walker and Gerhard Benecke writing on Germany have shown that in the same period in the Empire, there grew up a network of administrative entrepreneurs from the non-noble classes, ones who were not closely connected to the patronage networks of the nobility but who bought their jobs and looked upon government service as an investment and a career in and for itself.[18]

From the rulers' standpoint, the advantage might have been that this group was more politically neutral, did not have such great expectations and actually paid for itself by paying the princes about one-third of an office's worth. The same practice was initiated in Spain during the reign of Philip II and in Portugal itself during the reign of Philip III. But in Portuguese India, however, the system never supplanted the practice of government by *fidalgo*; it was tried in 1615-1616 and then quickly disappeared—no doubt because the viceroys and their henchmen had long been selling nominations—and did not want to start passing the receipts on to the treasury. The same seems to have held for the Portuguese courtiers in Lisbon, as well.[19]

It might therefore be argued that the *decadência* was connected with Portugal's failure to replace its warrior class in Asia with a group of men who might better fit the image of bureaucratized pen-pushers. More, I suspect, by accident than by deliberation, the conquistadores of Spanish America were nearly all phased out by the 1530's and supplanted with men who soon became accustomed to the ways of formulas, channels and, if not honest service, at least not collusive dishonesty. Meanwhile, Portugal not only seems to have continued patronizing its conquistador class, but institutionalized and entrenched them in the government of its Indian empire until a more modern bureaucratic evolution was impossible.

This up-to-date line of reasoning I pursued for a time, and though it did not ultimately seem applicable to Portuguese India, it did sharpen my awareness that the kind of aggressive behaviour and rapacity one observes there belongs to the military, not the civilian, to the nobility, not to the clerk. For ultimately the whole notion that the empire in Asia could have been run by clerks begins to break up when one considers that fortresses formed the backbone of the whole operation and that only in Goa was there anything like an administration not comprised of practising soldiers. And even the viceroys seems to have been chosen primarily for his grasp of military affairs. The pure administrators were all in subordinate roles, and only a civilian *audiencia* system could have given them enough influence to brake the military-*fidalgo* style of the government. The Philippine Hapsburg kings, however, did not attempt to introduce the *audiencia* into Portuguese Asia, while they did introduce the *residencia* and tried to effect the sale of offices. This might indicate that they, too, recognized that the whole nature of the Goan empire required a single authority, not a dual one, because it was always subject to attack.[20]

There, I think, the speculation must end about Portugal's "failure" to have built a professional bureaucracy in Asia. In the dawn of modern European history, the military meant the nobility—and vice versa—and so long as the crown operated an empire based upon conquest and threat of force, the *fidalgo* element was bound to dominate - even though the crown perhaps need not have gone so far as to guarantee the nobility a monopoly of all but the positions of minor command, both in the military and in the bureaucracy.

In any case it is to the nobility and its networks of inter-relationships that one must look to guess why the administration behaved as it did. Something in the background, opportunities and frustrations of this class must have given the officeholders a common behaviour. My guess was—and is—that, far from always being loyal to the crown, in India they set themselves almost in opposition to it. (Except, of course, openly).

In sixteenth century Portugal the nobility of all varieties numbered only around 20,000 and exercised great influence on both king and country, possibly more than in any other land of Western Europe. Its members occupied virtually all the administrative and military appointments of the crown ; judicial jobs were occupied by the smaller and almost equally exclusive group of *letrados*, a class of mixed *fidalgo* and non-noble origin with various kinds and degrees of legal training, both university and practical From this one may gather that the crown did not distrust the aristocracy so much as it did in neighbouring Spain or in France—or that if did, the remaining classes apt to be equally literate were not numerous enough to provide a real alternative. In any case, the country was small and sparsely peopled enough for the king to believe he could know whom to trust.

Around the middle of the sixteenth century, moreover, the economy of Portugal stagnated, and additions to the nobility slowed. Hence the pool of competent nominees for government service did not increase just as, probably, the ability of less wealthy parents diminished to educate their children for the higher levels of government service. Henrique Gama Barros, author of the monumental *Historia da Administração Pública em Portugal*, remarks that even the *letrado* class became nearly a closed caste.[21]

As in other countries, there were basically three kinds of nobles—court or *fidalgos da casa d'El-Rei*, country, and a small judicial group (of university trained lawyers, the *letrados*, who had risen to the top). There was also an unusual fourth group of traders, who may have had their origins in the national revolution of the 1380's. But in the 16th century, most nobles made their investments in commercial enterprises, and in the opinion of historian A.H. de Oliveira Marques, their activities may actually have hampered the growth of the bourgoisie.[22] Most of the higher administrative jobs went to members of the court nobility, posts at or above the *corregedor*, or district governor, level. Probably the lesser officials were a *mélange* of all aristocratic varieties, but it is doubtful whether there were representatives of the bourgeoisie in any but the municipal governments.

As indicated in the Introduction, however, aside from the highest positions, most India jobs went to members of the country nobility who had to pull strings to get them. One can imagine that *fidalgos* with any sort of rude education, achievement and connections at court could wangle and bribe a definite appointment to a particular post before embarking for India, but that *fidalgos* of the lower degrees with little influence, no special qualifications or who were otherwise feckless, merely registered with the *Casa da India*, had the fact of their *fidalguia* entered onto their *certidões*, and sailed as *soldados*, hoping to become an officer, or pick up an office in the course of their service.

The viceroy, or rather, the viceroy-designate, meanwhile assembled his personal staff. He had a certain allowance for such an entourage, but it was never adequate, just as none of the official salaries ever were, including his own. There is no information regarding just who these retainers were, but certainly a mixture of service personnel, gentleman-in-waiting, and perhaps a few private advisers. They were less likely to be interested in going to India *per se* than they were in serving their master, in what modern diplomatic jargon would term a "hardship area" —meaning they expected far more than the ordinary emolument. It may not have occurred to the viceroy-designate while still in Portugal that he would have to steal it for them.

When the viceroy arrived in Goa, therefore, it must have been disheartening to find his palace unfurnished, its contents removed by his antecessor and staff. Furnishing it in a style befitting his rank no doubt would have cost an year's income. The story told by Linschoten, incidentally,that neither a stick nor a stool was left behind seem to have been quite literally true, as witness what the Count of Óbidos wrote in 1654.[23] The Goan bureaucracy could, of course, have had a gorgeously furnished palace awaiting the incoming viceregent : no doubt they liked to give him a shock, one in some ways comparable to the shock the arriving *soldados* received when they disembarked and found only doorways in which to sleep. Then the furniture began to appear—and one can imagine every table, tapestry and chest bore the donor's name. It was virtually impossible not to accept, no doubt with individual thanks to each "benefactor." But once he had done so, the viceroy was compromised.

The three-year offices were all staggered, but it was not usual that *fidalgos* whose term had just expired and who wished to enter into a new office in India actually needed to return to Lisbon to petition the crown. Some appear to have done so, but homeward passages had to be paid for and were expensive; they were dangerous and time consuming, besides. There never could have been enough applicants at Lisbon for all the middling and lesser offices, anyway. Instead, officeholders and would-be officeholders no doubt "lubricated" the viceroy for a nomination to the king. The nomination by the viceroy was only a suggestion, of course, since for middling and major positions only the crown could actually nominate except on an interim basis, but the king complied in practically all cases and never seems to have known how many nominees were walking around with patents for the same lower or middling offices. Appointments for these were always made subject to a waiting list, anyway, a practice which left it in the hands of the Goan administration to fit nominees into sequence for the available jobs. The better jobs usually entailed nominations with a specified date for commencing service. Couto, of course, has told us that in actuality nobody could make a nomination from Portugal prevail unless the the Goan officials were pleased to honour it; if they did not, they would simply find a *falência*, a defect, in the way it was drawn up.[24]

The final result of all this was that not only did the bureaucracy compromise the viceroy upon arrival, but the viceroy and bureaucracy together then co-opted new members into their brotherhood only when these showed themselves compatible (or corruptible depending on one's viewpoint). In bucking the system Couto received what he deserved—or did not deserve—while Silveira, who was no *fidalgo*, never could break into it at all.

In effect, the patronage network extending from the country provinces and concluding in Lisbon was only a feeder to the network of officeholders already in Asia which culminated in the viceroy. As the ex-viceregent in Couto's dialogue is made to say, he had to accommodate himself to this bureaucracy, or no one would have served him. And one must not forget his own entourage, who expected him to enrich them. After all, why else would anyone in his right mind take all the risks entailed in sailing to Goa?

Thus it was that nobody who was already in India looked to the crown for anything further, save possibly trouble, in the case that a nominee not first designated by the viceroy should turn up from Lisbon with a conflicting appointment. It is likely that the same bureaucracy even saw the crown as their natural enemy because some new nominees coming out from the Portugal network seem to have held appointments exactly specified as for the next triennium and this could interfere with their own timetables; according to these they had to move over and make an extra place at the feeding trough, or else try to bring their own influence to bear and sting the rival with a *falência*, something the viceroy probably did not dare to do if he suspected the royal nomination concerned a candidate about whom the king really cared, like a fortress commander's post or one for an obviously well-connected individual. Besides this potential or real threat to their ladder-climbing, if officeholders went too far and committed a really blatant theft, or did so while an enemy was looking who was (un-)scrupulous enough to write Lisbon about it, then the king might direct the viceroy to investigate and punish them. Viceroys themselves were usually unobservant of evil bureaucratic behaviour but when a letter arrived from Portugal over the king's signature, saying "I am informed that great deviations have occurred in Chaul that the *Vedor*, Manuel velho Santos (or any other name), is reported to have shown great carelessness in the tranfer of my *fazenda*... I command you to suspend and imprison him pending investigation ...," then the Viceroy was duty bound to do so. He could usually get around the crown's distant authority for most things, but occasionally it would thus hang him up, and because that possibility was always in the back of everyone's mind, a *fidalgo* in office could hardly "kiss the royal hands" with any enthusiasm.

While it seems beyond question that the era of malfeasance preceded Couto and in fact did not have any special beginning, it is quite possible that governmental peculation indeed worsened after the late 1570's or early 1580's. The unspeakable disaster at Al-Ksar-el-Kebir in North Africa in 1578 resulted in the death or capture of practically all 140,000 men involved in the mad king Sebastian's expeditionary force, including thousands of land's fittest *fidalgos*. The fiasco cost half Portugal's annual state budget as it was, and when El Mansur, the emergent Moorish victor, got around to assessing ransoms on the surviving *fidalgos* (and even on their corpses), the payments all but ruined whole noble clans. El Mansur built El-Bedi, "The Wonderful," the most lavish palace of its time, with the proceeds and even had money left over to make loans to European monarchs.[25]

Two years later, even while the ransoming was still going on, King Philip II, or rather his general, the Duke of Alva, marched into Portugal to claim its vacant throne by force. The court nobility, those with bases in Lisbon, for the most part welcomed him and the Spanish connections, if only because his ambassador, Don Cristóbal de Moura, himself a Portuguese, had distributed moneys where they would most help to defray the heavy ransoms. To the court nobility the Spanish connection in itself must have promised far wider horizons and thus expanded opportunity, or at least they thought it did. Not so with the lower and middle classes and the country nobility, where national feeling burned brightly and continued to do so for sixty years. No doubt Don Cristóbal's largesse did not extend to the lasser *fidalguia*, and this may account for their indifference. They were also hard-hit by the Al-Ksar-el-Kebir aftermath, and all the signs read that the Portuguese rural economy remained in desperate condition throughout the 1590's and well into the seventeenth century.[26]

The gentry and the lesser classes were not merely depressed and disillusioned by the death of their king, their impoverishment and their subjection by a Spanish army, but the peasants even lost their sense of reality and expected Sebastian to return in miraculous form. The nobility were nct so naive as this, but theirs was a different reaction. Silveira, when he returned to

Portugal in 1598, was quick to notice the difference : the bureaucracy at home, in its own way, showed the same grasping, totally unfeeling hardness he knew all about in Goa—and he topped off his tract on the reform of India with one on reform in Portugal itself.[27]

King Philip II visited Portugal in 1581 and for a time made Lisbon his capital. One of his first major actions was to swear before the Portuguese *cortes* that he would in all respects conduct himself in Portugal as a Portuguese king and appoint only Portuguese to posts in the metropolis and Portuguese overseas colonies. He thus, of course, recognized the importance of patronage in maintaining allegiance.

But he forgot—or could not do anything about—the national feeling. While in Lisbon, he received the feudal homage of appointees to office personally. Normally, kneeling before the king and placing one's hands inside his must have a highly emotional experience; even today, royalty's presence has not lost its magic in Europe, much less in republican countries like the United States It is even probable that in bygone centuries such an act of fealty served to keep the basically honest on the narrow and straight path. One can also imagine, though, that officeholders already in India who had sworn allegiance to King Sebastian or to the Cardinal-King Henry and who did not return home to renew their oaths for different offices, but instead swore them before the viceroy, might hardly feel especially bounden. Nor, probably, did appointees who knelt before the Hapsburg viceroy in Lisbon after Philip had departed for Spain once again. The experience might only have served to remind them that they were serving an absentee foreigner.

Whether or not alienation from the Spanish monarchy had anything to do with it, the hard times in Portugal almost certainly did, and the crop of officeholders who appeared in India after 1580 may well have been more grasping than ever their antecedents were. Couto has a judge saying : " I pass sentence according to who gives me the most; I don't pay attention to (the right or wrong of) Bartolo or Baldo (John Doe and Joe Smith) because that would be living from hand to mouth and tied to a salary; after three years I intend to have twenty thousand cruzados."[28] No idealist. he ! All sense of responsibility (except to himself) and loyalty are absent. On the other hand this mentality is paralled by a story told fifty years earlier by Simão Botelho, the honest *vedor da fazenda* already mentioned : when accused of irregularities, the captain of Ormuz replied that, as a Noronha, he felt obliged to steal more than his predecessor, a Lima, who had made away with a mere 140,000 *pardaos*.[29] This was around 1550, and whether things demonstrably worsened after 1580 is hard to establish with any certainty.

One of the reasons that the Portuguese aristocracy may have been so adept at stealing from the royal treasury in India, is that the crown was uniquely indulgent of its high nobility, its foremost two or three per cent. Barring a few occasional deeds of treachery which the crown treated severely but individually, the Portuguese kings seem to have been exceptional in playing Father Christmas to their influential magnates and a few others without demanding very much in return. It would almost seem that the king, if not the world, owed them a comfortable living.

In fact, these trendsetters all received generous salaries from the crown on the basis of status alone, or status and past service: witness the 592 benefices, or *comendas*, which the crown handed out among the 500 or so foremost noblemen of the land, through inducting them into the Orders of Christó, Alcântara and Aviz, sometimes awarding more than one *comenda* to the same individual. Of these, 60 of the life time benefices, based on the Orders, lands, paid as much or more annually than the 600,000 *réis* nominal salary of the most important captaincies of Ormuz, Diu, Muscat, Bassein, Chaul or Columbo. Moreover, if one compares the benefices with Diogo do Couto's salary, at 120,000 *réis* per year, which was approximately that of an official at middle management rank, then of the 592 in total, there were 342 which equalled or exceeded his salary![30] In return, the recipients had to perform no real services whatsoever, despite the crusading origins of the brotherhoods and their high-sounding ideals. Philip III (IV of Spain) for instance, tried to induce members to go fight in Brazil against Dutch invaders in 1636—or at least surrender 1/4 to 1/6 of the incomes from their benefices for this purpose. Not only did the members resist vigorously, but the *Mesa de Relação*, or Portuguese high court, accused the king of exceeding his powers![31] In the end, the attempt came to nothing. It is noteworthy, by the way, that in Spain, most benefices no longer went to individuals, but were mortgaged to the Fuggers early in the reign of Charles V, along with the lands themselves.[32]

No doubt the spectacle of this preferment was not lost on the others, who though noble themselves, were not so fortunate as to have had such a sinecure tossed into their laps. Among them there could have been few of the third sons and poorer cousins who did not cherish the secret hope that he might one day fall heir to such a fat stipendium; it certainly would have beaten work as a royal overseer or treasurer. So, probably, when the lesser nobility did get an appointment to such a job, it was far more conscious of the salary and "perks" than in the duty involved. A case of (in modern psychological parlance) "role models".

I am of course dealing with imponderables and uncertainties, but the idea had entered my mind years ago that the kings of Portugal had made their most fundamental mistake when they awarded posts in the Indian empire, not on the basis of fitness or the expectation of competent performance, but as I wrote at the beginning of this chapter, as a lesser reward than the benefices for the nominee's status or previous service, including that of relatives. Thus the implication was that it was his to plunder. But I soon rejected the thought as holding much relevance for the time itself because it seemed to me a prime example of historian's hindsight: probably the age itself could not have thought that way at all.

But then, I came across this passage in one of the letters of Dom João de Castro from which I have previously quoted. It was written in 1539, to Dom João III:

> . . . you gave me licence to advise you on various things which seemed to me the breeders of trouble: the first and foremost would be that it seems to me very prejudicial for

> both your peace of mind and your treasury to give captaincies, factories and other offices in India as *payment* for services rendered. The proof of this is the destruction of your substance which we witness as following in its wake—that a captain or a factor having finished their terms each carry off a hundred thousand cruzados from their posts . . . though this damage could be greatly emended if it could be seen to that Your Highness might choose persons sufficient in themselves for the jobs. While this might seem the most difficult thing in the world to determine, still I think that if a number of people would go about it deliberately and upon advice, we would see things go much better.[33]

One could hardly do much better than that in putting one's finger on at least part of the real trouble. Of course, the choice of unfit persons for office was not peculiar to the Portuguese, but the giving away of offices as rewards for service and at such enormous distance from the metropolis may well have been so. After all no power in the sixteenth century ever had such distant offices to give away, and certainly not in areas which brought them into contact with such great wealth. In Spanish America, as already suggested, a royal employee was seldom in a position to prestidigitate much lucre on his own, if only because the natives were poor and trade was concentrated in a few hands.

Businessmen, like those found in the English and Dutch India Companies, were and are by nature realists, because their survival depends upon their just appraisal of their markets and their attunement to them. Noblemen, however, had to act businesslike only when managing their own estates; as soon as they could partake in a war or find a posh appointment at court, the only limit on their conduct might be how much they could carry off without being caught. Moreover, the social prestige lay in generosity and grandeur : how big an estate, how many hangers-on, how much influence, how big a party. Hence, in India "service," as at home in any sinecure, no amount of money was "enough." Save for the viceroy and his entourage, who were limited by an all-but-automatic cutoff of three years to their Asian possibilities, no doubt so long as a *fidalgo* once in India could arrange still another appointment for himself, he would stay to stuff his pockets, since sailing home would usually not have resulted in any job nearly as profitable. In fact, save for the viceroy and a few top officers whom the king may have wished to season for better posts at court, the lesser officials seem merely to have been "out of sight, out of mind." The metropolis held much less for them in future than India did.

Nor did Dom João de Castro miss the implications this held for the Estado da India :

> I observe everywhere that Your Highness awards all the offices of this land to men who have been out here many years. This might appear to be a fitting incentive that people should enjoy their rewards and benefits in the place where they serve. However, it would be better if Your Highness might pass these [favours] out in Portugal, for services rendered here [in India]—because I think it would constitute a great service to God that such persons should never return here once they had departed. Please forgive me Your Highness for not giving you more reasons for this opinion I hold.[34]

In other words, Dom João wanted to get rid of the "Old India Hands"—or rather, to prevent their formation as a reservoir of (bad) experience, influence and example. For he goes on to say :

> A thing I wish to impress upon Your Highness is that you should not allow men to grow old in this India, but you should oblige all the older men to leave here, because just as in other places they are the model and examples of virtue and good precept, here they found schools of vice and become teachers of scandals and discord and great spreaders of all kinds of detrimental talk of much tribulation to the commonwealth, without a single benefit to Your Highness of their services or to the Royal domain.[35]

It seems to me that the only possible conclusion one can draw is that the corruption is hardly result of a *decadência* which only set in after Portuguese India had been in existence for sixty years or so, as Couto implies. Rather, it seems really no more than the consequence of permanent conditions : patronage, the nature and attitudes of the Portuguese nobility and the distance from the metropolis. No doubt an otiose and privileged court nobility at home set the pace, or rather, non-pace, giving rise to the notion that the crown owed the *fidalguia* a living—and that the Indian administrative posts were rewards rather than responsibilities. With easy money available for those willing to suspend their scruples, the small group of *fidalgos* adventurous or desperate enough to make the long, dangerous trip eagerly did so. Moreover, as Dom João de Castro says, and as Couto intimates, the clique of experienced crooks already *in situ* corrupted the newcomers, no doubt in part to protect themselves and in part to gain confederates. This formed an ongoing society with the characteristics already described and witnessed. Hence (though I am not sure the term really has meaning here) the corruption was "structural" and not merely an aberration.

There remains one question of interest : would the consciousness of Portuguese Asia as a uniquely corrupt place-indeed that corruption was its most salient feature to many peoples' mind ever have emerged without the *Soldado Prático* ? I do not know, but I do believe that a book, a remark or an event can become famous only when it seems to epitomize a perception that many have experienced independently. Thus Sir Winston Churchill's "Iron Curtain" speech at Fulton, Missouri, in 1946, could never have become famous unless his listeners were already aware that the Russians were indeed behaving anti-socially toward western Europe and had effectively sealed off their own sphere of influence. The evidence for Portuguese corruption is certainly in the documents and chronicles for all to read; hence the *Soldado Prático* distills one's own observations and easily becomes accepted.

But, as I remarked in my preface, it has gone even further than mere acceptance among scholars in the field : it has created a "black legend" of Portuguese decadence in Asia because so many Portuguese—and even foreigners who know very little else about Portuguese Asia know that it was venal and corrupt. They "know" this at first-, or even second-or third-hand because the *Soldado Prático* has become a classic, one whose contents are familiar, but whose words are now seldom read.

NOTES

1. Justus Strandes, *The Portuguese Period in East Africa* (tr. Jean F. Wallwork and ed. J.S. Kirkman), Nairobi (East African Literature Bureau), 1961, pp. 267-296.
2. Richard S. Whiteway, *The Rise of Portuguese Power in India 1497-1550*, London and Santiago de Compostela (Susil Gupta), second edition, 1967, p. 297.
3. J. Hurstfield, "Political Corruption in Modern England," in *History*, no. 52 (1967), p. 19. Notice that in Chapter IV, Linschoten uses a similar criterion, which his translator has translated as "commonwealth."
4. Michael N. Pearson' "Corruption and Corsairs in Sixteenth Century Western India : A Functional Analysis," in Blair B. Kling and M.N. Pearson, jt. eds., *The Age of Partnership ; Europeans in Asia before Dominion* Honolulu (University Press of Hawaii), 1979, pp. 19 ff.
5. Jacob Van Klaveren, "Die historische Erscheinung der Korruption" in ihrer Zusammenhang mit der Staats-und Gesellschaftsstruktur betrachtet," in *Vierteljahrschrift für Sozial-und Wirtschaftsgeschichte*, no. 44 (1957), pp. 289-324.
6. Franklin C. Lane, "National wealth and Protection Costs," in *War as a Social Institution : the Historian's Perspective*, Jesse D. Clarkson and Thomas C. Cochran (jt. eds.), New York (American Historical Association), 1966, pp. 39-41.
7. As I have previously explained in Chapter II, note 36, sale of offices in Portuguese Asia was viceregal, not royal, and clandestine, not official. (That is, save for a very brief period after 1616.) Moreover, viceroys never possessed the actual power to appoint, except perhaps on an interim basis, and only to the minor jobs. The major posts, that of the viceroy himself, the *vedor da fazenda*, the *desembargador da coroa*, the principal *ouvidores*, or judges of the *relação* and the principal fortress captains were all appointed from Lisbon, and in event that they had died or were absent when their triennia began, these were alternate royal nominations, not only one but three or four in depth for each position. Whether open sale, as in the Spanish case, or *sub rosa* sale, as in the Portuguese Asian, afforded any benefits for the "commonwealth," i.e. the public interest, is hard to say. Probably both sets of officeholders worked equally hard on their "perks" to regain their investments and extract whatever profits were

inherent in performing their services. Only one aspect of the problem is clear : the Spanish crown at least could bank the purchase price, while the Portuguese viceroys enriched only themselves with moneys paid them for nominations to the crown. On the other hand, since the crown did not realize a gain from any sale of the more petty offices, it lacked the incentive to create unnecessary ones merely for the sake of selling them. Ultimately, this may have rendered the Portuguese system more "efficient," at least in this respect. My characterization of the Spanish New World system is chiefly based upon John Horace Parry, *The Spanish Seaborne Empire*, New York (Alfred A. Knopf), 1966, pp. 207-211. His more extended treatment of the subject is : *The Sale of Public Office in the Spanish Indies under the Hapsburgs*, Berkley (University of California Press). 1953. How the viceroys influenced the crown on nomination is illustrated in *Documentos Remetidos*, I, p. 366.

8. As set forth in Jorge Juan and Antonio de Ulloa's *Noticias Secretas*, alias *A Voyage to South America : describing at large the Spanish cities, towns, provinces, etc., on that extensive continent*, 2 vols., London, 5th edition, 1807, (or original Spanish edition, the *Relación historica del viaje a la América Meridional*, etc., 4 vols., Madrid, 1748).
9. I have chiefly employed A. Mervyn Davies' old but still serviceable biographies of Clive and Hastings (*Clive of Plassey ; a Biography*, New York (G.P. Putnam's sons), 1935 and *Strange Destiny : a Biography of Warren Hastings*, New York (Charles Scribner' sons) 1939. But I think more recent works do not alter the verdicts). See also vol. V of the *Cambridge History of India*, ed. Henry H. Dodwell, Cambridge (Cambridge University Press), 1929, and Peter J. Marshall, *The Impeachment of Warren Hastings*, London (Oxford University Press), 1965.
10. For some flagrant shenanigans, however, see A.K.A. Gijsberti Hodenpijl, "De Gouverneurs van Koromandel Christiaan van Teylingen, 1761-1765, en Pieter Haksteen, 1765-1771," in *Bijdragen voor Vaderlandsche Geschiedenis en Oudheidkunde*, V no X, pp. 134-157, 257-277 ; VII no II, pp. 109-123 ; VI no III, pp 281-300.
11. See Schwartz, *Sovereignty and Society in Colonial Brazil, passim.*
12. See *Ruth Pike, Aristocrats and Traders; Sevillian Society in the Sixteenth Century*, Ithaca and London (Cornell University Press), 1972, pp. 80-81.
13. Except, of course, for those of Castile itself, and in the New World proceeds from the *quinto real* and the Indian *servicio*, plus an occasional "voluntary" donation in time of acute crisis. See Koenigsberger, *Practice of Empire*, pp. 53-58 and 129 ff. ; John H. Elliott, *The Revolt of the Catalans; A Study in the Decline of Spain* (1598-1690), Cambridge (Cambridge University Press), 1963. pp. 182-193 ; Haring, *Spanish Empire in America*, pp. 274-297.

14. Steengaard, *Carracks, Caravans and Companies*, pp. 86-88.
15. In 1608, the king warned his viceroy that antecessors had used moneys intended for the contractual purchase of pepper. He says that in "no case whatsoever, no matter how stringent the necessity" must this be done. See *Documentos Remetidos* I, p. 191. Three years later, Lisbon complained that false weights used in Cochin resulted in a considerable shortfall. It ordered investigations and punishments. See *Documentos Remetidos* II, pp. 6-8.
16. See Chapter III, n. 35.
17. Charles R. Boxer, *Portuguese India in the Mid-Seventeenth Century*, Delhi (Oxford University Press), 1980, p. 11.
18. Mack Walker, *German Home Towns; Community State and General Estate, 1648-1871*, Ithaca (Cornell University Press), 1971; Gerhard Benecke, *Society and Politics in Germany*, 1500-1750, London (Routledge and Keagan Paul), 1974.
19. See letter of Frei Vicente de Laguna, in Silva Rego, *Documentação*, II, p. 194.
20. Couto, *Soldado Prático*, p. 130.
21. Henrique da Gama Barros, *História da Admtnistração Pública em Portugal nos Séculos* XII à XV (2nd edition, ed. Torquato de Sousa Soares), 9 vols., Lisbon (Sá da Costa), 1945, III, p. 257, n. 4.
22. A.H.R. de Oliveira Marques, *History of Portugal*, 2 vols., New York and London (Columbia University Press), 1972, vol. I *From Lusitania to Empire)*, pp. 180-181.
23. In Fitzler, *Cêrco de Columbo*, pp. 140-143.
24. Couto, *Soldado Prático*, p. 152. Royal nominations in favour of a *fidalgo* then in Portugal always stipulated that he must take up office in the next triennium; so, the temptation to derail him in favour of a local (and no doubt, paying) candidate must have been great. For an example of this, see *Documentos Remetidos* I, p. 382.
25. E.W. Bovill, *The Battle of Alcazar ; An Account of the Defeat of Don Sebastian of Portugal at El-Ksar el-Kebir*, London (the Batchworth Press), 1952, pp. 167-168.
26. See Joaquim Verissimo Serrão, *Historia de Portugal*, 6 vols.-date, Lisbon (Editorial Verbo), 1974-date, IV (1580-1640), 1979, pp. 342 ff.
27. Called *Discursos sobre a Reformoção de Justiça da Comarca da Beira e antre Douro e Minho em q se se descreveram os defeitos q ha na administração della, e os remedios verdadeiros e mais faciles pa. se emendarem com outras materias tocantes ao bem Universal deste Reino. Dirigidos a Elrey Catholico N. Snr. por Franco Roiz Silveira*, Document 49-XI-19 in the Ajuda Palace Library, Lisbon. The same text, with a few additions, follows the *Reformação da Milicia e Governo* of the same author in the British Museum Library copy. Ironically enough, it is even possible that the Hapsburgs purposely favored the country nobility over the court nobility in an attempt to cripple the central government and encourage regionalism. See Joel Serrão (ed.)

Dicionário de História de Portugal, 4 vols., Lisboa (Iniciativas Editoriais) 1971, III, pp. 154-155.

28. Couto, *Soldado, Prático* p. 155.
29. *Cartas de Simão Botelho* in *Subsidios*, p. 32.
30. Luíz de Figueiredo Falcão, *Livro em que contem toda a fazenda e reai patrimonio dos Reinos de Portugal, India e Ilhas Adjacentes*, (ms. of the 17th century), Lisboa (Imprensa Nacional), 1859, pp. 209-268.
31. Stuart B. Schwartz, "Luso-Spanish Relations in Hapsburg Brazil, 1580-1690," in *The Americas*, 25 (1968), no. 60, p. 47.
32. By the 17th century in Spain, the three orders had only 182 *encomiendas* in total, and those were mostly sold as investments. See Antonio Dominguez Ortiz, *La Sociodad Española en el Siglo XVII*, I, Madrid (C.S.I.C.), 1963, pp. 192-201.
33. Sanceau, *Cartas de Dom João de Castro*, p. 30.
34. Ibid., p. 31.
35. Ibid., p. 31.

9

A SECOND SIGHT

MODERN spectacles enable one to see modern sights very sharply indeed, but they may not penetrate farther into the past than do our modern concerns. Couto's *Soldado Prático* and Silveira's *Reformação* are after all only manuscripts, while the concept of a *decadência* was built upon their descriptions at a much later time. Which raises the problem : present-day government is more permeated than early modern polity was with high ethical values derived from Judeo-Christianity, and it is imbued, like Couto's and Silveira's writings, with ideas that officeholders ought to perform according to these standards (though they often don't). Are we, therefore, not seeing our own reflection in their writings and missing a lesson—an interesting one about how things were actually done in the past ?

I write this way because of two colleagues. One of them, the late D.J. Roorda, a distinguished Europeanist, was very skeptical of my definitions and ideas about corruption one night during a *stafdispuut* at Leiden University, but being the open-minded man he is, my argument half-convinced him that something must have been wrong in the period of which we had been talking, because if not, contemporaries like Couto and Silveira would never have seen fit to report it. I say "half convinced" because I think like Galileo in defeat he muttered something about their being "outsiders," even as he conceded my point. Professor Roorda, however, being a Europeanist, saw things only from a European standpoint.

My other colleague, Professor J.C. Heesterman, is an Indologist and he listened with fascination to all my ideas that night. Allegations about corruption left him unperturbed. "A very normal state of affairs...a fairly stable system," he said. "Fits very nicely into India," I heard him say to my amazement that the Portuguese imperium in Asia showed more broad similarities to than differences from that of the Mughals. The Portuguese did bring some features from Europe, true, he continued, but it was these which gave their operation the novelty to thrive. For instance, the naval organization and emphasis on sea fortresses provided it with new opportunities for the collection of tolls which did not interfere with anyone else's territory. Hence there was room for them as interlopers. Most aspects were startlingly similar, he thought. Both imperia depended upon a professional warrior class and were dedicated to conquests which, however, led to instability because the acquisition of new property only led to the addition of dependent clients who added to the drain on the treasury and increased vulnerability. Similarly, those who actually controlled the trade routes as often acted against as for the interests of the state (in the Portuguese case, the fortress captains), yet without their co-operation, the state would have no money. Both empires had too little food production in the lands they controlled;[1] this created an important opportunity for financiers and traders to preempt both the import of extra foodstuffs and the lending of moneys to sustain the peasants in lean years. But perhaps most importantly, the viceroy, like the Mughal, was not in a position to exercise anything like absolute authority : every officeholder, every captain and every merchant and financier exercised his own claim on the complex of power and economics that comprised the body politic. Heesterman also asserts that if any of these claims—call them "perquisites," if you like came into conflict with ruler's will, then it was he who usually suffered, not the claims or perquisites. But in practice, the roles of the various imperial participants were remarkably well attuned to one another, or at least well tolerated by one another, both in the Mughal and the Portuguese systems. Everyone enjoyed his *Lebensraum* though, in the Portuguese case, since the viceroy was not the ultimate (though he was the practical) authority, it was the king who always launched the investigations and punishments, not the viceroy.[2]

Heesterman went still further in his assertion that the Portuguese Asian empire was Indian in character. "Do you suppose," he asked, "that all of those dumb *fidalgos* were actually sitting at desks adding up port duties, tax receipts and the like ?" I replied that I didn't know about that, but that the local administration over the natives living under Portuguese rule was always in the hands of their own headmen, the *gancars*. I also remembered what the French jewel trader Jean-Baptiste Tavernier had written about the clever Kanarese in Goa and that he had said the Portuguese tended to prefer them to Portuguese themselves as lawyers, scribes and receivers. Tavernier, who twice visited Goa during the 1640's, said that some, in fact, were very wealthy, travelling about the streets with an entourage of their own slaves. He regrets that they were not employed to augment the strength of the state, meaning, no doubt, that they should have been given posts in the administration.[3] Certainly, they did not do literally possess them, but it would be surprising if they did not do much of the humdrum work for their masters. It is also more than likely that the Hindu merchants or *vanias*, were influenced and collaborated with the backbone of the Portuguese business class, the *casados*. For one might wonder, with whom were *casados* married? After all, practically no European women were available in Goa for matrimony. Probably, all the *casados* had Konkani or Gujarati brothers-in-law. And for these, having a Portuguese brother-in-law no doubt offered great advantages.[4]

It appears to have been a regular thing in the Mughal empire that moneys expropriated from the state were then cycled into the networks of the financiers, where that money then made more money. From what Tavernier says this happened in the Portuguese Asian empire, too :[5] the officials, the financiers and the merchants were doubtlessly all linked together, and for each group of *fidalgos* from Portugal, the crown inadvertently provided their investment source in the form of office. It is interesting that in Portugal itself, while the nobles regularly invested in trade, they seldom became merchants directly. In Goa they seem to have followed the same pattern : the holding of office comprised the prestige—and as we have seen, it offered its own unique monetary opportunities. The gains then were invested in the commercial networks surrounding the Portuguese fortresses to make more money.

Hence I might turn Heesterman's observation about Indianization another way, and say that the Portuguese Asian Empire was *literally* half Indian that is, *mestiço*, and that the European born *reinois* literally shaded off into the native population within the first generations, with money following bloodlines right through into the Indian economy. In other words, the Europeans' investments quickly became Indianized via the parallel economy, and the bridge between Europe and Asia was provided by their own relatives. And not only *mestiços* were involved : Hindu traders were as eager and acceptable as the *casado* merchants to the Portuguese investors.[6] It is interesting that the rural native Goan Christians even complained to the authorities that Hindus were often better treated than they.[7] Of course, one cannot blame the Hindu *vanias* for wishing to take Portuguese investments, because no doubt when a Portuguese official, the higher the better, gave them his money, he would see to it they were properly protected may be even from his government's own taxes.[8] Even their own relatives could not accomplish that.

From this line of reasoning it might well emerge that the European elements in Goan life were confined to the more formal aspects of the bureaucracy imposed by Lisbon, features common to the age, and also embodied in the Spanish and even Genoese and Venetian overseas organizations. But the organization itself was located in India and operated according to its peculiar possibilities and norms.

In its own way, the crown must have conceded that point, if grudgingly. At least it understood that, to find personnel to serve there, it had better not ask questions, or too many of them, and its occasional order for investigations and arrests were probably intended more to keep the officers in India from taking too much for granted than to effect any real house-cleaning. Besides it must be remembered, the metropolis was largely insulated from Goa by the independent financial systems. So long as the pepper trading on the king's account was on the whole decently managed, the crown, too, was inclined to be tolerant. Perhaps this was why no councillor in Lisbon paid much heed to Silveira on his return in 1598.

There seems to have been one other and highly dangerous—way in which the Portuguese Asian empire had become "Indianized," namely that of military defence. For while the original Portuguese conquerors had used round ships mounted with heavy naval guns to establish their supremacy, they soon found that they could easily maintain it with light galleys such as those used by the Indians themselves. When once their European rivals appeared, these naval forces, so well suited to their native enemies, were severely outclassed. One can observe the confusion in Rodrigues de Silveira's writings: he wrote that part of his *Reformação* dealing with upgrading of the Portuguese fighting vessels before the Dutch menace became apparent to him, and he does not clearly take into account in his later additions that even his own plans would have to be modified if *Ásia Portuguesa* were to meet the new challenge successfully. Probably even he did not clearly recognize the problem. and surely, most of his contemporaries learned only through bitter experience, and that when it was already too late. One can conclude that the Portuguese may have lost out in the struggle with their European rivals in part because they had adapted themselves too fully in India to Indian military norms.

Silveira and Couto were ambitious but honest Christians who, could not, or would not, accept the roles ordained for them. As Roorda remarked, they were "outsiders." They were above all "Europeans," at all times.

To change Roorda's perspective only slightly, it might well be that the "outsider" vs. "insider" concept really involves an early, a *point*, manifestation of opposing conceptions of the state. The *fidalguia* (and even the crown at times) could only think in terms of traditional networks of patronage and a ruling hierarchy based upon hereditary privilege. That is the way it had been for more than a thousand years ruling was the job of the upper classes and no one had challenged their basic right to rule. But now the outsiders, as represented by Couto and Silveira, have-and in the name of the crown itself questioned this monopoly, claiming that experienced commoners could serve the state more capably, and even faithfully. Silveira was the more imaginative and he goes on to propose something like a modern merit system coupled to a review board. Both of these are of course standard fixtures of our own present-day bureaucracies.

Obviously both men were trying to make room in the system for themselves and people like themselves, and to do so they had to change the shape of the state. Of course they didn't succeed – nobody did until the 18th century – and the aristocrats in Portugal were not about to move over just because a couple of dissidents had each written a manuscript. But I even wonder if it is not slightly more than coincidence that the date the *Soldado Prático* actually found its way into print was 1790, only one year after the beginning of the French Revolution ? Perhaps only by then was anyone in Europe ready for Couto's message. Still more interesting it is that the wholly common and more openly radical Silveira—or rather, his manuscript had a brush with a Portuguese nobleman as late as 1877 ! Roorda was thus right indeed ; his instincts as an historian of early modern Europe did not betray him. In fact it might not be going too far to assert that the whole Portuguese *decadência* was a concept grounded in middle class "outsiders." (Even the "witnesses" of Chapter IV fall into this category, when one comes to think of it).

At this point, one begins to wonder whether either Couto or Silveira would have written their *exposés* if they had been members of the noble inner circle and thus eligible to climb the ladder. Obviously, the question cannot be answered with any certainty, but it is fairly obvious that Couto craved recognition above all, and would have been happy to achieve it.[9] I do know that no *fidalgo* in Portuguese Asia or Europe ever seems to have addressed the problem other than in terms of trying to catch individual malefactors in cases where the law had been broken. Probably those on the inside simply lacked the perspective of an outsider, as though they had not only been "to the manor born" but never went out-of-doors to view it as a piece of architecture.

Of course if one considers the *decadência* itself on moral grounds— and may be it does belong there, too—the conduct of the people under scrutiny may only go to show that most of us humans indeed regulate our actions by what "others do" and not what our religion (virtually any religion) teaches us or our "still, small voices" dictate. In Portuguese India one could both observe and get away with far more than in Portugal, obviously because it was so distant from the mother culture and because the opportunities for self-enrichment existed there which no Portuguese had known at home.

Older writers all assumed that there was a direct connection between Portuguese official behaviour and Portuguese decline in Asia during the seventeenth century, and, of course no one can prove that there wasn't. But, as Professor Boxer has repeatedly pointed out, no one really needs corruption as an explanation wh n there are so many better ones at hand. As he wrote twenty years ago : "Apart from anything else, it is difficult to see how Portugal, with a population of a little over a million, could have developed effectively, or even maintained intact, her colonial settlements in three continents at a time when The Netherlands, France and England, with their far greater resources, were vying for colonial supremacy."[10] One would gather, therefore, that about all one could have expected from an efficient and well-run *Estado da Índia* would have been a somewhat lesser decline than it actually experienced. There, at least, that matter must rest, because it can be drawn out no further.

Nor do I wish, at this final stage, to be tempted into any set definitions of corruption, for I think I have shown that they are circumstantial, approximate and elusive. One can indeed perceive from my study, however, that things in the *Estado da Índia Oriental* did not run as they were supposed to, and that the divergence was wide enough to attract attention, even in the 16th and 17th centuries. I have merely tried to examine and explain this considerable problem—and for the simple reason that the "Black Legend" constantly gets in the way of all historians who work in Portuguese Asian history. In fact that "things did not run as they were supposed to" may be, after all, about the extent of this study's real findings. "Corruption," one discovers, is in the mind of the beholder at least as a political concept, and the unabridged Oxford and Webster's dictionaries take an abnormally large number of words to define nothing very definite. I can only hope that a future political scientist will arrive at a precise and satisfactory conclusion on the subject and that my name and the title of this little book will appear in his bibliography.

But all having been said, I do sincerely believe that the *Soldado Prático* and its study has afforded a ringside seat for the examination of human nature under highly colourful circumstances. The vista, of course, is really a reflection of ourselves, in one of our true dimensions.

NOTES

1. Cf. Disney, *Twilight of Pepper Empire*, p. 17.
2. I do not wish to become involved in a debate over the nature of the Mughal Empire here but merely to indicate how Professor Heesterman stimulated my thinking. See J.C. Heesterman's article "Was there an Indian Reaction? Western Expansion in Indian Perspective," in *Expansion and Reaction; Essays on European Expansion in Asia and Africa* (Comparative Studies in Overseas History, I), Leiden (Leiden University Press), 1978, pp. 31-58. Unless, Heesterman added, he had a personal feud to settle, or like the Counts—viceroy Linhares or Óbidos, he was determined to 'reform' the system in accordance with European ideas.' Óbidos, incidentally, tried the hardest in the 1650's and was rewarded by the first and only Portuguese Asian *coup d'état*, with himself as victim. See Winius, *The Fatal History*, pp. 133-139.
3. See Tavernier, Travels, I, pp. 187-193.
4. For a summary of the native Indian role in the Portuguese Indian Economy, see Boxer's *Portuguese India in the Mid-Seventeenth Century*, p. 43; also see Teotónio R. de Souza, S.J., "Glimpses of Hindu Dominance of Goan Economy in the 17th Century." *Indica*, XII, March, 1975, pp. 27-35 and Michael N. Pearson, "Wealth and Power: Indian Groups in the Portuguese Indian Economy," South Asia, III, pp. 36-44. Souza's and Prof. Pearson's articles fully corroborate Heesterman's instinctive guess. See also Pearson's *Coastal Western India: Studies from the Portuguese Records*, New Delhi (Concept Publishing Company), 1981, chaps. 3, 4, and 5.
5. Tavernier, *Travels*, I, 187. Although Garcia da Orta is no source for political or economic history, he does make one curious statement

which points in this direction. When Ruano, a character in his dialogue, says he has heard that the Portuguese rob the Indian natives, Orta says: "It is true that the Portuguese are not very curious, nor good writers: they are rather friends of action than of words. They work to acquire through their licit trading enterprises—but they do not treat the Indians badly—in fact, peaceful Indians are very much favored by the governors . . ." Orta, *Collóquio dos simples e Drogas da Índia.* (ed. Conde de Ficalho), 2 vols., Lisboa (Imprensa Nacional), 1891, II, p. 248.

6. Such a symbiotic relationship between Europeans and the *vanias* also existed in Bengal at a later date, in this case between (English) East India company and the Hindu merchants, who handled the money and operated under the European partner's privileges. See. Peter J. Marshall, *East India Fortunes, the British in Bengal in the Eighteenth Century*, Oxford (Oxford University Press), 1 76, p. 46.
7. Teotonio R. de Souza, *Medieval Goa; A Socio-Economic History*, New Delhi (Concept Publishing Company), 1979, p. 244.
8. This is a recurrent theme in the *Documentos Remetidos*, but for one good example see Vol. 1 of the printed series, p. 164.
9. One will remember, however, that this book began with a chapter on what is known of Couto's background. It is obvious that he was ambitious for recognition—and that he badly wanted a nomination to the order of Christ and the benefice that went with it As he wrote to Dom Francisco da Gama in 1608, about the time the *Soldado Prático* seems to have been written, or at least revised: "I am writing, year in and year out, for some sign, even a small one, that my services have been appreciated . . . ." Later on in the same letter, he put it in even a more graphic way: "I am amazed at how there is not one fidalgo in the whole kingdom who can argue and cry out my case that the ministers [of the king] owe me some honor, if only to improve my state of mind . . . ." Then he wrote the *Soldado Prático*, which amounted to a blast at the whole system. One wonders whether a habit of Christ, an award from the king of a benefice and membership, would not have caused him to forget his grievances entirely. There is, after all, that cynical, but far from untrue saying that "he who remains quietest has just had some" which should have been inverted to: "he who is most noisy has not had his payoff." Perhaps such reasoning is unfair, but Couto was hardly a saint. Though material gain meant little to him, he was apparently so eager for recognition that gratification of this need might well have acted as his own *sigillum silentio*, his own price for silence. Silveira seems to have had less choice in the matter, for, after all, he totally lacked the credentials of *fidalguia* in the first place. Both quotations are taken from Couto's letter of 1608, as reprinted in the *Revista Litteraria*, pp. 548-549.
10. Charles R. Boxer, "The Portuguese in the East, 1500-1800," in H. V. Livermore (ed.), *Portugal and Brazil; An Introduction*, Oxford (The Clarendon Press), 1963, p. 236.

APPENDIX

CORRUPTION IN THE DOCUMENTOS REMETIDOS OR BOOKS OF THE MONSOONS

No discussion of official corruption in Portuguese India could be complete without some reference to the *Livros das Moncões*, or *Books of the Monsoons*, which, beginning in 1605 and running into the 18th century, represent correspondence between the crown in Lisbon-Madrid and the viceroys or governors in Goa. When the viceregal letters to the king, the other side of this exchange, were destroyed in the great earthquake of November, 1755, in Lisbon, the ruling minister, the Marquês de Pombal, ordered the Goan set to be forwarded to Portugal in order to fill in the gap. Once in Lisbon, they were called the *Documentos Remetidos da India.* From 1880 on, these have been appearing in print at wide intervals. Nine volumes of them were scattered exactly over the spread of a century and reproduce the first eighteen of the original folios, or up to the year 1623. At the present rate of publication, the printed series will not be complete until around the year 2380 or thereabouts !

For the purpose of this study, centering around the career of Diogo do Couto, the present volumes are perfectly sufficient, since they reflect the polity of the Asian empire as Couto knew it. It had occurred to me almost from the beginning of my research to include them in my discussion, for they eloquently support everything and more, that Couto and his contemporaries recorded. Couto, in fact, must have seen the earliest volumes himself, for after all, he was their keeper in the original Goan Torre do Tombo. How to make the optimum use of them baffled me, though.

What I wanted was to give an example of their totality, not just write an essay about them, which was bound to be impressionistic and a bit lopsided. Nor did I particularly wish to translate a few documents from them—for after all, which ones? The baddest? The most typical?

Finally I came upon the scheme which I have utilized in the following pages, one which alone gives a kind of synopticon of what they record and is faithful to the variety and content. I simply took the editor's index describing the contents and called from it all the headings which dealt with malfeasance of some sort—excluding matters which touched upon the church participating in forbidden commerce, which I did not consider in the narrative scope of my study. I then assigned numbers to the various kinds of abuses described and added these to the descriptive index in order to give interested readers a better idea of what was actually being talked about. Then, finally, when I discovered that the document itself treated some misdeed not captured in the descriptive heading, I wrote a note about it. For readers who do not know Portuguese, the combination of these notes and the numbers will at least give them an idea of what is under consideration.

Diogo do Couto died in 1616, and I had originally planned to extend my treatment up to that year, that is through volumes I, II and most of III. I had already spotlighted some of the most spectacular and juicy instances up ahead as far as volume VII, in fact. But I soon discovered that sheer multiplicity of offences made reaching 1616 extremely tedious. I concluded that if I became bogged down after volume I (as I did), no doubt readers would, too. Moreover, I also discovered that, in studying corruption, I was dealing with a sort of commodity, like sausage, and that any decent sample was nearly identical to any other. The *Soldos velhos*, the old debts scandals and the embezzlement of fortress and treasury funds crop up monotonously over forty years, despite all attempts to curb them—as do nearly all the other categories. Only one thing almost tempted me on to volume II: the fact that on the very first page of documentation, a *carta régia* denounces the short-weighing and adulteration of the king's own pepper shipment from Cochin! Hence, should readers find their curiosity or skepticism—unslaked by the following pages, they can apply the system used here to the subsequent books of the series.

I should make one other observation. Namely, that for each abuse, the crown had an informant who tipped it off. Once in a while, this person is named in the document as a trusted overseer of finance or other officer, but he usually remains anonymous.

Key to the abuses listed in volume I of the *Documentos Remetidos da India*

1. Viceroy improperly influencing justice.
2. Other irregularities in the administration of justice, including illegal awards.
3. Abuses involving the *dívidas velhas.*
4. The underpayment, nonpayment or doing of violence to soldiers.
5. The *soldos velhos* scandal; or else, soldiers collecting pay on false pretences or certificates.
6. Abuses involving the despoiling of natives or the misuse of tribute moneys.
7. The overpricing of goods sold to crown and procurement from friends.
8. Officers, visitors or viceroys mulcting fortresses and/or their natural trade.
9. Officers neglecting or refusing to carry out orders, or else exceeding their authority, including by making unauthorized disbursals.
10. Unspecified kinds of disobedience and crime by officials.
11. Excessive patronage on part of Goan administrators and dealings proceeding therefrom; inserting own nominee above one from crown.
12. Embezzlement of funds or their illegal diversion to other purposes, specified or unspecified.
13. Irregularities in the administration of fortresses.
14. Unsuitable persons involved in the administration or justice, either through lack of training or reliability.
15. The viceroy overstepping his authority, either by diverting funds from their allotted usages or by arrogating functions belonging to others.
16. Illegal sale of offices.
17. The use of royal ships to further private trade without

permission, either by fortress captains or other crown officials.

18. Abuses in the coining or distribution of money from the mint, or from the supervision of mines.
19. Abuses involved in the withholding of pensions from dependents.
20. Abuses involving the confiscatory behaviour of the alfândegas, or customs houses.
21. The unauthorized leasing out of monopolies, concessions or customs posts for low costs, then taking kickback or sharing in profits.
22. Illegal transactions involving manipulation or abuse of the spice monopoly.
23. Illegal transactions involving slaves or prisoners.
24. Vacating of an office without paying off indebtedness of various kinds.

1605, Março ? Carta Regia ao vice-rei D. Martim Affonso de Castro. Manda observar a provisão que prohibe aos vice-reis irem mais de uma vez por mez a Relção, para não influirem nas decisões. 1.) Trata dos visitadores enviados às fortalezas, do ouvidor geral e superintendente da alfândega de Ormuz. 8.) Ordena que se proceda a respeito da desobediência de Lourenço de Brito na sua ida aos Rios de Cuama 10.) e que se tire nova residência a Nuno da Cunha, capitão que foi de Sofala. 2.) I, p. 39

1607, Janeiro 13. C. R. ao vice-rei D. Martim Affonso de Castro. Ordena-lhe que se dedique particularmente ao governo e administração da fazenda. 11.) Provê sobre desordens no pagamento de dividas velhas 3.), irregularidades do tribunal dos contos 12.), presentes que os reis da India mandarem ao de Portugal 6.), alfândegas de Malaca, Ormuz, Goa e Diu. 13.) Determina que o vedor da fazenda envie todos os anos os cadernos de receita e despeza do Estado 12.), que as pagas das praças a mais aos capitães das fortalezas, se arrecadem do vice-rei que as auctorisar, e que

Note : An asterisk (*) before a number indicates that the crown is not citing a specific case, but is warning against its repetition, or is legislating against such.

não se concedam aos vedores de Goa e Cochim mais homens que os permittidos pelo regimento. 13.) I, p. 62

1607, Janeiro 16. C.R. ao mesmo. Provem sobre o abuso de se nomearem ouvidores geraes sem serem desembargadores. 14.) Mande que se publiquem e cumpram todas as provisões régias idas do reino. 9.) Confirma a ordem para os vice-reis não serem juizes nas intrancias dos cargos. 15.) Trata...das irregularidades com que se tiram as residências dos capitães das fortalezas. 2.) Faz advertências a respeito do capitão de Moçambique, Sebastião de Macedo, de Nuno da Cunha, e Lourenço de Brito, e sobre as desordens de Gonçalo Rodrigues Caldeira, capitão de Barcelor, e Tomé Affonso Guedes, capitão que foide Cranganor 13). Proibe novamente ao capitão de Malaca e a quaisquer pessoas, que vendem roupas e outras fazendas aos jaos senão a troco de drogas. 13.) I, p. 70

1607, Janeiro 27. C. R. ao mesmo... e recommenda que se evitem os abusos no tomar as residências dos capitães e ouvidores das cidades e fortalezas. 13.) I, p. 124

1607, Janeiro 27. C. R. ao mesmo...Trata do desemparo dos soldados que chegaram á India no ano de 1605 e providenceia para que se não repita semelhante caso. 4.) I, p. 126

1607, Janeiro 30. C.R. ao mesmo...Ordena que se remitta a devassa das culpas de Paulo de Carvalho, que foi enviado para Portugal, onde está preso 10.); que se suspenda a nomeação de capitão ordinario para Macau, e se tire devassa sobre o venda de officios na India. 16.) I, p. 138

1608, Janeiro 2. C.R. ao mesmo. Provê sobre a nomeação sobre o capitão-mór e mais capitães da armada de Diu. 17.). (Note : this caption is not descriptive : the text involves the use of naval vessels for private trade by the associates of the captain of Diu, to the detriment of the state and treasury.) Lembra novamente as necessidades que padecem os soldados idos do reino. 4.)... e dos abusos dos capitães de Malacca, fazendo-se monopolistas das mercadorias que vão aquella praça. 8.) I, p. 164

1608, Janeiro 3. C. R. ao mesmo. Provê sobre as renuncias de cargos e falta de algumas formalidades em patentes e alvarás 16) ; trata do pagamento de tenças à viuvas e orfãos. 19) I, p. 169

1608, Janeiro 15. C.R. ao mesmo...e as representações da câmara dè Diu sobre diversos objectos 8.) e recommenda a vigia de sua fortaleza e a emenda dos abusos que se commetem na alfândega. I, p. 178

1608, Janeiro 23. Madrid. C. R. ao mesmo. Manda que dê ordem ao capitão de Macau para enviar munições ao governador das Filipinas, advertindo que o navio que levar este aviso ou as munições, não transporte nenhumas mercadorias, conforme a vigorosa prohibição de todo o commercio com as Indias occidentaes. (Note : while no actual abuse is directly mentioned here, it is well enough known that illicit trade between Macau and Manila in this period was rife.) 1, p. 186

1608, Fevreiro 12. C.R. ao vice-rei D. Martim Affonso de Castro....do abuso dos capitães, officiaes e marinheiros tomarem dinheiro a responder a risco do casco das naus. 17.) I, p. 187

1608, Fevreiro 23. C.R. ao mesmo. Prohibe que o dinheiro mandado para a carga da pimenta se empregue n'outra qualquer cousa. 12.) Trata do abuso no aforamento das rendas do bangue, sabão, etc., do Chaul 21.); do aforamento dos mandovis 21.) ; do rendamento da alfândega de Ormuz 7, 12. 13.) ; da prisão dos officiaes de moeda da Goa, por baterem moeda mais baixa do que manda o regimento 18.) ; dos bares de cravo e noz que se daram aos capitães de Goa nas naus que iam a Maluco e Banda. 22.) (Note : missing is a caption for a paragraph within the document concerning abuses of funds of the fortresses of Ormuz, Bassein and Diu, where unauthorized payments were made and others, unaccountably, were withheld. 12.) ...dos presentes enviados pelos reis de India aos de Portugal, concedidos aos Padres da Companhia, e abusos que d'ahi vieram. 6, 7.) Manda que os capitães das fortalezas não façam compras nem vendas de cousas pertencentes a fazenda real * 7). (Note : missing is a caption at this point for a paragraph within the document wherein the crown warns that the viceroy should not appoint the *executor dos contos* from among members of his entourage and then pay him an excessive salary, as viceroys have been accustomed to do. * 11, 15.)...e que a câmara não faça acórdãos para despesa da mesma fazenda, além do que está ordenado para presidios. 7,9.) I, p. 191

1608, Fevreiro 29. C.R. ao conde vice-rei Sobre a prohibição dos vice-reis irem mais de uma vez por mez a Relação, e sobre a jurisdicção dos ouvidoros. *1, 2, 15); trata dos inconvenientes dos capitães de Coulão e Cranganor sentencearem por si todas as causas sem appellação 13); das ouvidorias das terras de Salcete, Bardez, e Taná 14.) ; de provimento de logares na Relação 14.)...e tomar residência aos feitores que tenham servido de capitães mais de dois mezes 8.). (Note : missing is a caption here for a royal admonition that judges not solicit or accept *certidões* from *fidalgos* in return for not rendering justice. * 2.)

1608, Março 24. C.R. ao mesmo. Determina que a despeza para os arranjos do embarque dos vice-reis, quando vão a alguma empreza, não corra por mão de qualquer particular, mas pelos officiaes competentes* 11, 12) ; que as tenças concedidas sem informação régia saiam dos 30.000 cruzados que os vice-reis teem para distribuir annualmente 11, 15) ; e que estes não façam mercês aos capitães-móres e mais capitães das naus. * 21) Trata do vedor da fazenda de Cochim 12) ; das quitas aos rendeiros 3.) ; dos abusos na Ribeira Grande e na das Galés 9, 23.) ; da forma por que se deve fazer a despeza por ordem do vice-rei * 15.) ; que se tire informação dos abusos commetidos nos Rios de Cuama na arrecadação dos bens dos defuntos 12.) ; (note : caption is missing for a section on the *rey das Ilhas Maldivas*, in which the crown mentions that captains of the Malabar fortresses should not trade with their own funds in the Maldives, or with those of their subordinates, without paying crown duties. * 13.) and then asserts that there is not a crown official in those fortresses who does not violate the law through forcing loans to gain capital and then trading there without being permitted to. * 8, 17.). I, p. 230

1608, Março 26. C.R. ao mesmo...que se informe do abuso de estarem mais soldados dos que verdadeiramente andam no serviço 5.) I, p. 239

1609, Dezembro 24. C.R. ao vice-rei Ruy Lourenço da Tavora ...Recommenda que se cohibam os abusos de alguns officiaes de justiça 2.) (note : this caption covers four instances of judicial malfeasance : illegal payments by judges and scribes to their relatives and servants, the malpractice whereby *fidalgos* with cases pending before the Relação claim themselves beyond its jurisdiction due to family ties, often claimed or assumed for the occasion, jobs in the judiciary being given to untrained persons, especially friends and servants of the viceroy and the archbishop (14, 16 can be added !) and judges of the Relação issuing certificates to persons not entitled to them) I, p. 275

1610, Janeiro 23. C.R. ao mesmo...Ordena que se proceda contra D. Estevam de Ataíde, capitão que foi de Moçambique 13, 17.). Trata dos bares de cravo que os capitães de Goa tinham nas naus que iam a Maluco e Banda. 17.) I, p. 287

1610, no date. Apontamentos sobre a alfândega de Malaca. (Note : this is an appended document which discusses the illegal trade in spices between Portuguese and Javanese merchants and then asserts the involvement of the captains and their subordinates as well, who did not levy duties on outgoing vessels or declare the true amount of merchandise. 22.) I, p. 320

1610, Fevreiro 19. C.R. ao mesmo...(Note : editor fails to caption a passage wherein crown complains that *capitães-móres* of the *armada do norte* collude to allow enemy traffic to enter and depart. 17.) I, p. 338

1610, Feveiro 22. C.R. ao mesmo. Manda pedir informação do procedimento de Cristóvão Cotrim, provedor dos contos, e dá alguns ordens a respeiro d'aquelle tribunal, e sobre o visto das provisões de pagamentos e cousas pertencentes á fazenda real. 14.) I, p. 361

1610, Fevreiro 22. Alvará por que se ordena que o vedor da fazenda da India ponha o visto nas provisões e mandados que os vice-reis e governadores passarem fazer, e de cousas que são propriamente da fazenda real, etc. * 9.) I, p. 363

1610, Março 2. Alvará por que se manda cumprir uma provisão nelle incorporada sobra a capitania de Goa não se prover d'aqui em diante em pessoa alguma por satisfação de serviços, etc. * 11,&?16.) I, p. 366

1610, Março 8. Alvará por que se ordena que assim que os capitães das fortalezas da India acabarem de servir, enviem logo os feitores d' ellas ao tribunal dos contos todas as obrigações. * 13.) I, p. 368

1610, Março 10.C.R. ao mesmo. Provè sobre a merce de dois mil cruzados para embarcação aos capitaes que iam entrar nas fortalezas de Sofala, Ormuz e Malaca, e sobre a de 500 pardaus aos capitaes das viagens de Goa para Moçambique, e de Coromandel para Malaca. 11,9). Trata da carta que vem annualmente dos contos da Goa para se fazerem execucoes no reino a devedores á fazenda 11.); da desordem nos cadernos dos pagamentos dos soldados das fortalezas 5.); dos capitães das mesmas não se haverem de intrometter em cousa da fazenda real 5.) do modo por que davam contas o feitor e o thezoureiro de Goa e o recebedor de Salcete 12.) ; do alcance do fallecido feitor de Goa 12.) ; e de uma provisão do arcebispo primaz, sendo governador, para que nenhum capitao empreste dinheiro á fazenda * 12.). I, p. 377

1610, Março 12. C.R. ao mesmo. Sobre a nomeação feita pelo arcebispo primaz de criados seus para o cargo de corretor-mór de Ormuz, em que Simão Teixeira fora provido por el-rei. 11.) I, p. 382

1610, Março 16. C.R. ao mesmo. Manda annullar a acclamacão de um irmão segundo de Ferruxá como rei de Ormuz, feita pelo capitão d'aquella cidade, D. Henrique de Menezes. 10.) I, p. 382

1610, Março 19. C.R. ao mesmo...da desobediència da gente de guerra aos capitães. ? *4.) I, p. 387

1610, Novembro 12. C.R. ao vice-rei....das desordens de D. Christovam de Noronha em Moçambique com D. Estevam de Ataide, capitão da fortaleza, e dos capitães da armada do Conde da Feira que não guardaram o regimento que se lhes deu. 10.) I, p. 398

1610, Novembro 12, Alvará pelo qual se determina que nos casos em que pelo regimento da Relação da India se prohibe aos vice-reis poderem passar alvarás de perdão, nam se

admittam em maneira alguma petições para isso. 1.)
I, p. 401

1610, Dezembro 23. C.R. ao vice-rei Ruy Lourenço da Tavora. Manda tirar devassa do chanciller da Relação da Goa, Joao Freire de Andrade por ter aberto o maço em que ia uma das vias de successao do governo do Estado. 10.)
I, p. 401

1610, Dezembro 23. C.R. ao mesmo. Trata das devassas que se mandaram tirar todos os annos dos officiaes dos contos. * 2)...remette provisões para não se acceitarem papeis de dívidas velhas em pagamentos á fazenda. (Note : apparently not from citizens, but from crown employees. 3.) ; sobre satisfaçao de serviços.). Trata dos abusos do licenciado Francisco Gouveia, no pagamento de dinheiros aos moradores de Ormuz. 12.) Envia uma provisão sobre o registo de papeis de duvida da fazenda. 9.) Ordena a Jeronimo de Brito Pedroso que faça execução nos bens dos capitães que foram de Ormuz, Diu e Damão, D. Pedro Coutinho, Duarte de Mello e Ruy Mello de Sampaio, etc. 13.) Recommenda que se tome determinação sobre o desfalque nas pareas que paga o Melique, pelos feitores receberem quatro larins de prata por um pardão de ouro pagode, and so on (Note : it is difficult to know whether this item involves corruption or not; it concerns the annual underpayment to the crown of a tribute contract through the acceptance by the Portuguese crown officials of an exchange rate which was far below par. This may have been through oversight or incompetence on their part, but since the condition seems to have been of very long standing, it is also to be wondered whether the officials were not accustomed to accepting bribes in return for looking the other way. I have assigned no number to this, both because of the uncertainty and because no category quite seems to fit whatever abuse it might involve).
I, p. 405

1610, Dezembro 23. Lisboa. Alvara pelo qual se determina que aos fiadores dos rendeiros, capitães, feitores e officiaes de recebimento na India, não se acceitarem papeis alguns de dívidas velhas em pagamento do dinheiro que ficarem devendo á fazenda real. (Note : this pertains to the *carta régia* above. * 3.) I, p. 410

610, Dezembro 23. Alvará por que se determina que todas as provisões e papeis, dos quaes constem algumas dívidas da fazenda real, se registem em livro numerado pelo vedor da fazenda dos contos, e sem isso, não paguem. *9.) I, p. 411

1610, Dezembro 24. Alvará por que se determina que os soldados e pessoas residentes na India, que não estiverem matriculados na matricula geral, não vencem soldo, nem se lhes faça pagamento d' elle, ainda que provam que andaram nas armadas. *5.) I, p. 417

BIBLIOGRAPHY

[Anonymous], *Arte de Furtar*, Amsterdam, 1652.

Barros, João de and Diogo do Couto, *Da Asia*, 24 vols., Lisbon, 1778.

Bell, Aubrey F.G., *Diogo do Couto*, Oxford (Oxford University Press), 1924.

Benecke, Gerhard, *Society and Politics in Germany*, 1500-1750, London (Routledge and Keagan Paul), 1974.

Botelho, Simão, *Cartas de Simão Botelho*, in *Subsidios para a História da India Portuguesa* (ed. Rodrigo José de Lima Felner) Lisbon (Academia Real das Sciencias), 1868.

Bovill, E.W , *The Battle of Alcazar; An Account of the Defeat of Don Sebastian of Portugal at El-Ksar ef-Kebir*, London (The Batchworth Press), 1952.

Boxer, Charles R., *Portuguese India in the Mid-seventeenth Century*, Delhi (Oxford University Press), 1980.

——"The Portuguese in the East, 1500-1800, in H.V. Livermore (ed.) *Portugal and Brazil; An introduction*, Oxford (The Clarendon Press), 1963.

Cambridge History of India, vol. 5 (ed. Henry H. Dodwolt), Cambridge (Cambridge University Press), 1929.

Coimbra Martins, António, *Uma Questão de Mètodo sobre O Soldado Prático*. As yet unpublished paper offered to the Second International Seminar on Indo-Portuguese History, Lisbon, October, 1982. (It was copied photomechanically and offered to all participants and observers).

Corrêa, Gaspar, *Lendas da India*, 4 vols. Lisbon (Academia Real das Sciências), 1858.

Costa Lôbo, A de S.S. (ed. & comp.), *Memórias de um soldado da India, compiladas de um Manuscripto Portuguès do Museo Británnico*, Lisbon (Imprensa Nacianal), 1877.

Couto, Diogo do, Letters, in *Revista Litteraria*, Porto, 1893, pp. 450-466 and 529-549.

———, *Observações sobre as principaes causas de decadência dos portuguezes na Asia escritas por Diogo do Couto em forma do diálogo com o tĩtulo de Soldado Prático* (ed. Antonio Caetano do Amaral), Lisbon (Academia Real das Sciências), 1790.

———, *O Soldado Prático, ed. M. Rodrigues* Lapa, Lisbon (Colecção de Clássicos Sá da Costa), Lisbon, 1937.

Coutre Esteban de, (actual author, Coutre, Jacques de), *Vida de Iaques de Coutre,* MS 2780, Biblioteca Nacional de Madrid, Madrid.

Cunha Rivara, Joaquim Heliodoro da (ed.) *Archivo Portuguez Oriental,* 6 fascicles in 5 vols., Nova Goa, 1857-1876; V.

Davies, A. Mervyn, *Clive of Plassey; a Biography,* New York (G.P. Putnam's sons), 1935.

———, *Strange Destiny: a Biography of Warren Hastings,* New York (Charles Scribner's sons), 1939.

Diffie, Bailey W. and George D. Winius, *Foundations of the Portuguese Empire,* vol. 1. *1415-1580.* Europe and the world in the Age of Expansion series, ed. Boyd W. Shafer, Minneapolis (University of Minnesota Press), 1977.

Disney, Anthony R., *Twilight of the Pepper Empire; Portuguese Trade in Southeast India in the Seventeenth Century,* Cambridge, Mass. and London, England (Harvard University Press), 1978.

Documentos Remetidos da India ou Livros das Moncões, 9 vols. -date, Lisbon (Academia das Ciências), 1880 - date (to Livro 18 of manuscript volumes) the citations from vols. 55, 56 and 61 are from the manuscript volumes in the Arquivo Nacional da Torre do Tombo, Lisbon).

Dominguez Ortiz, Antonio, *La Sociedad Española en el Siglo XVII,* I Madrid (Consejo Superior de Investigaciones Científicas), 1963.

Elliott, John H., *The Revolt of the Catalans; A Study in the Decline of Spain,* Cambridge (Cambridge University Press), 1963.

Espinosa, Antonia Vázquez de, *Description of the Indies* (tr. Charles U. Clark) Washington D.C. (the Smithsonian Institution), 1968.

Falcão, Luíz de Figueiredo, *Livro em que se contem toda a fazenda e real patrimonio dos Reinos de Portugal, India e Ilhas Adjacentes*, Lisbon (Imprensa Nacional), 1859.

Fitzler, M.A. Hedwig (ed. & comp.), *O Cêrco de Columbo; Ultimos dias do dominio português em Ceilão. Rompimento das hostilidades pelos holandeses até a rendição de Columbo* (1652-1656) Coimbra (Coimbra University Press), 1928.

Gama Barros, Henrique da, *História da Administração Pùblica em Portugal nos seculos XII á XV* (2nd edition, ed. Torquato de Sousa Soares), 9 vols., Lisbon (Sá da Costa), 1945, III.

Gijsberti Hodenpijl, A.K.A., "De Gouverneurs van Koromandel Christiaan van Teylingen, 1761-1765, en Pieter Haksteen, 1765-1771." in *Bijdragen voor Vaderlandsche Geschiedenis en Oudheidkunde*, V no. X, pp. 134-157 and 257-277; VI no. II, pp. 109-123; VI no. III, pp. 281-300.

Godinho, Vitorino Magalhães, *Les Finances de l 'État Portugais des Indes Orientales (1517-1635)*; (Materiaux pour une Etude Structurale e Conjoncturelle), Paris (Fundação Calouste Gulbenkian; Centro Cultural Português), 1982.

Hanson, Carl A., *Economy and Society in Baroque Portugal, 1668-1703*, Minneapolis (University of Minnesota Press), 1981.

Haring, Clarence H., *The Spanish Empire in America*, Cambridge, Massachusetts (Harvard University Press), 1947.

Heesterman, Jan C. "Was there an Indian Reaction ? Western Expansion in Indian Perspective", in *Expansion and Reaction*; *Essays on European Expansion in Asia and Africa* (Comparative Studies in Overseas History, 1) Leiden (Leiden University Press), 1978.

Hurstfield, J., "Political Corruption in Modern England", in *History*, no. 52 (1967).

Juan, Jorge and Antonio de Ulloa, *A Voyage to South America: describing at large the Spanish cities, towns, provinces, and so on that extensive continent*, 2 vols., London, 5th edition, 1807. (The original Spanish version of 1748 was the *Relación historica del viaje a la America Meridional*).

Klaveren, Jacob van, "Die Historische Erscheinung der Korruption in ihrer zusammenhang mit der Staats-und

Gesellschaftstruktur betrachtet", in *Vierteljahrschrift für Sozial- und Wirtschafsgeschichte*, no 44 (1957).

Koeningsberger, Helmut G., *the Practice of Empire*, Ithaca (Cornell University Press), 1969.

Lane, Franklin C., "National Wealth and Protection Costs", in *War as a Social Institution: the Historian's Perspective*, Jesse & Clarkson and thomas C. Cochran, jt. eds., New York (American Historial Association), 1966.

Linschoten, Jan Huyghen van, *The voyage of Jan Huyghen van Linschoten to the East Indies* (from the English translation of 1598, ed. A.C. Burnell and P.A. Thiele), 2 vols., London (the Hakluyt society), 1885, I.

———, *Itinerario, Voyage ofte Schipvaert van Jan Huygen van Linshoten naer Oost ofte Portugaels Indien*, Amsterdam, 1596.

Mandelslo, Jan Albert von, *The Voyages and Travels of J. Albert de Mandelslo*, tr. John Davies of Kidwelly, London, 1662.

Marques, António Henrique Rodrigo de Oliveira, *History of Portugal*, 2 vols., New York and London (Columbia Universty Press), 1972, I (*From Lusitania to Empire*).

Marshall, Peter J., *The Impeachment of Warren Hastings*, London (Oxford University Press; Oxford Historical Series), 1965.

———, *East India Fortunes. The British in Bengal in the Eighteenth Century*, Oxford (Oxford University Press), 1976.

Matos, Arthur Teodoro de, *O Estado da Índia nos Anos de 1581-1588: Estrutura Administrativa e Económica. Alguns Elementos para o seu Estudo.* Ponte Delgada (Universidade dos Açores) 1982.

Mocquet, Jean, *Voyages en Afrique, Asie, Indes Orientales & Occidentales*, Paris, 1617.

Orta, Garcia da, *Colloquio dos Simples e Drogas da India* (ed. Conde de Ficalho), 2 vols., Lisbon (Imprensa Nacional), 1891.

Parry, John Horace, *The Sale of Public Office in the Spanish Indies under the Hapsburgs*, Berkeley (University of California Press), 1953.

———, *The Spanish Seaborne Empire*, New York (Alfred A. Knopf), 1966.

Pearson, Michael Naylor, *Coastal Western India; Studies from the Portuguese Records.* New Delhi (Concept Publishing Company), 1981.

———, "Corruption and Corsairs in Sixteenth Century Western India: A Functional Analysis", in Blair B. Kling and M.N. Pearson, jt. eds., *The Age of Partnership; Europeans in Asia before Dominion*, Honolulu (University Press of Hawaii), 1979.

———, *Merchants and Rulers in Gujarat.* Los Angeles and Berkeley (University of California Press), 1977.

———, "Wealth and Power: Indian Groups in the Portuguese Indian Economy", *South Asia* III.

Pike, Ruth, *Aristocrats and Traders; Sevillian Society in the Sixteenth Century*, Ithaca and London (Cornell University Press), 1972.

Pissurlencar, Panduronga S.S., *Regimentos das Fortalezas da Índia*, Bastorá, Goa (tipografia Rangel), 1951.

Pyrard, Francois, *The Voyage of François Pyrard of Laval to the East Indies* (ed. & tr, Albert Gray), 2 vols. in 3, London (the Hakluyt Society), 1887-1889, II.

Rebello da Silva, Luís Augusto, *Historia de Portugal nos Séculos XVII e XVIII*,5 vols., Lisbon, 1860-1871, III.

Rego, António da, *Documentação para a História das Missões do Padroado Português do Oriente*, 12 vols., Lisbon (Agência Geral das Colónias/Agência Geral do Ultramar), 1947-1958.

Rodrigues, José Maria and Afonso Lopes Vieira (jt. eds.), *Lírica de Camões, Coimbra (Coimbra University Press)*, 1932.

Sanceau, Elaine (ed.), *Cartas de D. João de Castro*, Lisbon (Agência Geral do Ultramar), 1954.

Schurhammer, Georg, S.J. and Josef Wicki, S.J. (jt. eds.), *Epistolae S. Francisci Xaverii aliaque eius scripta. Nova editio*, 2 vols., Rome (Monumenta Historica Societatis Jesu) 1944-1945.

Schwartz, Stuart B , *Sovereignty and Society in Colonial Brazil; the High Court of Bahia and its* Judges, 1609-1651, Berkeley. *Los Angeles and London* (the University of California Press), 1973.

———, "Luso-Spanish Relations in Hapsburg Brazil, 1580-1640, "*The Americas* 25 (1968).

Serrão, Joaquim Veríssimo, *Historia de Portugal*, 6 vols.-date, Lisbon (Editoral Verbo), 1974-date, IV (1580-1640), 1979, pp-342ff.

Serrão, Joel (ed.), *Dicionário de Historia de Portugal*, 4 vols., Lisbon (Iniciativas Editoriais), 1971,III.

Silveira, Francisco Rodrigues da, *Discursos sobre a Reformação da Justiça da Comarca da Beira e antre Douro e Minho em q̃ se descreveram os defeitos q ha na administração della, e os remedics verdadeiros e mais faciles p. a se emendarem com outras materias tocantes ao bem Universal deste Reino. Dirigidos a Elrey Catholico N. Sñr. pro Franco Rois da Silveira.* codex 49-XI-19 Ajuda Palace Library, Lisbon; also follows folio 204 of author's Add. ms. 25:419, British Museum Library.

———, *Reformação da Milicia e Governo do Estado da India Oriental*, Ms. no. 25:412, Additional Manuscripts: Portuguese, British Museum Library, London.

Solis, Duarte Gomes de, *Alegación en Favor de la Compañia de la India Oriental* (ed. Moses Bensabat Amazalak), Lisbon (privately printed), 1955.

———, *Mémoires Inédits* (ed. Léon Bourdon), Lisbon (privately printed), 1955.

Souza, Teotónio R. de, S.J., "Glimpses of Hindu Dominance of Goan Economy in the 17th century", *Indica XII* (March, 1975).

———, *Medieval Goa: A Socio-Economic History*, New Delhi (Concept Publishing Company), 1979.

Steensgaard, Niels, *Carracks, Caravans and Companies; the Structural Crisis in the European-Asia Trade in the Early 17th Century*, Scandinavian Institute of Asian Studies Monograph Scenes, number 17. Copenhagen (Studentlitteratur), 1972.

Strandes, Justus, *The Portuguese Period in East Africa* (tr. Jean F. Wallwork and ed. J.S. Kirkman), Nairobi (East African Literature Bureau), 1961.

Tavernier, Jean Baptiste, *Travels in India* (tr. v. Ball), 2 vols., London, 1889, I.

Tovar, Franciso Javier Allendesalazar y Aspirox, conde de,

Catalogo dos Manuscritos Portugueses Relativos á Portugal no Musea Británnico, Lisbon (Academia das Ciências), 1932.

Walker, Mack, *German Home Towns; Community State and General Estate, 1648-1871*, Ithaca (Cornell University Press), 1971.

Whiteway, Richard S., *The Rise of the Portuguese Power in India, 1497-1550*, London and Santiago de Compostela (Susil Gupta), second edition, 1967.

Winius, George D., *The Fatal History of Portuguese Ceylon; Transition to Dutch Rule*, Cambridge, Massachusetts (Harvard University Press), 1971.

INDEX

Portuguese names are alphabetised by the last name in a combination; thus, J.H. da Cunha Rivara is listed under the "R's" as "Rivara, J.H. da Cunha," even though the text might refer to him as "Cunha Rivara." Modern authors' names are printed in light-face type.

KIND HEARTS!

GAURANGA DARSHAN DAS

ILLUSTRATIONS
CHARBAK DIPTA

SCHOLASTIC
New York Toronto London Auckland
Sydney New Delhi Hong Kong

Published by Scholastic India Pvt. Ltd.
A subsidiary of Scholastic Inc., New York, 10012 (USA).
Publishers since 1920, with international operations in Canada, Australia, New Zealand, the United Kingdom, India, and Hong Kong.

For information regarding permission, write to:
Scholastic India Pvt. Ltd.
A-27, Ground Floor, Sigma Centre
Infocity-1, Sector 34, Gurgaon-122001 (India)

First edition: May 2026

ISBN-13: 978-93-5954-694-0

Printed in India at: VK Global Digital Private Limited

*Every child carries seeds of golden virtue,
a noble heart waiting to bloom.
Nurture them with timeless wisdom, and
watch them shine with character and grace.*

Author's Note

In a world overflowing with gadgets, noise, and fast content, the quiet glow of a sound character is what truly makes a person shine.

Think of a bridge: if every plank is strong, it safely carries everyone across, but if even one plank is weak, the bridge breaks. Our character is like that bridge. Its planks are not our wealth, looks, or popularity—they are our values, virtues, and principles. When we compromise on them, the bridge of trust begins to crack. I have learnt these virtues from the scriptures, my beloved guru, and by observing the lives of many saintly people whose actions speak louder than their words.

Kind Hearts! was born from a simple wish—to help children discover that true greatness doesn't lie in what we own, but in who we are within. Each virtue in this book is like a golden thread woven into the fabric of our hearts. When we nurture these threads our lives become brighter, happier, and deeply meaningful.

The stories, examples, and reflections in these pages draw on timeless wisdom, rooted in the teachings of the Bhagavad Gita, the Ramayana, the Srimad-Bhagavatam, and the lives of noble souls. Yet they are presented in a way that today's young minds can easily relate to—through simple tales, playful situations, and heartfelt lessons that gently awaken understanding.

With love, prayers, and best wishes for your bright future,

– Gauranga Darshan Das

What is 'Kind Hearts'?

Kind Hearts! is a gentle journey—from the heart, to our relationships, to the world around us. Each virtue builds upon the other, helping children grow from within and express goodness in every thought, word, and action.

1. **Virtues of the Heart—The Inner Foundation**
   Before we can be kind to others, we must be peaceful and strong inside. Gratitude, satisfaction, integrity, and humility teach us to appreciate what we have, stay calm within, act righteously, and be humble, even when no one is watching. These are the roots of character—the invisible strengths that nourish every other virtue.
2. **Virtues in Relationships—The Art of Living Together**
   Once the heart is steady, we can build beautiful bonds with others. Respect, tolerance, forgiveness, and compassion show us how to think, speak, and act with care. True strength lies not in shouting louder, but in loving deeper. These virtues turn our interactions into opportunities for understanding and harmony.
3. **Virtues in Action—The Outer Expression**
   Finally, our inner goodness must shine through what we do. Determination and cleanliness remind us that discipline is devotion. Determination helps us keep trying even when things are hard, and cleanliness keeps our body, mind, and surroundings pure so that everything we touch becomes brighter.

Together, these virtues form a circle of goodness—to think purely, feel kindly, act wisely, and live beautifully.

How to Use This Book

Kind Hearts! is not just a book to read—it's a book to live.
Each chapter is a small journey, filled with stories, lessons, reflections, and simple practices that help you grow in your heart, mind, and actions.

1. Read Slowly, Reflect Deeply: Take one virtue at a time. Pause after the story and ask, 'When have I felt like this?' or 'How can I practise this today?'

2. Discuss and Share: Talk about what you read—with your parents, teachers, or friends. When you share your thoughts, virtues grow stronger inside you and inspire others, too.

3. Revisit and Reflect: At the end of every chapter, you'll find simple questions to help you look within. Write your answers in a journal or talk about them. Reflection turns knowledge into wisdom.

4. Practise and Live the Virtues: Each chapter ends with a short call to action—to be grateful, to forgive, to stay clean, and so on. Try living that virtue for a week. Notice how it transforms your thoughts, friendships, and peace of mind.

5. Repeat and Remember: Virtues grow like plants—they need daily care. Revisit these pages whenever you feel confused, sad, or proud. Each time you reread, you'll discover something new blooming in your heart.

Virtues are not rules—they are lights. The more you walk in their glow, the brighter your world becomes. Cultivate a heart that is kind like a flower, strong like a tree, and steady like the sun. Let the wisdom of the Gita guide your choices, the compassion of Lord Rama fill your heart, and the grace of Lord Krishna protect and empower you.

Contents

1 Gratitude: Seeing Gifts Everywhere

The Two Lunchboxes

It was field trip day at Sunrise School. The air buzzed with excitement as the buses rolled towards the city museum. Madhavi sat beside her cheerful friend, Riya, humming a tune and soaking in the thrill of the adventure.

By lunchtime, everyone was hungry. The teacher called, 'Find a nice spot under the trees and open your tiffin boxes!' The rustle of wrappers and bursts of laughter filled the park.

Madhavi flipped open her lunchbox and frowned. 'Ugh, vegetable parathas again,' she muttered. 'Couldn't Mom pack something new for once?' She poked the food without enthusiasm.

Next to her, Riya opened her box with a bright smile. 'Wow—rice, dal, and an apple. Just perfect! Thank you, Mom,' she whispered.

Madhavi rolled her eyes. 'That's the same thing as yesterday. Aren't you bored?'

Riya shrugged. 'It's warm, tasty, and made with love. Those are three gifts already. Sure, there's nothing wrong with wanting yummy food. But we can still be grateful for what we get. By God's grace, we eat hot meals every day—many people can't afford that. We can compromise on the menu sometimes, right?'

Just then, a gust of wind toppled Madhavi's water bottle. The water spilt into her lunch, soaking the parathas. 'Great,' she grumbled. 'Now even this is ruined.'

Riya quietly tore her napkin in half and handed it over. 'Here—use this.'

'Thanks,' Madhavi said, still a little irritated.

'Try some of my dal,' Riya offered, scooping a little into Madhavi's box. Madhavi tasted it, and her expression softened. 'It's really good.'

'Thank you for trying it,' Riya replied.

Madhavi blinked. 'Why are you thanking me? I should thank you!'

Riya smiled. 'My parents taught me that one level of gratitude is to thank the person who helps us. A higher level is to thank someone for allowing us to serve them. So...thank you, Madhavi, for letting me share.'

Madhavi fell quiet. The breeze rustled the leaves above, and the moment felt gentle and bright.

'Once,' Riya added softly, 'someone shared something with me when I was upset. Gratitude grows when we pass it on.'

On the ride back, Madhavi unwrapped a leftover corner of her paratha, took a bite, and smiled. *Mom woke up early to make this*, she thought.

That evening, she hugged her mother. 'Thanks, Mom. And I'm sorry for grumbling this morning.'

Her mother smiled. 'I knew you'd understand someday.'

That night at dinner, Madhavi silently thanked Riya, her mother, and even the spilt lunch that taught her a lesson:

Gratitude doesn't always change what's in your lunchbox—but it turns ordinary moments into gifts.

What Is Gratitude?

The Sanskrit word for gratitude is *krtajña*—'krta' means 'what has been done', and 'jñah' means 'to remember'. Gratitude means remembering and honouring what others have done for us—recognizing the love behind every favour and reciprocating it through our thoughts, words, and actions.

Takeaways from the Tale

- Complaining closes doors; thankfulness opens them.
- A 'thank you' can be for the chance to serve, not only for being served.
- Small acts of kindness—sharing food, giving a napkin—carry a lot of warmth.
- Focus on gifts, not gaps.
- Gratitude spreads when you pass it on.
- Even a mishap can teach a sweet lesson if your heart is open.
- When something goes wrong, quickly list three things still going right.

It isn't pretending that everything we receive is perfect. It is valuing the heart behind it. Gratitude is like wearing special glasses: with them on, even small things look beautiful—a drink after a tiring day, a teacher's patient explanation, or a parent's hug when you're sad.

Without gratitude, life feels dull and incomplete. With gratitude, every moment becomes a blessing waiting to be noticed. Even difficulties become teachers when viewed through a thankful heart.

Why Gratitude Matters

Gratitude is like sunlight for the heart—under its warmth, many other virtues bloom.

1. **Brings Humility:** 'I received more than I deserve.'
2. **Earns Respect:** 'Others do so much for me.'
3. **Encourages Service:** Gratitude inspires us to give back.
4. **Provides Contentment:** It makes 'enough' feel like 'plenty'.
5. **Gives Forgiveness:** Counting blessings makes faults feel smaller.
6. **Fosters Positivity:** A thankful heart heals faster from disappointment.
7. **Strengthens Faith:** Gratitude reveals God's grace even in trials.

Like the unseen roots of a tree, gratitude quietly nourishes your character. From it grow the fruits of simplicity, joy, and kindness. The more you water this root, the stronger your life-tree becomes.

Gratitude Transforms Relationships

Gratitude turns interactions into connections. When we are grateful, even a small 'thank you' carries warmth. When we are ungrateful, even close relationships feel cold and transactional.

An ungrateful person sees others as tools to use. A grateful person sees them as gifts from God. Gratitude reminds us:

'People are not ladders to climb higher—they are lights that help us see farther.'

When you express gratitude sincerely—to parents, teachers, friends, and to God—life stops feeling like a list of demands and becomes a garden of blessings. Grateful people don't wait for big miracles—they notice small blessings and thank God for them daily.

Even God Is Grateful

In the Bhagavad Gita, Lord Krishna declares:

patraṁ puṣpaṁ phalaṁ toyaṁ
yo me bhaktyā prayacchati
tad ahaṁ bhakty-upahṛtam
aśnāmi prayatātmanaḥ

'If one offers Me with love and devotion a leaf,
a flower, a fruit, or even a little water, I accept it.'

Bhagavad Gita (9.26)

This verse reveals a divine truth: Even God is grateful. Krishna is *krtajña*—He never forgets an act of love. No offering is too small when made with sincerity.

Krishna and Sudama: The Grateful Friend

Krishna's childhood friend Sudama, a poor Brahmana, once came to Dvaraka to see Him. His wife gathered a handful of flattened rice (poha) by begging from neighbours. When Sudama shyly offered it, Krishna's eyes lit up.

'Is this for me?' He smiled. 'This is the most precious gift I've ever received!'

He ate it joyfully, moved by Sudama's devotion, not the gift itself. In return, He blessed Sudama with prosperity; yet the real blessing was an eternal place in His heart.

The Lord never forgets even the smallest act done with love.

Rama's Gratitude to His Devotees

After defeating Ravana, Lord Rama said, 'This victory belongs to Hanuman and my vanaras (monkey warriors) who helped me.'

Although all-powerful, He shared the glory with His devotees. Rama's gratitude extended even to the tiny squirrel that rolled in sand to help build the bridge. He gently stroked its back and blessed it—leaving the sacred lines seen on squirrels today.

Rama's example teaches that what counts is not the size of our offering but the sincerity behind it.

God values not what we give, but the heart with which we give it.

The Weight of Ingratitude

Ingratitude burdens the heart; gratitude lightens it. Ingratitude is like carrying a stone of pride and forgetfulness; gratitude is like carrying a flower—it adds fragrance to every step.

Once, the wise Vidura advised King Dhritarastra to return the kingdom unjustly taken from the Pandavas. Duryodhana, burning with arrogance,

insulted and banished Vidura—forgetting his decades of loyal service. That single act of ingratitude closed his eyes to wisdom and hastened his ruin.

Ingratitude blinds us to goodness; gratitude keeps us humble and protected.

How to Practise Gratitude?

How do we live this virtue? Here are simple, powerful ways to cultivate gratitude in daily life.

1. **Gratitude in Success**
   Behind every victory stand many helping hands—parents, teachers, friends, and the Lord who arranged it all. Celebrate your efforts, but remember those who made them possible. Gratitude keeps success graceful and fame humble.
   A truly successful person says, 'I worked hard, yes—but I also received help, guidance, and grace from those around me.' What is the use of success if it makes us forget the very people who helped us rise?
2. **Gratitude in Failure**
   Failure hurts, but a grateful heart sees it as a lesson, not a loss. 'Yes, I failed—but this failure is my teacher.'
   Gratitude in the face of failure turns a setback into a stepping stone. When you thank life for its lessons, not just its gifts, failure loses its sting, and you grow wiser and steadier.

3. **Adjust Expectations**
   One of gratitude's biggest enemies is unrealistic expectations. When we expect constant attention or perfect help, we end up disappointed. Reasonable hopes are fine; demands are not. Here's the secret:
   - High expectations, unmet → Frustration.
   - Modest expectations, kindness → Gratitude.

   The situation may be the same; your heart's setting changes the outcome. Instead of 'I deserve this,' say, 'If I receive this, I'll be thankful.' Gratitude begins where your sense of entitlement ends.
4. **Acknowledge Kindness Sincerely**
   If someone does even a small act of kindness—shares food, gives advice, holds a door—say 'thank you' sincerely, and mean it. Let your thanks come from the heart, not just habit. A genuine 'thank you' is sunshine for someone's day, and yours.
5. **Make Gratitude a Daily Practice**
   Gratitude grows stronger when it becomes a habit—part of your nature and values.
   - **Morning Thanks:** When you wake, thank the Lord for another day—to learn, serve, and be happy.
   - **Evening Reflection:** Before sleeping, recall three things—one joy, one struggle, and one kindness you experienced. Thank the people involved, and finally thank God for arranging your day.
   - **Mealtime Pause:** Before every meal, pause. Thank your parents who prepared it, the farmers who grew the crops, the rain and sunlight that nurtured them, and the Lord who arranged it all. Many people sleep hungry—don't complain about the menu; celebrate the blessing of having food.
6. **Express Gratitude Through Action**
   At first, gratitude is a feeling; then it becomes words; finally, it becomes service. Use your talents to uplift someone who's struggling. Be selfless. When gratitude flows into action, it becomes love in motion—strengthening relationships and bringing deep inner joy.

What you do for others today becomes someone else's reason to say 'thank you' tomorrow.

7. **Connect Gratitude to the Divine**

   Behind every blessing and every lesson stands the Lord. Thank Him for your family, health, school, talents, and the countless chances to grow.

   When something good happens, say, 'Thank You, Krishna, for this joy.'

   When challenges appear, say, 'Thank You, Krishna, for this chance to grow.'

   Gratitude to people leads to gratitude towards God. A grateful heart is never empty—it overflows with blessings.

   Gratitude doesn't just count blessings—it multiplies them.

8. **Gratitude Towards Parents**

   Parents sacrifice more than we can see. They stay awake when we're sick, work hard to provide for us, and often hide their own worries behind smiles so we can study, play, and grow in peace. A thoughtful child recognizes the love behind every effort—a packed lunch, a paid school fee, a word of advice, even a firm correction meant to guide.

   A grateful child doesn't wait for a special occasion to say 'thank you'. Gratitude shows up as helping hands at home, respectful words, thoughtful choices, and conduct that makes parents proud. Gratitude towards parents is the foundation of strong character.

9. Gratitude Towards Teachers

True teachers give more than lessons—they offer time, patience, and encouragement. They rejoice in their students' successes and hold steady when students struggle.

An ungrateful student may think, 'It's their job to teach me.' A wise student realizes that real teaching is an act of love. A grateful learner listens with attention, practises sincerely, and thanks teachers through improvement.

Wise Gratitude vs. Blind Gratitude

Gratitude is beautiful, but it must be guided by wisdom. Sometimes, gratitude is misunderstood and misused.

Blind gratitude means repaying help by doing wrong. Imagine a friend lends you an eraser and later demands, 'Let me copy your test.' Feeling thankful for the eraser doesn't mean you should help them cheat. That's not gratitude—it's misuse of gratitude that causes harm.

Wise gratitude recognizes kindness but responds in the right way:

'Thank you for your help, but I cannot do something unfair.'

Karna and Duryodhana: The Misuse of Gratitude

In the Mahabharata, Duryodhana honoured Karna even as others mocked him. Out of deep gratitude, Karna pledged lifelong loyalty. But Duryodhana's motives were selfish and unjust. Karna's unquestioning loyalty led him to fight against virtue and to stand with *adharma* (unrighteousness). His gratitude—misapplied—led to tragedy.

Gratitude should never make us blind to right and wrong. If gratitude makes us ignore truth, it becomes weakness. If gratitude strengthens our goodness, it becomes wisdom.

True gratitude says: 'I remember your kindness, but I will never forget my conscience.'

Reflection Corner

- Who are three people I'm most thankful for today—and how will I show it?
- How can I express gratitude through action, not just words?
- Have I ever shown blind gratitude? What will I do differently next time?
- What challenge can I thank Krishna for today?
- What daily habit will help me notice more blessings?

Lets Be Grateful

Gratitude is the sunshine of the heart. It warms everything it touches.
See gifts in every corner: a meal, a smile, a helping hand.
When you thank others, you grow richer in spirit.
When you thank God, your heart becomes light and joyful.
Count blessings, not troubles, because what you notice grows.
A grateful heart turns ordinary days into a festival of blessings.

A grateful person finds lessons in loss, smiles in struggle, and joy in giving.

TRY THIS OUT!

Tomorrow (or any school day), do this:
Before opening your lunchbox, guess:

- Who packed it
- How long it might have taken
- One thing that could have gone wrong while making it

Now open the box and eat.

When you finish, try answering this question: Is this meal simply ingredients put together or is it much more? Observe the feeling of gratitude as you answer all these questions in your mind.

The Toy Store Lesson

For the past few weeks, little Kavya had been enjoying a toy-receiving spree. In just one month, she had been gifted a singing doll, a jigsaw puzzle, a doctor set, and even a shiny pink scooter. But none of them seemed to keep her happy for long.

Every few days, a new wish popped up, 'I'm bored with this! Can I have something new?'

One Sunday, her parents took her to the mall. As they passed a big, bright toy store, Kavya's eyes widened. 'Papa! Look! That talking robot can dance and sing. I really, really want it!' she cried, tugging at his sleeve.

Her father chuckled. 'Didn't we just get you that scooter last week?'
'Yes, but this one's different,' she insisted. 'I promise, this time I'll be happy forever!'

Her mother smiled kindly. 'Sweetheart, you said the same thing about the doll and the scooter. Are you sure you need another toy?'
Kavya crossed her arms and pouted. 'But everyone in my class has something new. I just want one more.'

Her father gently said, 'Let's walk around the mall first. If you still want it later, we'll talk again.'

As they walked, they passed a bookstore. A little girl sat beside her father on a bench. She had no fancy toys, just a paper puppet her father had folded from an old magazine. Yet she was laughing joyfully, clapping her hands as he made the puppet dance.

Kavya stopped to watch. The girl's laughter echoed with such

happiness that it made Kavya's heart warm—and a little puzzled. How could she be so happy with just a paper puppet?

That evening, back home, Kavya quietly opened her old puzzle set. As she fit the missing pieces together, she smiled without realizing it. Her mother peeked in. 'No robot today?' she teased gently.

Kavya shook her head. 'No, Mom. I think I already have enough toys. I just forgot to enjoy them.' Her mother hugged her. 'That's wonderful, my dear. You've just learned something very special—the feeling of satisfaction.'

She added, 'If our hearts remain greedy for more, even a palace feels like a prison. But if we are satisfied, even a hut feels heavenly.'

That night, before sleeping, Kavya whispered a small prayer to her favourite Lord: 'Thank You, Krishna, for my toys, my parents, and even for helping me see how lucky I already am.'

Satisfaction doesn't come from owning more; it comes from enjoying what you already have.

What Is Satisfaction?

The Sanskrit word for satisfaction is *tusti*, which means to feel content with what comes by God's grace.

Satisfaction doesn't mean having everything; it means being happy with what you have obtained by your honest efforts and God's grace, and trusting that what you need will come at the right time.

Sometimes we think, 'If only I had better clothes, tastier food, or a cooler gadget, then I'd be happy.' But saints explain that even if someone owned the whole world, their heart would remain restless until they learned to control their mind's unwanted desires.

Takeaways from the Tale

- Appreciate what you already have instead of constantly hankering for more.
- Comparison steals joy, but appreciation brings it back.
- Chasing joy outside leads to dissatisfaction; seeking it within satisfies.
- Gratitude is the seed, and satisfaction is the flower that blooms from it.
- Satisfaction lies not in the number of toys, but in the number of smiles.
- Satisfaction is a journey from 'I want more' to 'This is enough'.

A satisfied heart is free from unnecessary attachments, envy, pride, and greed. It doesn't compete for name, fame, or praise. A satisfied person is grateful for what one has and what one is—everything feels like a gift from God.

A satisfied person is content with what one has, and never tries to take what belongs to another—their things, their opportunities, and their spotlight. They know that the Lord arranges everyone's portion, and no one can take away what He intends for us.

Why Satisfaction Matters

Cultivating genuine satisfaction yields great, enlivening results in our lives. Few of them are:

1. **Freedom from Misery:** Troubles may come, but they no longer shake us.
2. **Clear Thinking:** Like still water reflects the sky, a calm mind reflects truth.
3. **Joy Everywhere:** When your heart wears the shoes of contentment, even rough roads feel smooth.
4. **Inner Strength:** You stop begging for happiness and start sharing it.
5. **Closeness to God:** A peaceful heart naturally remembers Krishna in all things.

The Calm Ocean of the Gita

In the Bhagavad Gita, Lord Krishna compares a wise person's peace to the steady ocean:

āpūryamāṇam acala-pratiṣṭhaṁ
samudram āpaḥ praviśanti yadvat
tadvat kāmā yaṁ praviśanti sarve
sa śāntim āpnoti na kāma-kāmī

'Just as the ocean remains steady and full even when many rivers flow into it, a wise person remains peaceful and satisfied even when many desires enter the mind. But one who keeps chasing desires never finds peace.'

Bhagavad Gita (2.70)

The ocean doesn't overflow with more rivers—it stays vast, deep, and calm. Similarly, a satisfied person doesn't lose balance when life brings pleasures or problems. Desires may flow in, but the heart remains steady because it knows: 'My happiness doesn't depend on more—it depends on me.'

Rama's Joy in the Forest

In the Ramayana, when Lord Rama was about to be crowned king, the people of Ayodhya rejoiced. But just then, Kaikeyi asked that He be sent to the forest for fourteen years. Everyone expected Rama to be heartbroken. Instead, He smiled calmly and said, 'If this pleases My father, it pleases Me.'

He wore tree bark instead of silk, walked on foot instead of riding a chariot, yet His heart was peaceful. In the quiet of the forest, He found joy in serving sages, protecting the innocent, and living close to nature. Rama showed that true happiness doesn't depend on comfort—it blooms from contentment and gratitude in every situation.

Five Levels of Satisfaction

Satisfaction is the quiet music of a heart that knows its genuine needs, relies on honest efforts, and trusts God's arrangement in life. It is like a candle glowing steadily when protected from the wind of undue desires.

Satisfaction is not just one feeling—it exists on many levels. Each level touches a deeper part of who we are.

1. **Bodily or Sensory Satisfaction**
   At the most basic level, we feel satisfaction through our senses.
   When we see something beautiful, our eyes are satisfied.
   When we hear something melodious, our ears are satisfied.
   When we taste something delicious, our tongue is satisfied.
   When we touch something soft, our skin is satisfied.
   When we smell something fragrant, our nose is satisfied.
   All these forms of satisfaction are on the bodily plane.
2. **Mental or Emotional Satisfaction**
   Deeper than the body is the mind, which seeks warmth and affection. When we experience love, friendship, appreciation, and care, our hearts feel satisfied.
   Simple things—a friend's encouragement, a parent's hug, or a teacher's kind word—bring this type of joy. This satisfaction lasts longer than physical pleasure.

3. **Intellectual Satisfaction**
   At another level, the intellect feels satisfied when it understands, learns, and solves problems.
   Finishing a tough puzzle, finding the answer to a question, or understanding how something works gives a special joy—the satisfaction of using our intelligence well.
4. **Ego-based Satisfaction**
   Still subtler is the satisfaction of the ego—our sense of identity in this world. People often feel happy about their roles and designations—being a good student, a teacher, a responsible leader, or even holding an important post or position.
   When such identity inspires us to act with integrity and service, it's positive satisfaction. But when it grows into pride or envy, it turns unhealthy.

5. **Spiritual Satisfaction—The Highest Level**
We certainly need all the above types of satisfaction to a reasonable extent. But beyond all these is the most profound, purest joy—spiritual satisfaction, which comes from our eternal relationship with the Lord, our supreme Father. Lord Krishna says in the Bhagavad Gita:

ahaṁ bīja-pradaḥ pitā

'I am the seed-giving father of all living beings; they are all My children.'

Bhagavad Gita (14.4)

The joy we derive from this relationship is on the spiritual plane. It is the fulfilment we feel when we hear about the Lord, chant His holy names, worship Him, and serve others selflessly.

This satisfaction is not limited by body, mind, or circumstance. It stays steady through success or failure, praise or blame, gain or loss. Spiritual satisfaction doesn't depend on what we get; it grows from what we give—our love, service, and devotion.

It is the serene happiness that fills the heart when we realize: 'I belong to Krishna, I am cared for by Him, and my joy lies in serving Him.'

The Path of Progress

We don't have to reject the lower levels of satisfaction; they all have their place in a balanced life. But we can rise gradually—from enjoying physical comfort to cherishing emotions to using our intellect wisely to serving with humility, and finally to finding deep contentment in spiritual connection.

Just as a tree grows from roots to trunk to branches to flowers, our satisfaction grows from the senses to the spirit. When we nourish all levels—especially the spiritual—we live a truly fulfilled life.

Learn to enjoy your senses without being controlled by them. Use your intellect for truth. And most of all—find your ultimate satisfaction in remembering and serving Krishna.

Then, no matter what comes or goes, your heart will remain peaceful, grateful, and full of joy.

In devotion, satisfaction deepens joy. The devotee thinks, 'God has given me everything I need—a body to serve, a voice to sing, hands to give, and a heart to love.'

Greed—The Opposite of Satisfaction

If satisfaction is calm water, greed is a fire that never stops burning. Greed whispers, 'Just one more toy, one more medal, one more like, one more praise.' But every 'more' only makes the fire hotter.

A greedy person is like someone drinking salty water—the more they drink, the thirstier they become. Greed promises joy but delivers exhaustion. It replaces peace with pressure and kindness with comparison.

Greed makes friends into rivals and blessings into burdens. It pushes people to grab, lie, and forget gratitude—and in the end, even victory tastes bitter.

Duryodhana's Needle of Greed

When the war between the Pandavas and Kauravas seemed inevitable, Lord Krishna Himself went to Hastinapura as a peacemaker.

He said to Duryodhana, 'You promised to return the kingdom after the Pandavas' exile. Yet they are not demanding it back. Just give them five small villages—enough for them to live in peace.'

But Duryodhana's eyes burned with pride. He thumped his chest and declared, 'I will not give them even as much land as can fit on the tip of a needle!'

Krishna looked at him with compassion. The Lord offered peace; Duryodhana chose possession. His greed made him blind to wisdom, deaf to reason, and empty of joy.

In trying to keep everything, he lost everything—his kingdom, his family, his peace, and his life. True wealth lies not in what we hold, but in what we can let go. Greed fills the hands but empties the heart.

A Short Parable: The Greedy Farmer

Once, a farmer received a magical offer: for every patch of land he walked across before sunset, he could keep it. Excited, he began running across fields, forests, and hills. But he wanted more, so he kept running faster and farther, until the sun started to set. He collapsed from heavy breathing and exhaustion before he could return. The only land he ultimately received was the small patch required to bury him.

Greed makes us run for miles and lose what really matters—peace, health, and love.

The Cure for Greed

Remember: Krishna provides what we truly need, not always what we want.

- Say 'thank you' before saying 'I want.'
- Replace getting with giving.
- Pause before a purchase: 'Do I need this, or do I just crave it?'
- Think of what you already have that once felt like a dream.

Greed demands, 'I want more.'

Satisfaction smiles, 'I already have enough.'

When you realize that, the heart becomes free—light, open, and joyful.

Balancing Satisfaction and Ambition

Satisfaction doesn't mean we stop trying or growing. We must avoid stagnation and continue to improve ourselves and serve others—but without anxiety, comparison, or greed. Real satisfaction is a calm balance between effort and acceptance.

While satisfaction keeps us peaceful, ambition keeps us purposeful. Real success lies in balancing both.

A satisfied person says, 'I am thankful for what I have.'

An ambitious person says, 'I will use what I have to become better.'

A wise person says both.

Sometimes people misuse the idea of satisfaction as an excuse for laziness. For example, a student who scores poorly and says, 'I'm satisfied; I don't need to improve,' isn't showing peace—just indifference.

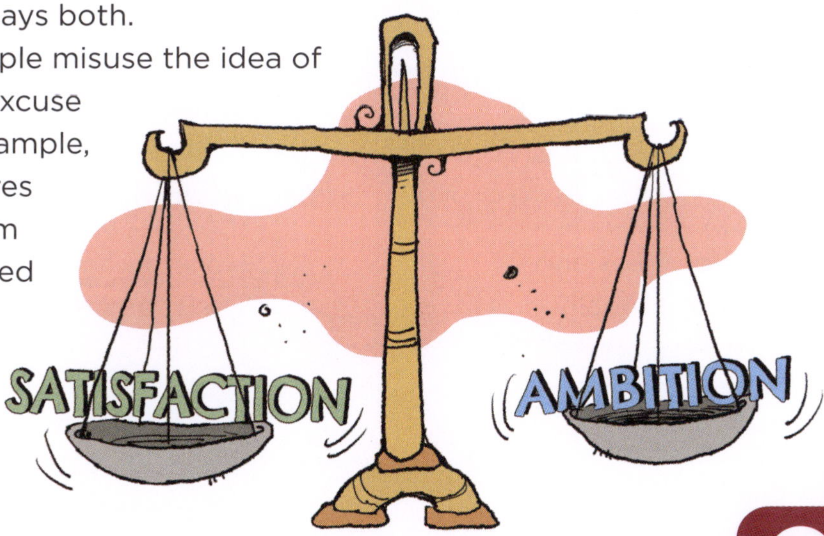

Real satisfaction says, 'I'm not upset with my marks obtained by honest effort, but I'll study better next time.' It's calm on the inside and sincere in effort on the outside.

We can have ambitions, but they should never harm ourselves or others—not mentally, physically, or spiritually. It's fine to dream big, but our dreams should rest on honesty, compassion, and faith. This is called sattva, or the mode of goodness. It helps us work enthusiastically without anxiety or greed.

Reflection Corner

- What things already make my life rich and joyful?
- When was the last time I said, 'This is enough'?
- How can I improve myself without losing peace?
- Do I work hard out of love or comparison?
- What can I thank God for right now?

Lets Be Satisfied

Satisfaction is the quiet smile of the soul.
It whispers, 'I have all I need—right here, right now.'
Chasing more brings restlessness; thanking more brings peace.
True wealth is not in possessions but in peaceful contentment.
It neither envies nor boasts—it simply trusts God's plan.
Satisfaction isn't giving up dreams, but giving up restless wanting.
It teaches us to grow with grace, work with honesty, and smile with peace.

TRY THIS OUT!

The 'Enough' Experiment

Have you noticed how wanting more often steals the joy of what we already have?

1. Pick one area today where you usually want more: food, screen time, toys, praise, winning, or attention.
2. Decide your 'enough' limit in advance (for example: two sweets, one episode, two games, one compliment).
3. Stop when you reach that limit, even if you feel tempted to continue.
4. Replace wanting with thanking: Silently say, 'Thank you for what I received.'
5. At the end of the day, reflect: Did stopping early make me calmer or happier? Did I feel lighter inside?

You'll discover something surprising—contentment feels richer than excess.
True satisfaction isn't about having less—it's about needing less.

3 Integrity: Do Right Even When No One's Watching

The Lost Wallet

The lunch bell rang at Bright Hearts School, and children ran to the playground. Atul, a wise and cheerful student, loved cricket. After finishing his lunch, he was heading towards the field when something shiny caught his eye.

He bent down and found a wallet lying near the bench. Curious, he opened it slightly—it contained some cash and a few cards. He looked around. The playground was empty. None of his friends has arrived yet. No one had seen him.

For a moment, Atul's thoughts raced. 'No one knows I found this. I could buy a new cricket bat or some chocolates. Who would ever find out?'

But another voice whispered inside him, *That's not right. What if someone lost it and is anxious about it right now?*

Atul stood still, thinking. Then he quietly took the wallet to the teacher's office and handed it over. 'Ma'am, I found this near the playground,' he said.

The teacher smiled. 'Thank you, Atul. You didn't use the money, even though you had the chance. I appreciate you, dear child. You did the right thing. This is called integrity. A person's character is known by what they do when nobody is watching. Many behave well when others see them—but true integrity is choosing the right thing even when you could get away with wrong.'

Later that afternoon, a parent came to school, worried and searching for the lost wallet. When he got it back from the teacher, his eyes filled with gratitude. 'Whoever found this is truly honest,' he said. Atul didn't say anything—but his heart felt peaceful and light.

That night, Atul's mother noticed him smiling as he finished his homework. 'Why are you so happy?' she asked. 'I just feel good inside,' Atul replied. 'I did the right thing today.'

That quiet, deep joy that comes from choosing right over wrong is called integrity.

What Is Integrity?

Integrity is being consistent in our thoughts, words, and actions—even when no one is watching. It includes straightforwardness, honesty, and sincerity. People with integrity say what they mean and do what they say, regardless of who is watching or applauding.

Integrity is inner strength—doing the right thing when it is not easy, convenient, or popular. It is not about appearing righteous; it is about being righteous.

Takeaways from the Tale

- Integrity means doing the right thing even when no one is watching.
- It gives peace to the heart and strength to the mind.
- Integrity builds trust—others know they can depend on you.
- A small, honest act today builds great character tomorrow.
- True integrity shines even when no one claps for it.

Integrity includes:

- Keeping promises even when you don't feel like it.
- Admitting mistakes instead of hiding them.
- Returning what doesn't belong to you.
- Being the same person in private as in public.

Integrity includes honesty, but it is more than honesty.

- Honesty = aligning words with reality (speaking the truth about what happened).
- Integrity = aligning life with truth (doing what is right and what you promised).

The Three Pillars of Personal Integrity

1. **Discern** what is right and what is wrong.
2. **Act** on what is right, even at personal cost.
3. **Declare** your stand truthfully—without fear or hypocrisy.

Integrity is not perfection; it is being principled.

Integrity on the Spiritual Plane

True integrity is deeply spiritual—it reflects a life aligned with *dharma*.

We behave carefully when we see a sign: 'CCTV: You are under surveillance.' But what about when no camera is around? In our heart, there is a far more perfect 'camera': the *Paramatma* (Supersoul)—the Lord who lovingly witnesses all thoughts, intentions, and actions.

Lord Krishna explains in the Bhagavad Gita that He is situated within everyone's heart as *Paramatma*, guiding and witnessing our wanderings. He is all-pervading; nothing is beyond His awareness. He remembers not just what we did but why we did it. When we remember His presence, integrity becomes natural: we choose what is right, not merely what is comfortable.

This awareness is not about fear; it is about love and accountability. We don't act properly just to avoid punishment. We avoid wrongdoing because we don't want to displease the Lord who cares for us. We act truthfully because we value His presence, not merely because someone on earth might catch us.

Why Integrity Matters

People may admire your talent, beauty, or cleverness, but what they trust is your integrity.

1. **Builds Trust:** When your word can be relied on, relationships grow strong.
2. **Brings Peace:** Nothing to hide, nothing to fear—guilt fades, calm increases.

3. **Strengthens Courage:** Doing right grows confidence; doing wrong drains it.
4. **Inspires Others:** One honest act often ignites honesty in those who see it.
5. **Earns Lasting Respect:** Fame fades; character remains.

Integrity is the invisible foundation of every virtue. Without it, even great talent becomes risky. With it, a person becomes dependable—like a deep root holding a tree steady in storms.

Scriptural Emphasis

True success is not measured by victory, but by virtue.

Dharmo rakṣatzi rakṣitaḥ—Mahabharata
(Dharma protects those who protect it.)
Satyam eva jayate nānṛtam —Mundkopanishad
(Truth alone triumphs, not falsehood.)
Dharmasya tattvaṁ nihitaṁ guhāyāṁ, mahājano yena gataḥ sa panthāḥ.
—Mahabharata, Vana Parva; Madhya 17.186
(The essence of dharma lies hidden in the hearts of the great; follow the path they walked.)

ye tu dharmyāmṛitam idaṁ yathoktaṁ paryupāsate
śhraddadhānā mat-paramā bhaktās te 'tīva me priyāḥ

'A person who performs their duty without selfish motives, with sincerity and truthfulness, is dear to Me.'

Bhagavad Gita (12.20)

Integrity protects us from fear and confusion. When we act truthfully, there's nothing to hide. Our mind stays calm, and our heart shines clear—like a clean mirror reflecting sunlight. Never let fear or greed push you to lie or cheat. Even when the world doesn't see—Krishna sees—and He values integrity more than any outer success.

Integrity and Self-Respect

Real self-respect rests on integrity.

- If you have integrity—even if others misunderstand or disrespect you—you can still respect yourself. You stood by the truth. You won't be overwhelmed even by failure when you have integrity.
- If you lack integrity—even if the whole world praises you—you'll struggle to respect yourself, knowing the praise wasn't earned rightly. You cannot truly rejoice in success without integrity.

Integrity gives a quiet, durable dignity. It lets you look anyone in the eye with a clear mind and a peaceful heart. True self-respect is not pride—it is peaceful confidence born from living in truth.

Think About It!

Imagine you're writing an exam. The invigilator isn't watching, and your classmate's answers are clearly visible. Everyone around you is busy writing. Will you copy the answer you don't know—or rely on your own effort and be satisfied with the honest marks you earn?

That single choice reveals how much integrity you have. Even if cheating earns a high score, you cannot fully rejoice. Deep inside, anxiety whispers. *What if someone finds out? What if I'm asked to explain something I don't actually understand?* But when you refuse to copy and trust your honest effort, you may get fewer marks, yet you feel confident, calm, and unafraid.

Integrity isn't about what others see—it's about who you are when no one is watching. The reward is priceless: a quiet, calm joy no one can take away.

Integrity vs. Duplicity

The opposite of integrity is duplicity or hypocrisy. Integrity is living truthfully—thinking, speaking, and acting in line with what is right. Duplicity is thinking one thing, saying another, and doing a third.

Integrity is steady and simple; duplicity is exhausting—keeping track of lies, props, and performances. Integrity frees the mind; duplicity chains it to fear.

Integrity is truth in action; duplicity is falsehood in disguise. One builds trust; the other breaks it.

Aspect	INTEGRITY (One face, one standard)	DUPLICITY (Different faces, changing stories)
Values	Consistent everywhere	Shift with audience
Behaviour	Aligned and steady	Contradictory, inconsistent
Promises	Keeps commitments	Breaks commitments
Dealings	Honest, transparent	Deceptive, manipulative
Character	Trustworthy, dependable	Unreliable, unprincipled
Attitude	Admits mistakes, seeks help	Hides faults, blames others
Inner State	Peaceful, confident	Fearful, restless

Outcomes

Results of Integrity	Results of Duplicity
Trust and cooperation	Mistrust and conflict
Personal and interpersonal growth	Stagnation and guilt
Strong relationships	Damaged relationships
Inner peace and confidence	Anxiety and insecurity
Respect from others	Loss of credibility

Integrity is the root of every healthy friendship, partnership, and community. Duplicity may bring short-term gains, but it always costs long-term respect.

How to Practise Integrity

Integrity isn't shown only in grand moments—it shines through small, daily choices:

- Finish homework and assignments without cheating or excuses.
- Admit you broke a glass instead of blaming your sibling.
- Accept full responsibility for your words and actions.
- Communicate openly and clearly.

- Keep promises and honour commitments.
- Avoid hidden motives or selfish agendas.
- Have the courage to lead with fairness and humility.
- Be honest with yourself—in mind, word, and heart.

Think in simple roles:

1. **Promise Keeper:** Do what you said you would.
2. **Truth Detective:** Admit mistakes and learn from them.
3. **Do the Right Thing:** Return what you find, even if it's small.
4. **Consistent Kindness:** Let actions match words.
5. **Invisible Hero:** Do good quietly—God notices even when people don't.

Every small act of honesty strengthens your inner foundation. Integrity is not just about truth-telling—it's about truth-living.

When Integrity Is Tested

Integrity often faces trials. You may lose comfort, face criticism, or stand alone—but those moments reveal your true strength.

If everyone cheats and you don't—you may lose a few marks, but gain lifelong confidence and satisfaction.

If a friend forgets your book and you forgive—you choose peace over pride.

If you admit your mistake—you might face correction now, but you earn lasting trust.

Integrity may not bring quick rewards—but it builds a reputation that glows forever.

Integrity with Wisdom (Not 'Blunt Honesty')

Honesty must walk hand in hand with wisdom and kindness.

- Speaking the truth harshly can harm. Telling a sad friend, 'You always mess up!' isn't integrity—it's insensitivity.
- Integrity leads to confidence—but not arrogance. Rigidly upholding your standards while looking down on others strains relationships. True virtue makes our hearts softer, not harder.
- Share values without shaming people. Be firm on principles and gentle with persons.

Integrity means doing what is right and beneficial, not just 'telling it straight'. It combines truth with compassion.

A helpful question you can ask yourself while talking things out with someone: 'Will this help—or will this hurt?'

That keeps integrity balanced with wisdom.

When Others Lack Integrity

When you see dishonesty around you, it's easy to feel discouraged—but integrity means staying right even when others aren't.

- Don't copy their behaviour just to fit in.
- Don't insult or expose them harshly—guide kindly.
- Keep your standards high; your example may inspire change.

Real integrity doesn't just protect you—it uplifts everyone around you.

Examples of Integrity from the Scriptures

1 **Lord Rama—Keeping His Father's Promise**

When Rama was to be crowned, he accepted exile instead—simply to keep his father's word. He gave up his throne without anger or complaint. His integrity shines brighter than any crown.

Sometimes doing right costs comfort—but wins character.

2 **King Śibi—The Protector of the Dove**

A frightened dove sought refuge in King Sibi's lap. A hawk demanded its prey. Sibi protected the dove even at the cost of his own flesh. The gods revealed themselves and blessed him for steadfast truth.

Integrity is keeping your promise even when it hurts.

3 **Yudhisthira—The King of Truth**

Yudhisthira never lied, even in the face of loss, exile, and war. He proved that integrity isn't about always winning—but about never betraying truth.

Truthfulness is the victory of the heart.

4 **Bhisma—Loyal to His Vow**

As a young prince, Bhisma took a lifelong vow to never marry so that his father could fulfil his love for Satyavati. He remained faithful his entire life, facing loneliness, hardship, and even battle wounds. His integrity gave him immense spiritual power and respect from friend and foe alike.

Integrity gives strength that no weapon can defeat.

5 Hanuman—Promise Keeper

When Lord Rama gave Hanuman the mission to find Sita, Hanuman promised, 'I will not rest until I find Her.' He crossed oceans, faced demons, and searched tirelessly—all to keep his word. Hanuman's integrity made him fearless and unstoppable.

When we keep our promises, no matter how small, we earn the trust of others and the blessings of God.

Reflection Corner

- Do I do what's right even when no one sees?
- Do I keep promises when it's inconvenient?
- Do I tell the truth kindly, not harshly?
- Do I live the same way in private as in public?
- Do I respect myself by being honest?

Let's Be Honest

Integrity is the bridge between what we believe and how we behave.

It turns honesty into strength, promises into action, and values into character.

People may forget your words, but they will remember your truthfulness.

Like Lord Rama and King Sibi, let your word be as firm as truth itself.

Do right even when no one is watching—for when you live with integrity, God is smiling.

Truth may not always be easy, but it is always peaceful.

Let your thoughts, words, and actions walk together—steadily, sincerely, and firmly.

TRY THIS OUT!

THE OUT-OF-SYNC MOVIE

Have you ever watched a movie where the actor's lips move—but the words don't match? It feels strange, confusing, and a little irritating, doesn't it?

Integrity works the same way in real life. When our words say one thing but our actions do another, people feel uncomfortable—and trust breaks. Integrity is about keeping our life in sync—so our words, actions, and intentions match.

Your Integrity Challenge:

1. Choose one promise or statement you make today (for example: 'I'll finish my homework,' 'I'll help my friend,' or 'I won't use my phone during study time').
2. Write it down or say it clearly.
3. Act exactly according to it, even when no one is watching, it feels inconvenient, or you feel tempted to do otherwise.
4. At night, reflect quietly: Did my actions match my words? How did I feel when they did?

4 Humility: Bowing Low, Growing High

The Unsung Hero of Service Day

Vidya Public School celebrated its annual 'Service Day' just before the Diwali vacation. The teachers and coordinators invited students to volunteer to help with various aspects of the arrangements—stage decoration, lighting, seating, cleaning, and performances.

Soon, the sign-up sheet filled up. Most students rushed to grab the glamorous roles—anchoring, singing, and dancing. Amid the excited crowd, a quiet boy named Arjun slowly walked up to the notice board and wrote his name under 'Floors and Lamps'.

That was just like him—calm, sincere, and humble. Arjun's parents had always taught him that no work is small and that real joy comes from serving quietly. Coming from a simple background, they had trained him to respect even the smallest acts of service.

Since the celebration was happening just before Diwali, the principal decided to decorate the auditorium with rows of traditional oil lamps to give it a festive, spiritual glow. Arjun was thrilled. He loved the idea of polishing and lighting lamps for his beloved Lord Krishna, of whom an idol would be placed on the stage.

All week, he came to school early. He swept and mopped the hall, polished every brass lamp until it shone, and diligently cleaned corners others had missed. He didn't tell anyone what he was doing, nor did he seek praise. He simply worked with love.

Finally, the big day arrived. The lamps flickered like little stars across the hall, the decorations sparkled, and everything looked radiant. The event went perfectly—students performed beautifully, teachers smiled proudly, and the whole school felt festive and bright.

The principal went on stage and praised the singers, dancers, and speakers. But no one mentioned Arjun. He didn't mind. He smiled, offered a silent prayer to Lord Krishna in his heart, and rejoiced that the event had gone so well.

Suddenly, Arjun noticed a few drops of oil that had spilt near the glowing lamps. Without saying a word, he quietly fetched a cloth and began wiping the floor carefully.

Just then, the principal noticed him cleaning the floor so attentively. She called him forward. Arjun looked a little shy and nervous as he stood before the students and staff.

She smiled warmly and said, 'Many students shone brightly on stage today—but this boy made the whole stage shine.'

The hall echoed with applause. Arjun blushed, folded his hands, and softly said, 'Thank you, Ma'am. Everyone did their part. I just did mine.'

The principal nodded, then turned to the students. 'Do you know what makes every dish delicious?' she asked. 'Salt! When you eat

paneer or any other tasty dish, you praise the cook, the spices, and the vegetables. But without salt, even the best dish tastes bland. And yet, no one ever praises the salt—it quietly does its work, making everything complete.

'Our Arjun is like that salt—silent, unseen, but essential. Without such humble helpers in the background, even the grandest event loses its sweetness.'

The students clapped again, some looking thoughtful, others inspired. Arjun smiled gently, bowed to the principal, and quietly returned to his duties.

That night, before going to sleep, Arjun folded his hands and prayed softly, 'Dear Lord Krishna, please let me serve like this always—quietly, sincerely, and with love.'

Humility, like Arjun's, is the sweetness of service—the silent light that makes everything shine. Just as a mango tree bends closer to the earth as its fruits ripen, truly great hearts bow down so that others can reach and be happy.

Takeaways from the Tale

- Even unnoticed acts done with sincerity please both people and God.
- No work is small when done with love and devotion.
- Real humility is strength–it shines quietly, without needing attention.
- Recognition fades; contribution remains.
- Just like salt in a dish, humble service may go unseen–but it makes everything around it better.
- When we serve without pride, our hearts become lamps that spread light everywhere.

What Is Humility?

The Sanskrit words for humility are *vinaya* or *amanitvam*, which means freedom from the desire for honour—a state of gentleness, modesty, and freedom from pride.

To be humble doesn't mean to think of yourself as low or useless. It means not being self-absorbed or obsessed with yourself. You don't need to prove that you're the best or that others are wrong. You stay grounded, willing to listen, learn, and help.

Humility is not weakness or shyness—it is quiet strength based on truth. A humble person understands both their strengths and their limits. They don't develop a false sense of pride in their abilities. Instead, they respect others' talents and recognize that God is the ultimate controller of everything.

When you're humble, you respect everyone—teachers, parents, helpers, and even those younger than you. You understand that nobody is too big to learn and nobody too small to teach.

Humility is the soil in which all other virtues grow. Just as rich soil allows plants to flourish, a humble heart allows kindness, knowledge, and happiness to thrive. Without humility, knowledge turns into pride, power into arrogance, and talent into showing off. But with humility, even the smallest act becomes beautiful.

Humility is not about feeling small or weak—it's about remembering that the world doesn't revolve around 'me,' but around truth, goodness, gratitude, and God.

Real humility is the awareness that:

- God is the source of all strength, talent, and intelligence.
- We are His instruments, meant to serve and contribute to the world with gratitude.
- Everyone has a significant role to play in this creation—I am just one of them!

Why Humility Matters

Humility keeps both the heart and mind healthy. It helps us relate kindly, learn constantly, and grow beautifully.

1. **Builds Friendships:** Nobody enjoys being around people who always boast or look down on others. Humble people make everyone feel respected.
2. **Helps Us Learn:** When we admit that we don't know everything, we remain open to new ideas and grow wiser.
3. **Keeps the Heart Peaceful:** Humility removes the pressure to always impress others. You stop comparing and start improving.
4. **Earns Respect Naturally:** The more you respect others, the more others respect you.
5. **Turns Success into Gratitude:** When you win, you thank those who helped you instead of thinking you did it all alone.

Even in spiritual life, humility is the foundation of growth. Sri Krishna begins His list of the twenty qualities of knowledge with *amanitvam*—humility (Bhagavad Gita 13.8). Without it, all other virtues fade away.

A humble person doesn't crave applause or titles. They admit mistakes quickly, learn gladly, and say 'thank you' easily. They see every talent, opportunity, and success as a gift from God, not a personal trophy.

What Isn't Humility

Humility is sometimes misunderstood as weakness—but it is not fear, self-pity, or lack of confidence. It doesn't mean thinking, 'I'm useless', or allowing others to treat you unfairly.

True humility is inner strength guided by wisdom.

- It is not feeling worthless.
- It is not letting others insult or exploit you.
- It is not pretending to be small while secretly feeling proud of being 'humble'.

Humility doesn't mean letting wrong things continue. If someone bullies others, it's not humility to stay silent. Real humility stands for truth—with respect but firmness.

A humble person stands for what's right, but without arrogance. They don't shout to prove their point—they speak calmly and act wisely. They accept appreciation gracefully but don't crave it.

It also doesn't mean hiding your talents. If you draw, sing, or lead well, do it confidently—but with gratitude, not pride. Use your gifts to inspire, not to impress.

A humble person shines without shouting, 'Look at me!'

Even great heroes like Hanuman and Yudhisthira were known for their humility. They stood for truth, served with devotion, and fought for justice—but never allowed pride to control their hearts.

Pride—The Opposite of Humility

The opposite of humility is pride—a constant focus on 'me, my success, my desires, my opinions, my talents'. A proud person is absorbed in their own achievements, while a humble person appreciates the greatness in others and ultimately understands that God is the greatest. A humble person doesn't deny their abilities; they just don't claim ownership of them.

Pride Says...	Humility Says...
'I'm always right.'	'I'm ready to listen.'
'I don't need advice.'	'I can learn more.'
'I did it all by myself.'	'I'm thankful for the help I got.'
'I deserve more.'	'I'm grateful for what I have.'
'I'm better than you.'	'We all have different strengths.'
'Why should I do small tasks?'	'Every job matters.'
'I never make mistakes.'	'Sorry, that was my mistake.'

Examples of Humility from the Scriptures

Yudhisthira and Duryodhana

In the Mahabharata, Yudhisthira was known for his humility. Though a powerful and wise king, he always bowed to his elders, spoke gently to everyone, and never claimed credit for victory. When praised, he would say, 'Whatever I achieve is by Krishna's grace and the support of my brothers.'

However, Duryodhana was the opposite. He was proud, arrogant, and stubborn. He refused to heed the wise counsel of elders like Bhisma, Vidura, and even his own father, Dhrtarastra. Instead, he followed flatterers like Sakuni and Karna, who fed his ego. His pride closed his eyes to truth—and in the end, that arrogance led to his destruction.

Pride makes you blind; humility helps you see.

Hanuman's Humility

Hanuman is one of the greatest examples of humble strength. He leapt across the ocean, found Sita Devi, and gave her courage by assuring her that Lord Rama would soon rescue her.

When Sita asked, 'You crossed this vast ocean so easily, Hanuman! Will the other vanaras be able to do it, too?' Hanuman bowed and said, 'Mother, I am just Rama's messenger. Usually, the weaker ones are sent as messengers. There are many vanaras stronger and braver than I. Surely they will all come across the ocean with Lord Rama to rescue you soon.'

Though he had performed a miracle, Hanuman never boasted about his achievement. He considered himself the weakest in Rama's army, even though he was the greatest hero.

Later, when Lord Rama praised him for his unmatched service, Hanuman folded his hands with humility. 'My strength, courage, and wisdom all come from You, my Lord. Without Your grace, I couldn't even lift my tail.'

That is real humility—greatness without pride, service without ego.

How are Knowledge and Humility Related?

Knowledge and humility are closely connected. Humility is the foundation of learning and growth. Only a humble person can truly learn and grow. Proud people think they already know everything, but a humble individual remains open to new lessons. When we are humble, our understanding expands; when we are arrogant, our growth stops.

In every culture, humility is seen as a divine quality. In the Bhagavad Gita (13.8), Lord Krishna lists *amanitvam*—humility—as the first sign of true knowledge. He explains that those who are humble, grateful, and free from pride live peacefully because they see life as a gift.

Vinaya (humility) + Jnana (knowledge) = Vijnana (realization)
Ahankara (arrogance) + Jnana (knowledge) = Ajnana (ignorance)

When we realize we didn't create the sunrise, the rain, or even our own heartbeat, it becomes easy to stay grounded and kind. Humility connects us to something higher—it reminds us that life isn't just about 'me' but about how we can serve and uplift others.

Albert Einstein once said, 'The more I learn, the more I realize how much I don't know.'

That's true humility—not pretending to know everything, but being eager to keep learning.

When you're humble, teachers enjoy teaching you. You ask questions freely, and even feedback feels like a gift.

In ancient times, great scholars like Socrates and Chanakya were known not just for their brilliance but also for their humility. They believed that real wisdom begins when pride ends.

Knowledge must always be accompanied by humility. Without humility, knowledge becomes like a sword without a handle—it ends up hurting the one who holds it.

How Humility Empowers Us

If we think about our place in this huge universe, we'll see how small we really are. But pride makes us forget that. It makes us feel like we are the biggest and best—as if everything happens because of us.

When we become proud, God steps back. But when we become humble, He steps forward to help us. When we bow our heads, He lifts us.

Being humble means remembering that we are not the owners or controllers of everything—we are instruments in God's hands. And when we realize that, God fills us with strength, wisdom, and courage to do amazing things.

Humility doesn't make us weak; it makes us ready for God's power.

Practical Ways to Cultivate Humility

1. **Start with Gratitude**
   Begin and end your day by thanking those who help you—parents, teachers, friends, and God. Gratitude naturally melts pride.
2. **Listen Before Speaking**
   Give others a chance to express themselves. Listening is silent respect, and everyone loves to be heard.
3. **Admit Mistakes**
   If you make a mistake, don't cover it up. Apologize and learn from it. Admitting wrong doesn't make you small—it makes you strong.
4. **Let Others Shine**
   If your friend wins a prize, be the first to clap for them. When you celebrate others' success, your heart grows lighter and happier.

5. **Serve Quietly**
   Do small acts of kindness—help clean the classroom, share your lunch, or assist someone struggling—without expecting recognition. True service needs no audience.
6. **Remember the Bigger Picture**
   When you feel too proud or too upset, remind yourself: 'I'm part of something bigger. What matters is being kind, not just being right.'
7. **Chant the Names of God**
   Usually, people think, 'I'm the one who does everything. I make things happen. I'm in control.' This kind of thinking makes the heart proud and restless. But when we chant Krishna's names, we slowly realize a wonderful truth: Krishna is the one who gives me strength, ideas, and success. I am not the controller—I am cared for by Him. He is the master, and we are His helpers. He is the source of everything, and we are His children.

By repeatedly chanting Krishna's names, this understanding grows in our heart, and pride naturally melts away. We come out of our self-absorption. We stop feeling, 'I'm so great', and start feeling, 'Krishna is so kind'. That gentle feeling is called humility.

Chanting doesn't just calm the mind—it shapes our attitude. It reminds us that we are not the centre of everything—Krishna is. When we remember this through chanting, our heart becomes soft, peaceful, and filled with love—and that is the true beginning of humility.

Therefore, if you can, daily chant the following mantra prescribed in our scriptures:

Hare Krishna Hare Krishna Krishna Krishna Hare Hare
Hare Rama Hare Rama Rama Rama Hare Hare

Chanting helps us remember that we're cared for, not in control—and that memory makes our hearts humble.

Reflection Corner

- When was the last time I said 'thank you' with real feeling?
- Do I listen carefully to others, or wait for my turn to speak?
- How do I handle success—gratefully or proudly?
- Do I look down on people who do smaller jobs?
- Can I use my talents to serve others more sincerely?

Let's Be Humble!

Humility bows—but never breaks.
It shines without shouting and wins hearts without fighting.
Humble people don't think less of themselves—they think of themselves less.
Like a tree heavy with fruit, bend low with grace.
Pride builds walls; humility builds bridges.
When you stay humble, you stay close to wisdom and to God.

Humility opens the door of the heart through which love, wisdom, and God's grace enter. And the one who bows low...grows high.

TRY THIS OUT!

The Invisible Helper Challenge

An aspect of humility is to do good without desiring credit.

1. Choose one helpful act you can do today: clean something at home or school, help a classmate understand a lesson, carry something for an elder, or arrange books, shoes, or chairs without being asked.
2. Do it quietly. Don't announce it. Don't wait for praise. Don't tell anyone what you did.
3. If someone notices it and thanks you, simply smile and say, 'It's okay.'
4. At the end of the day, ask yourself: Did I feel lighter or happier even without appreciation? Did helping quietly make my heart calmer?

You may notice something beautiful—when ego steps aside, joy steps in.

5 Respect: Seeing Value in Everyone

The Missing Wire

The corridors of Lotus International School buzzed with excitement. The annual science exhibition was just a day away, and students were adding the final touches to their projects. Tables were filled with wires, charts, glue sticks, and colourful posters.

Among all the students, Vivaan Mehta, the son of a very wealthy businessman, stood out. He was talented, intelligent, and confident, but also slightly arrogant. He often boasted about his ideas and had little respect for anyone he thought was 'less important'.

Vivaan's team was working on a model of a solar-powered house for the exhibition. His teammates—Arya, Kabir, and Ritesh—were sincere and hard-working, but Vivaan dominated them and rarely let them contribute. He often dismissed Arya's suggestions and ignored Kabir's calculations. He even spoke curtly to his teachers, as if he knew everything.

One afternoon, while setting up their model, the school sweeper, Ramesh Uncle, accidentally spilt a little water near their table. Vivaan frowned.

'Can't you see what you're doing? You'll ruin my project!' he snapped.

Ramesh quietly wiped the floor and said softly, 'Sorry, *beta*.' His gentle humility made Arya uncomfortable, but Vivaan didn't notice.

Finally, the day of the exhibition arrived. The principal, teachers, parents, and judges went from table to table admiring the projects.

When it was their turn, Vivaan stood proudly beside his model. 'Good morning, respected judges,' he said, brimming with confidence. 'Our project demonstrates how solar energy can power a home efficiently.'

He flipped the switch to light up the model. Nothing happened. He tried again—still nothing. The lights didn't glow; the fan didn't move. The judges looked on patiently as his confidence melted into panic.

Arya quickly bent down to check. 'Vivaan, one wire is loose—it needs a connector!' she whispered.

Just then, Ramesh's Uncle, who was mopping nearby, noticed the situation. He gently came forward and said, 'Beta, I have a small tool. May I help?'

Vivaan hesitated. His pride held him back. How could he let a sweeper fix his science project? But Arya whispered, 'Please, Vivaan. Let him help.'

Vivaan swallowed his pride and nodded. Ramesh Uncle took a tiny screwdriver from his pocket, bent down, and fixed the wire in seconds. 'Now try,' he said with a smile.

Vivaan pressed the switch again—and this time, the house came alive! The tiny bulbs glowed, the fan turned, and the judges clapped. 'Wonderful model,' one said appreciatively.

Vivaan smiled, but this time it wasn't pride—it was gratitude. The man he had disrespected had just saved his project.

After the event, Vivaan quietly walked up to Ramesh Uncle and said, 'I'm really sorry for how I spoke earlier. Thank you for helping me and my team.'

Ramesh Uncle smiled kindly. 'It's alright, beta.'

That evening, Vivaan reflected deeply. He realized that respect wasn't just for teachers and principals, but also for all those who serve quietly behind the scenes.

The next morning, he greeted Ramesh Uncle and spoke kindly with his teammates.

When a friend asked, 'What changed you, Vivaan?' he replied, 'I learned something important. Everyone deserves respect—from the person who cleans the floor to the one who walks on it. Without others, none of us can truly shine.'

Takeaways from the Tale

- Respect means seeing value in everyone, not just those above us.
- When we disrespect others, we lose more than we gain.
- Accepting help is a sign of strength, not weakness.
- The missing wire in many hearts is respect—once connected, everything shines.
- Pride makes us forget people; respect helps us remember their worth.

What Is Respect?

The Sanskrit words for respect are *satkara* or *mana*, which mean honouring or valuing someone or something. Respect means treating others—and everything around us—with care, appreciation, and dignity. When we respect someone, we are silently telling them, 'You matter. You have worth. I value you for who you are.'

Respect applies to people, things, time, and even nature.

- We respect people by listening, speaking kindly, and valuing their feelings.
- We respect things by using them carefully and avoiding waste or damage.
- We respect time by being punctual, responsible, and not wasting it.
- We respect nature by protecting it rather than exploiting it.

Just as a mirror reflects what we show it, life reflects the respect we give.

Why Respect Matters

Respect is the foundation of all relationships—at home, at school, and in society.
It keeps our hearts peaceful and our surroundings harmonious.

- **Builds Trust:** People feel safe and comfortable around those who respect them.
- **Strengthens Bonds:** Respectful behaviour brings warmth to friendships and family ties.
- **Enhances Learning:** When you respect your teachers, you absorb knowledge better.
- **Reduces Conflict:** Respectful words calm arguments before they begin.
- **Earns Respect:** The more you give, the more you receive.
- **Brings Inner Peace:** A respectful person sleeps with a calm heart.
- **Nurtures Gratitude:** You begin to value what you have instead of complaining about what you don't.

When we don't respect others, they eventually stop respecting us.
Even when someone disrespects you, don't respond with the same behaviour.

If we answer disrespect with disrespect, there's no difference between them and us.

But being respectful doesn't mean letting others walk over you. It means standing firm—with calmness and dignity.

Respect flows both upward (to elders) and downward (to the young).

Three Levels of Respect

Respect grows as our understanding deepens. There are three primary levels:

1. **Respect for Age, Position, and Guidance**
   This is the basic level of respect—towards parents, teachers, elders, and those positions of authority. They've reached where they are through hard work, discipline, and sincerity.
   When we show them respect, we honour their experience and contribution.
   Respect also comes with age. Elders carry the wisdom of years we haven't yet lived. When we listen to them, greet them, and speak gently, we show that we value their experience.
   Standing when

elders enter, not interrupting while they speak, or following teachers' advice are small gestures that reveal significant character.

2. **Respect for Character and Conduct**
   This is a deeper level. It's not about someone's status but their values. We respect people for honesty, kindness, patience, or generosity, even if they hold no big title. A humble cleaner, a hard-working driver, or a helpful classmate deserves as much respect as anyone in power.
   Virtue is real royalty. When you admire people for their goodness rather than their greatness, you are growing wise.
3. **Spiritual Respect—Seeing God's Presence in All**
   The highest form of respect comes from spiritual understanding. We see everyone as a child of God and every object as God's creation. Therefore, nothing and no one is 'ordinary'.

Krishna says in the Bhagavad Gita:

vidyā-vinaya-sampanne brāhmaṇe gavi hastini
śuni caiva śvapāke ca paṇḍitāḥ sama-darśinaḥ

'The truly wise see with equal vision—a learned Brahmana, a cow, an elephant, a dog, and even a dog-eater.'

Bhagavad Gita (5.18)

Even the greatest form of self-respect is to identify oneself as a child and a servant of God. After all, that is our eternal identity, beyond all the temporary designations we hold in this world.

This vision teaches us that all life is sacred. We don't kick doors, scribble in books, waste food, or throw away things casually. Everything has value because it exists by God's will.

Respecting people for their divine origin brings peace to our hearts. Respecting things as God's gifts teaches gratitude and responsibility.

When we respect the world as sacred, we naturally respect ourselves.

Examples of Respect from the Scriptures

Lord Rama—Respect Beyond Duty

Lord Rama is an eternal example of respect. He obeyed His parents without hesitation, honoured His teachers, and treated citizens with kindness. Even when exiled to the forest, He bowed to His father's command and left peacefully. Rama respected everyone—from sages to soldiers—and was loved by all.

When Lord Rama and His army were building a bridge to Lanka, all the mighty vanaras were carrying huge boulders. Among them, a tiny squirrel brought in sand and shook it off near the rocks to fill the gaps. Lord Rama gently stroked the squirrel's back. Its effort may be small, but its love is great. Every act done with devotion counts and is respected by the Lord. Rama's respect teaches us that no one is too small to matter—every sincere effort deserves honour.

The Pandavas—Respect for Teachers

The Pandava brothers respected their gurus, Dronacharya and Kripacharya, even when those teachers fought on the opposite side in the war. Yudhisthira went to the elders on the opposite side for their blessings before the Kurukshetra war began. When Arjuna won the great archery contest, his first act was to bow before his teacher. True respect doesn't depend on perfection—it honours the role others play in shaping our lives.

Respect means honouring people's roles, even when we differ in opinion.

Lord Krishna—Respecting All

Lord Krishna was the Supreme Lord Himself, yet He humbly bowed to His parents, Devaki and Vasudeva. He welcomed guests with devotion, washed the feet of sages, and served them personally. He even showed affection and respect towards animals, such as cows, recognizing that all creatures are sacred.

Prahlada—Disagreement Without Disrespect

Prahlada was a young devotee whose father, Hiranyakashipu, opposed his devotion to Lord Narsimha. Even when threatened, Prahlada spoke respectfully and calmly. He disagreed with his father's views, but never insulted him. Respect and courage can walk together. We can disagree without being disrespectful.

Respect in Daily Life

Respect is not a once-a-year action—it's a daily practice shown through our words, habits, and gestures.

At Home

- Listen when parents speak—don't interrupt or roll your eyes.
- Help elders with small tasks; assist grandparents when they are in need.
- Speak gently to siblings, even when you disagree.

At School

- Stand up to greet teachers and elders.
- Thank the staff who clean, cook, or maintains your school's premises.
- Don't mock someone who answers wrong in class—encourage them.

With Friends

- Don't tease a person about looks, marks, or clothes.
- Listen when they share something important.
- Avoid gossip and rude jokes.
- Value your friend's feelings.

With Things

- Don't kick doors or throw objects in anger.
- Use pens, books, and refills till they're finished—wasting is disrespect.
- Don't scribble in books—they give you knowledge.
- Don't buy and discard gadgets too quickly.

When we waste or misuse objects, we disrespect the effort, material, and energy that went into creating them.

A respectful heart values usefulness, not just newness.

Respect for Time

- Be punctual—it shows regard for others' schedules.
- Don't keep people waiting unnecessarily.
- Avoid idle gossip and distractions.

Every minute of life is a gift. Using it wisely is a way of respecting both yourself and the Creator.

When Others Disrespect

If someone mocks you, smile and walk away. Their behaviour shows their nature, not yours. When we stay respectful, we protect our dignity—and sometimes even inspire them to change.

But sometimes, people may speak rudely, ignore, or cross tolerable limits. How should we respond?

- Don't copy their disrespect—that makes you like them.
- Don't allow repeated disrespect—set gentle boundaries without hatred.
- Stay calm, not cruel. Firm, not furious.

Respect is strength under control.

Respect and Responsibility Go Together

Respect is not just a feeling—it's a responsibility.
When we respect:

- Teachers → We study sincerely.
- Nature → We save and reuse resources.
- Friends → We keep their trust.
- Ourselves → We choose honesty and effort.

Respect turns ordinary work into meaningful service. It transforms duty into devotion.

Reflection Corner

- Do I speak respectfully even when I'm upset?
- Do I thank the helpers and teachers who serve me daily?
- Do I waste time on things that others worked hard to provide?
- Do I respect all people—rich or poor, strong or weak?
- Do I respect myself by acting with integrity?

Let's Respect!

Respect is seeing God's grace in every heart.
It begins with manners, grows through kindness, and ends in love.
Speak gently, listen carefully, act thoughtfully—that is true respect.
It builds bridges where pride builds walls and turns arguments into understanding.
When we value people for their goodness and things for their purpose, life feels peaceful and bright.
True respect begins with gratitude—to parents, teachers, helpers, nature, and God.

To bow low is not weakness but wisdom.
For those who respect all, are the ones who truly rise high.

TRY THIS OUT!

The Respect-in-Action Challenge

Respect begins with how we treat people and things—especially in small moments.

- Choose one person you usually take for granted (a parent, teacher, helper, sibling, classmate). Show respect through action by doing one of these:
  1. Listen without interrupting
  2. Speak politely even if you disagree
  3. Say a sincere 'thank you' or follow their advice without complaining.
- Choose one object you use daily (a book, desk, bag, uniform, gadget). Handle it carefully today—no throwing, scribbling, or wasting.
- Reflect for a Moment: Did respect make my actions calmer? Did people respond more positively when I was respectful?

Flip the Cool Switch

Aarav's favourite part of the day was dessert time. That night, there was one piece of strawberry cake left in the freezer. He had carefully saved it for after dinner, planning to enjoy it after finishing his homework.

But when he opened the freezer—empty! The cake was gone. He turned around to see his little sister, Anvi, happily enjoying the last bite, her mouth smeared with cream.

'ANVI!' Aarav shouted. 'That was mine!'

Anvi froze. 'I—I didn't know,' she stammered.

Aarav was furious. 'You always do this! You never listen!' He slammed the fridge door and stormed off to his room.

Their mother comforted little Anvi, and a few minutes later, she entered Aarav's room.

'Aarav,' she said softly, 'I know you're upset. But yelling won't bring back the cake, will it?'

Aarav crossed his arms and muttered, 'She took what was mine. She deserves to get scolded.'

His mother sat beside him on the bed. 'I'll make the cake again tomorrow. Don't worry. But tell me—who is suffering more right now?'

Aarav blinked. 'Me, I guess. I'm the one who lost it.'

'Yes,' she said gently. 'You're not only upset because you lost the cake, but you're suffering even more because of your anger. Feeling disappointed is natural, but when we become intolerant and lose our cool, we only increase our pain.

'When anger takes over, it burns us from within. Anvi ate it unknowingly. She already said sorry and has forgotten it—but you're still boiling. My dear, we must learn to tolerate small inconveniences caused by others, especially when they're unintentional. Tolerance means choosing a calm response instead of an angry one.'

'But it's so hard, Mom,' Aarav said, his voice softer now. 'I just get mad quickly. And why should we stay calm, even when life feels unfair?'

'Because anger and complaining cannot change the past,' his mother explained. 'But tolerance gives us the strength to move forward. As you grow older, life will throw bigger challenges. If you can't tolerate small things now, how will you handle those later? Tolerance is like a muscle—the more you use it, the stronger it becomes. When things don't go your way, you have a special power—a quiet, cool switch inside you. You can flip it anytime to calm yourself down.'

'Like magic?' he asked, smiling a little.

'Almost,' she laughed. 'But it's real. Every time you flip that cool switch, your mind settles, your words become kinder, and your actions become wiser. Remember, shouting doesn't make you strong. Staying calm does. Sometimes, peace tastes sweeter than cake. So, please practise tolerance.'

Aarav nodded slowly. 'OK, Mom. I'll try.'

Takeaways from the Tale

- Losing your cool burns you first.
- Tolerance means responding wisely, not reacting impulsively.
- Every provoking situation is a chance to practise patience.
- Real victory is winning over your own anger.
- You can't control situations, but you can control your response.
- Patience today brings peace tomorrow.

What Is Tolerance?

Tolerance (*titiksa*) means staying calm and peaceful even when something unpleasant happens. It's your ability to 'stay cool' when emotions heat up.

A tolerant person doesn't complain or fight about every little thing. Instead, they stay composed, think clearly, and choose their response wisely.

Tolerance doesn't mean ignoring problems—it means facing them without being overwhelmed.

When you're tolerant, you're like a captain steering your ship through rough waves. The storm is real, but you still hold the wheel.

Why Tolerance Matters

Tolerance may sound simple, but it's actually a powerful virtue that separates strong kids from impulsive ones. Here's why:

1. **Peace of Mind:** When you stay calm, you protect your happiness.
2. **Better Decisions:** You think clearly and make smarter choices.
3. **Stronger Friendships:** Friends trust someone who doesn't explode easily.
4. **Inner Strength:** When you can control anger, you grow strong within.
5. **Wisdom:** You stop wasting time reacting and start solving problems.

Tolerance is not weakness—it is inner strength. It means being steady inside so that minor troubles don't shake you. When you are tolerant, you act like a smart kid who chooses peace over anger.

Lord Krishna teaches Arjuna the art of tolerance in the Bhagavad Gita:

mātrā-sparśās tu kaunteya
śītoṣṇa-sukha-duḥkha-dāḥ
āgamāpāyino 'nityās
tāṁs titikṣasva bhārata

'O son of Kunti, happiness and distress come and go like summer and winter. They are temporary. So learn to tolerate them without being disturbed.'

Bhagavad Gita (2.14)

Just as we tolerate the heat of summer and the chill of winter—because we know they'll pass—we should also learn to accept the ups and downs of life. When you face disappointment, remind yourself: 'This is just a passing season—it won't last forever.'

Three Levels of Tolerance

Lord Krishna encourages us to develop tolerance on three levels—the body, the mind, and the ego. Wise people learn to stay balanced in all three.

1. **Bodily (Physical) Level:** We need to tolerate the physical dualities—like heat and cold, comfort and discomfort. Just as we don't skip school on a hot day or stop playing because of a bit of sweat, we learn to adjust and continue our duty.
2. **Mental (Emotional) Level:** We must tolerate happiness and distress that come and go. When something pleasant happens,

we rejoice; when something unpleasant happens, we feel sad. But by practising tolerance, we remind ourselves that both are temporary visitors.

3. **Ego Level:** We need to tolerate honour and dishonour, success and failure, praise and criticism. These touch our sense of self-worth the most, but smart kids remain steady. They don't become proud when praised or broken when blamed—they stay balanced and peaceful inside.

These dualities—heat and cold, joy and sorrow, gain and loss, victory and defeat—are part of everyone's life. They are unavoidable, but we can choose a balanced response instead of being swept away by them.

Tolerance doesn't mean feeling nothing; it means remaining calm and steady in the middle of changing situations. When we master this art, we live every season—sunny or stormy—with grace and strength.

Complaining doesn't stop life's rain; it only makes more noise. But tolerance helps you carry an umbrella and keep walking peacefully.

A Four-Step Formula for Practising Tolerance

Whenever your 'anger volcano' starts rumbling, do these four things:

- **Pause:** Stop for a few seconds before reacting. (Even a five-second pause can save a friendship!)
- **Breathe:** Take deep, slow breaths to cool down.

- **Think:** Ask, 'What really happened? Was it on purpose or an accident?'
- **Respond:** Choose what's best, not what's easiest.

Tolerance doesn't mean ignoring problems or being weak. It means facing difficulties with a calm mind, a kind heart, and the courage to do what's right.

Each time you flip your cool switch, you train your mind to choose peace over anger, patience over panic, and wisdom over reaction. That's what makes you, not just a smart kid, but a truly strong kid.

TRY THIS OUT!

TOLERANCE THERMOMETER

Draw a thermometer labelled from Calm to Boiling. During the day, check where you are and cool down when needed.

When to Tolerate—and When Not To

Tolerance helps us stay calm, patient, and kind even when things are difficult. But does it mean we should accept everything, even when it's wrong? Not at all!

Tolerance doesn't mean letting others hurt, cheat, or be unfair to us. It means being peaceful in small problems but courageous and wise when serious wrongs happen.

A thoughtful and kind person learns to tolerate minor inconveniences, mistakes, or teasing with patience. When someone annoys us or makes a silly comment, we can choose not to react angrily.

By doing so, we achieve two good things:

- We keep our peace and patience instead of losing control.
- We give the other person a chance to realize their mistake and improve.

Often, a calm response can even melt someone's heart and prompt them to apologize.

However, if someone crosses the line, tolerance doesn't mean silence. Being tolerant doesn't mean being weak or quiet—it means being wise and balanced. When something unfair happens, speak up calmly but firmly.

What to tolerate?	What not to tolerate?
Accidents or unintentional mistakes	Intentionally caused harm
Small teasing or irritating comments	Bullying, and cruelty
Losing a game, waiting in line, or facing delays	Dishonesty or cheating
Weather changes, simple food, or minor disappointments	Disrespect or humiliation of yourself or others

Tolerance and courage together create a heart that is both peaceful and strong.

The Smart-Kid Formula of Wise Tolerance

Here's your practical four-step plan for handling any problem:

Example:

If your classmate keeps teasing you, tolerate it the first few times. Then communicate gently. If it continues, escalate the matter by telling your teacher. If it still doesn't stop, create some distance or change your seat.

That's wise tolerance—calm, firm, and smart.

Wise Tolerance vs. Blind Tolerance

Even the scriptures teach that tolerance must be guided by wisdom, not weakness.

The Mahabharata gives us a powerful example of wise tolerance. The Pandavas tolerated Duryodhana's cruelty many times. They remained patient, sought peace, and avoided conflict for years. But when he crossed all limits—burning their house, cheating them in the dice game, and insulting Queen Draupadi—they realized silence was no longer the answer.

Under Lord Krishna's guidance, they finally took a stand to fight for justice. Krishna told Arjuna, 'Tolerate the temporary pains and emotions that come with duty, but do not tolerate injustice—even if it comes from your own relatives.'

Even Lord Shiva showed the difference between wise tolerance and blind tolerance. King Daksha, who was Sati's father, did not like Shiva's simple lifestyle. In a big gathering, Daksha spoke very rudely about Shiva and tried to insult him in front of the crowd. But Shiva stayed calm. He didn't get angry or argue. He quietly left the place because he knew that reacting in anger would only create more problems. Later, Daksha organized a grand sacrifice and invited everyone except Shiva. Sati wanted to go, hoping her father would change. But when she arrived, Daksha again spoke harshly—this time insulting Shiva in front of her. Sati's heart broke. She couldn't bear to hear her beloved husband spoken of so severely, and she gave up her life in deep pain. When Shiva heard what had happened, he was deeply saddened. His patience was not from weakness—it was from wisdom. But now, the insult had gone too far. It was no longer about his own honour; it was about *dharma* and respect. Shiva sent his mighty follower, Virabhadra, to stop Daksha's arrogance and restore peace.

In the Bhagavad Gita, Lord Krishna reminds Arjuna to stay steady through life's ups and downs—pleasure and pain, success and failure—but also to act firmly when truth and goodness were at stake.

That is the secret of wise tolerance: stay calm in ordinary troubles but to stand strong when faced with real wrongs.

When you balance tolerance with courage, you become both gentle and powerful—like a cool breeze that can also move mountains.

Smart kids stay peaceful and protect their safety by setting clear boundaries.

Be calm like water, but strong like a wave when needed.

Everyday Practice of Tolerance

Here are real-life moments where tolerance helps—and how to practise it wisely:

- **Teasing in Class:** Pause and breathe. Say calmly, 'I don't like that. Please stop.' If it continues, inform your teacher.

- **Losing a Game:** Say, 'Good match! I'll practise and try again.' Use your energy to improve, not complain.
- **Food You Don't Love:** Remember that food is a gift. Eat with thanks and suggest your favourite dish next time.
- **Difficult Homework:** Tolerate the first wave of frustration. Break it into small steps and reward yourself after each one.
- **Cancelled Plans:** Feel disappointed, then send a friendly message and reschedule.
- **Borrowed Things:** If a sibling borrows without asking, say kindly, 'Please ask next time,' and show them where to keep things.
- **Bad Weather:** Turn it into fun—board games, reading, or indoor storytelling.
- **Unfair Criticism:** Listen to what helps you grow. Let go of what doesn't.
- **Waiting in a Queue:** Use the time to observe, smile, or say a short prayer.
- **When Technology Fails:** Don't yell at your gadget; instead, take a short break. Stretch, drink water, or help around the house.

Each time you choose patience, your tolerance muscles grow stronger.

When you learn to tolerate wisely, every challenge becomes your teacher—and every calm choice makes you stronger.

Reflection Corner

- When was the last time I stayed calm instead of shouting?
- What helps me cool down when I start to get angry?
- Do I react quickly or respond thoughtfully?

- How can I strengthen my 'cool switch' each day?
- Am I patient with people who make mistakes, just as I want them to be patient with me?
- What can I learn from moments when I lost my temper?

Let's Be Tolerant

Tolerance is the art of staying peaceful in a noisy world.
It doesn't mean we feel nothing—it means we choose calm over chaos.
When your mind is calm, your words heal; when it's hot, your words hurt.
Every time you stay patient, you win an invisible battle within yourself.
Like Krishna told Arjuna, joy and sorrow come and go—so learn to stand steady through both.
Let minor troubles pass, forgive easily, and smile often.
True strength isn't in shouting the loudest—it's in staying quiet when anger shouts inside you.
Flip your 'cool switch', and let peace, not anger, lead your life.

TRY THIS OUT!

THE COOL-SWITCH CHALLENGE

1. When something annoying or disappointing happens (waiting, teasing, mistakes, delays, losing a game), pause for 10 seconds.
2. Take three slow breaths and silently say: 'This will pass.'
3. Choose one calm response:
   - Stay quiet and walk away
   - Speak politely instead of shouting
   - Let go and move on, or ask for help without anger
4. Notice how your body and mind feel after choosing calm.

7 Forgiveness: Let Go and Grow Strong

The Choice to Forgive

Sunrise School's Sports Day was buzzing with cheers, music, and a thousand bright colours. Aarav felt ready. He had trained for weeks for the 200 metre race. As he stood at the starting line, he whispered to himself, 'Run your best. Be your best.'

The whistle blew.

Aarav sprinted. The wind rushed past his ears, the track flew under his feet, and the finish line drew closer. Ten metres to go—victory felt near.

Then it happened.

A runner from the next lane—Rohan—brushed Aarav and stumbled into him. Aarav lost his balance and fell hard. The world spun around him. By the time he pulled himself up, the race was over.

His knee stung. But his heart hurt more.

Anger surged like a storm. 'He ruined my race! This isn't fair! Aarav's fingers curled into fists. He wanted to shout, complain, and blame the other participant.

But then he remembered Mom's words from last night: 'Shouting doesn't make you strong. Choosing calm and kindness does.'

Rohan ran back, breathless and wide-eyed. 'Aarav, I'm so, so sorry! I slipped and bumped into you. I didn't mean to—please forgive me.'

Aarav looked at Rohan's worried face. Inside, the storm still rumbled. He took a slow breath. He remembered the cool switch and gently flipped it on.

'OK,' Aarav said quietly. 'No worries, Rohan. You didn't do it on purpose.'

Rohan's shoulders dropped in relief. 'Thank you. I'll be more careful.'

The principal overheard the honest exchange and smiled approvingly.

Later, during the assembly, the principal announced a special honour. 'This year, the Sportsmanship Award goes to Rohan.'

As Rohan walked to the stage, Aarav felt a tiny pinch of sadness. But he chose to clap wholeheartedly, cheering for his friend.

When Rohan returned with the cup, he smiled and said, 'If I hadn't bumped into you, this would've belonged to you.' Aarav grinned. 'No worries. Congratulations!'

Then, to everyone's surprise, the principal added, 'We also have a

Takeaways from the Tale

- Choosing to forgive won't undo what happened–but it releases the pain.
- Forgiveness heals friendships and makes you stronger inside.
- You can't control every situation, but you can control your response.
- Forgiveness turns a bad moment into a brave moment.

Special Recognition Prize today. He may not have crossed the finish line first, but he showed kindness and forgiveness on the track. The special prize goes to Aarav.'

The hall burst into applause. Aarav didn't win the race—but he had won something greater: a peaceful heart and a friendship strengthened by forgiveness.

What Is Forgiveness?

The Sanskrit word for forgiveness is *kshama*. It means letting go of hurt and resentment and opening your heart to peace. Forgiveness is not pretending nothing happened, and it's not saying that wrong is acceptable. It is choosing kindness over grudges and peace over punishment.

Our scriptures like the Bhagavad Gita and the Srimad-Bhagavatam praise a heart that forgives. Anger and grudges are like tiny thorns stuck in your foot—they keep hurting as long as they stay inside. Forgiveness removes those thorns so you can walk happily again.

Forgiveness is not weakness; it is spiritual strength—the power to keep your mind peaceful, your actions thoughtful, and your relationships strong.

Forgiveness often grows like a seed. Sometimes you can forgive quickly; other times it takes days or weeks. That's OK—seeds take time to become trees. Your heart is learning.

Forgive Others to Be Forgiven

Whenever we make a mistake—knowingly or unknowingly—we hope others will forgive us and still care for us. If they stop talking to us or keep their distance, it hurts even more. Similarly, when others make mistakes and genuinely regret and apologize, we should be kind enough to forgive them.

Let's treat others the way we want to be treated!

Forgiving someone doesn't mean approving their wrong actions—it means freeing our own heart from the heavy burden of anger and negativity.

When we forgive, we let go of the weight of grudges and feel light again.

Why Forgiveness Matters?

1. **Light Heart:** Grudges feel heavy; forgiveness makes you feel free and peaceful.
2. **Better Friendships:** Letting go keeps love and trust alive.
3. **Wiser Choices:** Calm minds decide better than angry ones.
4. **Brave and Strong:** It takes real courage to say, 'I forgive you.'
5. **Happier You:** Forgiveness reduces stress and makes room for joy.
6. **Closer to Divinity:** A forgiving heart is pleasing to the Lord.

Tolerance and Forgiveness: How They Work Together

Sometimes we may choose to tolerate minor inconveniences caused by others—by staying calm and not reacting harshly. But if we keep anger and resentment inside, it won't last long. Suppressed hurt bursts out later.

True peace comes when external tolerance is joined by internal forgiveness.

At other times, the opposite may be true—we must not tolerate harmful behaviour on the outside (we should set boundaries and seek help), but we can still forgive in our hearts so we don't grow bitter.

You can be a well-wisher internally and still be firm externally.

A perfect example of this balance is a mother's love. A caring mother may not tolerate a child's mischief—she corrects, sets limits, and even scolds when needed—but her heart forgives instantly. The correction comes from love, and forgiveness keeps the relationship warm.

That's the model: firm on the outside when needed, soft on the inside always.

Examples of Forgiveness from the Scriptures

Yudhisthira and Duryodhana: In the Mahabharata, the Pandavas tolerated Duryodhana's cruelty many times. But when his actions became unbearable, they had to fight the Kurukshetra battle to reclaim justice. Yet, King Yudhisthira never held hatred or bitterness in his heart towards Duryodhana. Even after victory, he felt compassion and wished Duryodhana peace.

Lesson: True forgiveness doesn't mean accepting injustice—it means keeping your heart free from hatred even when you stand for what's right.

Rama and Ravana: In the Ramayana, Ravana kidnapped Mother Sita. When Rama reached the shores of Lanka, He told His army, 'Even if Ravana himself comes and sincerely seeks forgiveness, I will forgive him.' Rama's heart was always guided by *dharma*. His forgiveness showed that even justice can be carried out with compassion. **Lesson:** Forgiveness is noble. It doesn't cancel justice, but it welcomes a change of heart.

Krishna and Indra: Once, Indra, the king of heaven, became angry with Krishna and the people of Vrindavan for not worshipping him. In pride, he sent heavy rains to destroy the village. Krishna calmly lifted the Govardhana hill to protect everyone. Later, when Indra realized his mistake and apologized, Krishna forgave him and taught him humility. **Lesson:** Even great people make mistakes. Admitting wrong and seeking forgiveness brings peace—and the one who forgives grows greater, not smaller.

Forgiveness doesn't mean forgetting or allowing harm. It means releasing anger, choosing peace, and giving others a chance to improve.

When we forgive, we not only help others grow—we free our own hearts too.

Simple Ways to Practise Forgiveness

1. **Heart Talk:** Close your eyes and say in your mind, 'I forgive you. I release this. May we be peaceful again.'
2. **Prayer for Strength:** 'Krishna, please help me let go of this anger. Give me a forgiving heart.' Even trying to forgive counts—Krishna sees your effort.
3. **Forgiveness Journal:** Write what hurt you, how you felt, and one kind thought you can choose now. When you read it later, you'll see how your heart has grown.

A Simple Forgiveness Framework

When your feelings are hurt, try the **4Rs**:

- **Recognize:** Name the feeling: 'I'm hurt, angry, or sad.'
- **Reflect:** Breathe and ask, 'Was it an accident or on purpose?'
- **Respond:** Speak kindly but clearly: 'That hurt me. Please don't do it again.'
- **Release:** Let go inside, so you don't carry the pain everywhere.

If the hurt keeps repeating, use the Tolerance chapter's safety steps: Communicate → Escalate → Set boundaries. You can forgive—and still keep distance—for your peace.

What Forgiveness Is and Isn't

Forgiveness Is	Forgiveness Isn't
Letting go of anger and grudges inside you	Saying the wrong was acceptable
Choosing peace and kindness over revenge	Ignoring that a wrong happened
Giving yourself and others a chance to start again	Allowing others to harm you repeatedly
A sign of inner strength	Blindly trusting someone who hasn't changed

Forgiveness and Trust: What's the Difference?

- Forgiveness is about your heart—letting go of anger.
- Trust is about their actions—it grows back slowly through honesty and change.

You can forgive someone today and still say, 'I need time before I can trust you again.'
That's not rudeness—that's wisdom.

Everyday Practice: Quick Examples

- **At School:** A friend forgets to invite you. You talk, understand, and forgive. Next time, you ask them first—you lead with kindness.
- **At Home:** A sibling breaks your model. You forgive, then set a new rule about asking before touching.
- **In Teams:** A teammate blames you unfairly. You stay calm, share your side, and forgive—but also improve your skill.
- **Teasing in Class:** Breathe. Say, 'That hurt. Please stop.' If they apologize, forgive and move on.
- **Breaking Promises:** 'I forgive you. Let's plan better next time.'
- **Accidental Spills:** 'It's OK. Let's clean it together.'
- **Unfair Comments:** 'That wasn't kind. But please don't repeat it.'

Forgiveness doesn't make you smaller—it makes your heart bigger. Each time you forgive, your heart becomes a little braver and a little brighter.

Forgiveness doesn't erase what happened—but it heals what remains.

When you forgive wisely, you grow lighter, kinder, and closer to Krishna—strong enough to let go and truly grow strong.

Reflection Corner

- When someone hurts me, do I hold on or let go?
- What feels heavier—anger or forgiveness?
- Have I ever been forgiven by someone? How did it feel?
- Do I forgive quickly, or wait until anger fades?
- Can I pray for someone who hurt me and wish them peace?
- How does forgiveness make my heart lighter and my friendships stronger?

Let's Forgive

Forgiveness is not about approving misdeeds—it's about freeing your heart. It doesn't mean saying 'It's OK' to wrongdoings—it means saying 'I choose peace.'

When you forgive, you drop the heavy stones of anger and walk freely again.

Like Rama forgiving Ravana, and Krishna forgiving Indra, learn to release hurt, not hold it.

Even if others forget to act properly, let your heart remember to act kindly.

Forgiveness is strength in softness, courage in calmness, victory in letting go.

Each time you forgive, your heart grows bigger—and God smiles within it.

Because when you forgive others, you heal yourself.

TRY THIS OUT!

The Heavy Bag – Light Heart Activity

- Think of one small hurt you're still carrying (a rude word, a broken promise, being left out, or an argument).
- Imagine that hurt as a heavy bag you're carrying on your back.
- Close your eyes and ask yourself: 'Is this bag helping me... or hurting me?'
- Now imagine placing the bag down. Say silently: 'I choose peace over pain. I forgive and let go.'
- Take a deep breath and notice how your heart feels lighter.
- If possible, do one kind act towards that person (a smile, a kind word, or simply no bitterness).

Did holding the hurt make me happier or heavier? How did it feel to let go, even a little?
Forgiveness doesn't change the past but it frees your heart for the future.

The Sparrow in the Rain

One stormy evening, the streets of Vrindavan were quiet. Raindrops fell in silver streams, and the sky growled softly with thunder. A little girl named Meera stood by the window, watching the rain. Suddenly, she noticed a small sparrow fluttering helplessly on the ground. Its wings were soaked, and it was shivering in the cold.

'Oh no!' she gasped and ran outside, holding an umbrella. The ground was muddy, and her shoes splashed through puddles, but she didn't care. She gently picked up the trembling sparrow and carried it inside.

Using an old towel, she dried its wings and placed it near a warm lamp. She gave it a few drops of water and a few grains of rice.

For a while, the little bird sat still. Then it chirped softly—once, twice, and finally fluttered its wings again. It looked at Meera as if to say, 'Thank you.' Meera smiled, her heart glowing.

Her mother walked in and asked, 'Why are you all wet, dear?'

Meera pointed at the tiny guest. 'He needed me.'

Her mother smiled warmly. 'You gave more than comfort to that bird—you gave love.'

Later that evening, as the sparrow flew away into the slowly darkening pink sky, Meera felt a strange sense of joy. She had not received anything in return—yet her heart felt full. That's the quiet power of compassion. It's love that moves—not for fame, not for reward, but because the heart cannot help but care.

Takeaways from the Tale

- Compassion is caring even when you gain nothing in return.
- Small acts of kindness can make big differences.
- Helping others brings more joy than receiving.
- True compassion doesn't wait for applause.
- A caring heart is stronger than a proud one.

What Is Compassion?

The Sanskrit word for compassion is *daya*, which means to feel and share another's feelings. Compassion or kindness is more than saying, 'I feel bad for you.' It is love in action—a heart that not only feels another's pain but also wants to ease it.

Imagine your friend trips and falls. Instead of just saying, 'Oh no!', you run to help, pick up their bag, and offer a hand. That is compassion. Or think of a classmate who forgot their pencil. You could ignore them and say, 'Not my problem.' Instead you share yours—that, too, is compassion.

Sometimes, compassion doesn't even need words—like helping your mother when she's tired, or quietly giving your father a glass of water before he asks. It gently says, 'I see you. I care for you.'

Every being—from a tiny ant to a great king—wants love and kindness. Toys, medals, or sweets may bring short bursts of happiness, but the joy that fills the heart forever is the one that comes from giving and caring. Compassion is love that moves—it connects, heals, and uplifts.

Why Compassion Matters

Compassion is like a soft cushion within your heart. It makes room for others' pain and joy. It turns selfishness into sharing and transforms loneliness into belonging.

When you show compassion:

- People feel safe and valued.
- Your own heart feels peaceful and light.
- The world becomes a little gentler and brighter.

Every small act of compassion is like a drop of rain cooling the ground on a scorching day—and together, those drops can form an ocean of goodness.

Divine Compassion

Ultimately, God is the greatest example of compassion. In the Bhagavad Gita, Lord Krishna explains that He descends into this world again and again to establish *dharma*, protect the righteous, and uplift the fallen. These divine descents are not just acts of duty—they are acts of compassion.

Even when people forget Him or act against *dharma*, the Lord never gives up on them. Instead, He lovingly guides, forgives, and gives them another chance to grow.

Godly souls and saints, following His example, travel far and wide to uplift others with wisdom and devotion—that too is compassion in action.

True compassion, therefore, means to love, forgive, and uplift, even when others falter.

Lord Krishna teaches that real compassion means being kind to all living beings—not just to our friends and family, but also to humans, animals, and even the tiniest creatures.

A compassionate person never hates, hurts, or looks down upon anyone, for they see every life as part of the same divine family.

Five Levels of Compassion

Just as satisfaction is felt at many levels, compassion, too, can be expressed in many ways—from the physical to the spiritual.

1. **Compassion on the Bodily Level**
   When we help someone physically—like feeding the hungry, tending to the sick, giving medicine to the ill, or supporting someone in financial distress—we express compassion through service to the body. Such acts comfort the suffering and show genuine care.

2. **Compassion on the Emotional Level**
   When someone feels sad, lonely, or discouraged—perhaps after a failure or being spoken to harshly—we can express compassion with kind words, encouragement, and listening with empathy. Lifting someone's heart is one of the sweetest forms of kindness.
3. **Compassion on the Intellectual Level**
   Sometimes people struggle with confusion or problems they can't solve. When we patiently share our understanding, explain lessons, or help someone find clarity, we express compassion through our intelligence and knowledge.
   Teaching a classmate who finds a topic difficult, or helping a friend think through a tough decision, is compassion at work on the level of intellect.
4. **Compassion on the Level of Identity (Ego)**
   Here, ego means one's sense of self-worth. Many people just long to feel valued and respected. When we appreciate someone's efforts, recognize their abilities, and make them feel important, we heal their heart.
   This is not flattering false pride, but nourishing healthy self-worth. Respecting others' dignity is a subtle yet powerful form of compassion.
5. **Compassion on the Spiritual Level**
   This is the highest and purest form of compassion. Every living being is a part of God, and the greatest kindness we can offer is to help others remember their divine connection with God. When we share spiritual wisdom, encourage prayer, help others chant God's names, or inspire goodness in their hearts, we express compassion for the soul—which is eternal.
   To guide others spiritually, we must also be sincere and grounded in our own spiritual life. Only then can we inspire others to rise towards the Divine.

A compassionate heart sees the soul, not just the skin. It doesn't judge by appearance, wealth, or background. It understands that everyone—rich or poor, strong or weak, young or old—has the same inner longing to love and be loved.

As the wise say, 'True wisdom is not how much you know, but how deeply you care.'

The Compassion of the Great

Lord Buddha and the Wounded Swan

When Lord Buddha was a young prince named Siddhartha, he once walked through the royal gardens with his cousin, Devadatta. Suddenly, a swan fell from the sky—an arrow had struck its wing. The bird fell weakly on the grass, flapping its broken wing in pain.

Siddhartha immediately ran forward, gently lifted the bird, and removed the arrow. He tore a piece of his robe to wrap its wound and softly comforted it until the trembling stopped.

Just then, Devadatta arrived with his bow. 'That's my swan!' he argued. 'I shot it, so it belongs to me!'

Siddhartha calmly replied, 'Brother, you may have caused its pain, but I have given it life. A living being belongs to the one who protects it, not to the one who harms it.'

The matter was taken to the royal court, where the wise ministers listened carefully. They decided that life belongs to the one who saves, not the one who wounds. Siddhartha smiled and released the healed swan into the sky. The bird circled above him as if blessing him for his kindness.

This gentle act of compassion became the seed of the great mercy that later blossomed in Lord Buddha's heart. As he grew, he walked from village to village, teaching people to be kind, peaceful, and gentle towards all living beings.

He taught that true strength lies in compassion, and that real religion is to live without hurting any creature—in thought, word, or deed.

Lord Shiva's Compassion

When the gods and demons churned the ocean of celestial milk to obtain nectar, a deadly poison called *halahala* emerged first, threatening to destroy the entire world.

Not knowing what to do, they all approached Lord Shiva for help. Out of pure compassion, Lord Shiva stepped forward and drank the poison to save all living beings.

It turned His neck blue, earning Him the name Nilakantha, 'the blue-throated one'. Because of Lord Shiva's compassion, the universe was saved.

Of course, we cannot imitate Lord Shiva's level of sacrifice. But within our capacity, we, too, can express compassion—by helping those in need. If we see someone hungry, thirsty, or struggling, we can offer food, water, or words of comfort. Even small acts of kindness reflect divine compassion.

Srila Prabhupada's Compassion

In recent times, Srila Prabhupada showed what real compassion looks like in action. At the age of sixty-nine, he left India alone on a cargo ship bound for America with no wealth, no friends, and no comforts. His only treasure was his devotion and love for Lord Krishna.

He endured sickness, storms, and even heart attacks at sea, but never gave up. Why? His heart overflowed with compassion for people suffering in ignorance of their spiritual identity.

He crossed oceans not for fame or profit, but to share Krishna's love with the world. Through his compassion, millions found a path of joy, peace, and devotion.

We may not cross oceans, but we can cross the small distances between hearts—by being kind, patient, and helpful to others. Even a few words of care can carry someone from darkness to light.

Misplaced Compassion

Compassion is powerful—but like other virtues, it must be guided by wisdom. Sometimes, helping in the wrong way can harm instead of heal.

Imagine your friend has eaten too many chocolates and asks for more. You feel sorry and give in. That's not compassion—it's indulgence!

Or suppose a drunkard or smoker asks for money, but you know it will only harm them. Giving that money isn't kindness—it's carelessness.

Real compassion doesn't mean saying 'yes' to every request or fulfilling unreasonable desires of others. It means doing what is truly good for the other person, even if it requires saying 'no' with gentleness. That's what parents often do. They are always kind towards their children, but forbid them when needed.

If your friend bullies someone, it's compassionate to stop them and explain why it's wrong. If someone cheats, guiding them towards honesty is also an act of compassion.

Kindness without wisdom becomes weakness; Compassion with wisdom becomes strength.

True compassion corrects without condemning—it uplifts without humiliating.

Practising Compassion in Daily Life

You don't need superpowers to be compassionate. You only need a caring heart and the willingness to act.

1. **Be a Good Listener:** When a friend is sad, don't rush to speak. Listen patiently. Sometimes, quiet attention is the best comfort.
2. **Help Without Being Asked:** If your parents look tired, clean your room, fill water bottles, or help set the dinner table. Silent help speaks loudest.
3. **Be Kind to Animals:** Give water to a thirsty bird, feed an old beggar gently, or avoid stepping on ants. Every life, big or small, deserves kindness.
4. **Share What You Have:** If you have an extra snack, pencil, or toy—share it. Compassion grows when shared.
5. **Forgive Quickly:** Everyone makes mistakes. Forgiving others is compassion in its purest form.
6. **Pray for Others:** Even if you can't

always help physically, you can always wish well. A compassionate heart whispers, 'May everyone be happy.'

When we correct others, it too can be compassion—if done with empathy and kindness. Correction should aim to uplift, not embarrass. True compassion heals hearts, not hurts them.

Everyday Practice: Compassion in Action

- **At School:** Help a classmate struggling with lessons.
- **At Home:** Smile at siblings even when they irritate you.
- **In the Community:** Help elders or feed stray animals.
- **Towards Nature:** Water plants, avoid waste, and protect the environment.
- **In Prayer:** Wish peace for those suffering, even if you don't know them.

Each small act adds light to the world—and that light never goes out.

Reflection Corner

- When did I last help someone without being asked?
- Have I ever corrected someone kindly instead of scolding?
- How can I show compassion when it's inconvenient?
- How can I express compassion towards animals and nature?
- How does compassion connect me with God?

Let's Be Compassionate

Compassion means feeling others' joys and sorrows as your own.

True compassion acts, not just feels.

Wise compassion helps without harming.

Every being deserves love and care.

Compassion connects us with Krishna, making our hearts divine.

The smallest act of kindness is greater than the grandest intention.

TRY THIS OUT!

1. **SEE**: Look around today and notice one person who may be struggling—a sad friend, a tired parent, a lonely classmate, or a hungry animal.
2. **FEEL**: Pause and imagine how they might feel. Ask yourself: 'How would I feel if I were them?'
3. **HELP:** Do one small kind act—a smile, a kind word, sharing food, helping with work, or simply listening.

In this world if you can be anything, be kind.

9 Determination: Keep Going, Keep Growing

The Mountain of Effort

Mira sat at her study table, her notebook open, pencil tapping restlessly. Numbers danced before her eyes, and the maths problem refused to make sense. 'I've tried again and again,' she sighed. 'I just can't do it!'

Her grandfather, seated nearby, looked up from his newspaper. 'What's the matter, Mira?'

'This problem is impossible!' she groaned. 'No matter how many times I try, it doesn't work. I think I'll just give up.'

Grandfather smiled gently. 'Hmm... You remind me of someone who attempted an almost impossible task, but managed to do it.'

'Who?' Mira asked curiously.

'Hanuman,' said her grandfather. 'During the great battle in Lanka, Lakshmana fell unconscious. Only a rare herb called Sanjivani from a mountain in the Himalayas could save him. Hanuman was sent to bring it. He flew across the sky with great determination, but when he reached the mountain, he couldn't recognize which herb it was.'

Mira's eyes widened. 'So what did he do?'

'Did he sit down and cry?' Grandfather chuckled. 'No. He didn't give up. He used his strength to lift the entire mountain and bring it back! Because of his determination, Lakshmana's life was saved—and so was the entire vanaras' army.'

Mira leaned forward, fascinated. 'He carried the whole mountain? Just because he couldn't find one herb?'

'Yes,' said Grandfather softly. 'Sometimes in life, when we can't find the exact answer, we must bring the whole mountain of effort. Hanuman's determination turned an impossible task into a miracle.'

He patted Mira's head affectionately. 'You may not lift mountains, dear, but in your little world—your studies, your projects, your duties—you can still show the same spirit. Don't give up so easily. Try one more time... maybe two, or even three. Each effort brings you closer to the solution.'

Mira smiled slowly, turned back to her notebook, and started again. This time, she worked with calm determination. After a few minutes, her face lit up—she had found the answer.

Grandfather nodded proudly. 'There it is—the sanjivani of patience and perseverance.'

Takeaways from the Tale

- Determined people try again even when things seem impossible.
- Every effort counts–sometimes success hides just behind one more attempt.
- Hanuman's example teaches that true strength lies in not giving up easily.
- We may not lift mountains, but we can overcome our own obstacles through steady effort.

What Is Determination?

The Sanskrit word for determination is *dhrti* or *drdha-niscaya*—unshakable resolve. It means continuing to do what is right, even when it is difficult, uncomfortable, or slow.

Determination isn't stubbornness or unwanted passion—it's steady strength. A determined person says, 'I'll try again, no matter how many times I fail.' It's not about never falling; it's about rising each time you fall.

Determination is the bridge between dreams and reality, plans and results. Without it, even the best ideas remain incomplete. With it, even small steps lead to great achievements.

In the Bhagavad Gita, Lord Krishna says:

vyavasāyātmikā buddhir ekeha kuru-nandana
bahu-śākhā hy anantāś ca buddhayo 'vyavasāyinām

'Those who are resolute in purpose have one-pointed determination. The thoughts of the indecisive are scattered in many directions.'
Bhagavad Gita (2.41)

This verse defines true determination—single-minded focus on a righteous goal. A determined person doesn't get lost in confusion, temptation, or distractions. They think clearly, choose wisely, and move steadily.

Determination, in spiritual terms, means staying fixed in *dharma*—doing one's duty sincerely, without giving up in the face of obstacles.

Determination vs. Stubbornness

Aspect	Determination	Stubbornness
Motive	Rooted in reason and higher purpose	Rooted in pride or ego
Response to Guidance	Listens, learns, adapts	Rejects advice blindly
Emotion	Calm, patient, disciplined	Angry, restless, rigid
Outcome	Leads to growth and success	Leads to frustration and isolation
Example	Arjuna focusing on the bird's eye	Duryodhana refusing to make peace

Determination is courage guided by wisdom; stubbornness is pride guided by ignorance.

Why Determination Matters

1. **Gives Direction:** When the goal is clear, energy doesn't scatter.
2. **Builds Confidence:** Each small victory strengthens the will to continue.
3. **Conquers Fear:** A determined person may feel afraid—but moves forward anyway.
4. **Inspires Others:** When people see your persistence, they believe they can persist, too.
5. **Earns the Lord's Grace:** Krishna helps those who help themselves with steady effort.

Without determination, talent is wasted potential. With determination, even a simple soul can move mountains.

Determination and Patience

Many confuse determination with restlessness or unwanted passion—working in a rush, losing peace when results don't come quickly. But true determination walks hand in hand with patience.

Determination says, 'I'll keep trying.' Patience says, 'I'll wait for the right time.'

A seed grows into a tree not by shouting at the soil but by staying planted, nourished, and patient. Similarly, a determined person isn't discouraged by delays; they trust that steady effort always bears fruit in time.

Determination without patience becomes frustration. Patience without determination becomes laziness. Balance both, and success blossoms naturally.

The Opposite of Determination: Laziness

Laziness (*alasyam*) is the enemy of determination. It whispers, 'I'll do it later,' until later never comes. A lazy person has dreams but no direction, goals but no grit. They wait for the 'perfect time', not realizing that today is the perfect time to begin.

The Bhagavad Gita (18.39) says that laziness arises from ignorance—it dulls the mind, weakens enthusiasm, and keeps one stuck in mediocrity.

Laziness promises comfort but delivers regret. Determination demands effort but brings peace.

The difference between ordinary and extraordinary is just a little extra determination.

Examples of Determination from the Scriptures

1. Arjuna's Focus

When Guru Drona wanted to test his students, he placed a wooden bird on a distant branch and asked each prince what they saw.

Bhima said, 'I see the tree.'

Nakula said, 'I see the sky.'

Yudhisthira said, 'I see the bird and the branch.'

Finally, Arjuna said, 'I see only the bird's eye.'

Drona smiled. 'Then shoot.'

Arjuna's arrow hit the target perfectly.

That focus—seeing the goal and nothing else—is determination. It's not that Arjuna's eyes were sharper; it was his mind that was steady. Krishna later blessed him with the wisdom of the Gita because Arjuna had the determination to listen, learn, and fight for righteousness even when he was afraid.

2. Dhruva's Resolve

Long ago, little Dhruva was just five years old when he was hurt by his family.

His father, King Uttanapada, lovingly lifted his stepbrother onto his lap but pushed Dhruva aside. The child's heart burned with sadness and rejection.

His mother, Suniti, gently said, 'If you want true happiness, seek the Lord. Only He can give you what no one else can take away.'

So Dhruva left the palace and went alone into the forest to meditate.

He faced hunger, fear, and harsh weather, but he never gave up.

Guided by Sage Narada, he chanted the holy names of the Lord with complete faith.

After months of determination, Lord Vishnu personally appeared before him, blessing him with divine vision and eternal peace. Dhruva didn't just win a kingdom—he won spiritual strength. His story teaches that no pain is too great when determination is guided by devotion.

3. **Bhagiratha's Perseverance**

Long ago, King Bhagiratha wanted to bring the sacred river Ganga down from heaven to purify the ashes of his ancestors. For thousands of years, he performed austerities, prayed, and meditated. Finally, Mother Ganga appeared and said, 'I will descend, but my force will destroy the earth unless someone holds me.' Bhagiratha then prayed to Lord Shiva, who agreed to catch her mighty waters in His hair.

Even after Ganga's descent, Bhagiratha guided her across forests, mountains, and plains until she reached the ocean and touched the ashes of his ancestors—freeing them at last. Bhagiratha's unbreakable will gave the world the holy river Ganga. That's why when a person shows great persistence, we still say, 'He has Bhagiratha-like determination.'

How to Build Determination

1. **Set a Clear Goal:** You can't stay steady if you don't know where you're going. Write your goal, big or small, and remind yourself why it matters.

2. **Start Small but Stay Consistent:** Reading one page a day or practising a skill for ten minutes regularly is better than a single big burst followed by long breaks.
3. **Expect Obstacles:** Every worthwhile goal has challenges. Don't see them as roadblocks—see them as training.
4. **Avoid Comparisons:** Everyone's pace is different. The tortoise reached the finish line not by running fast but by moving steadily.
5. **Seek Inspiration:** Read stories of great achievers like Dhruva, Arjuna, and Hanuman. Their strength came not from comfort, but from conviction.
6. **Pray for Endurance:** When your energy fades, close your eyes and pray: 'O Krishna, please give me the strength to continue doing what is right.' Determination grows when devotion fuels it.

When Determination Is Tested

Determination is not proven in comfort but in challenge.

- If everyone around you gives up and you continue—that's determination.
- If results come late and you stay patient—that's determination.
- If failure visits and you welcome it as a teacher—that's determination.

Each test strengthens your inner will.

Like iron shaped by fire, a strong character is formed by enduring difficulty. The more you are tested, the stronger your spirit becomes.

Determination in Daily Life

- **At School:** Keep studying subjects you find hard instead of quitting.
- **In Bhakti:** Chant, read, and serve with steadiness even on restless days.
- **In Relationships:** Be patient with people. Determination isn't only for work—it's for love and kindness too.

- **In Sports:** Play fair, even if it means losing a match.
- **At Home:** Finish chores even when you feel lazy.

Reflection Corner

- Do I finish what I start?
- Do I quit easily when things don't go my way?
- Am I patient when progress feels slow?
- Do I confuse determination with stubbornness?
- How can I strengthen my willpower through faith in Krishna?

Let's Be Determined

Determination is the quiet fire that keeps the heart alive during storms. It turns failure into experience and effort into excellence.

When guided by patience and purpose, determination becomes divine.

When ruled by pride, it becomes destruction.

So, fix your mind on what is right, walk steadily towards it, and never let temporary setbacks stop you.

Like Dhruva's meditation, Arjuna's focus, Hanuman's leap, and Bhagiratha's prayer, let your efforts be steady, sincere, and sacred.

Slow progress is still progress.

The Lord sees your effort, not just your result.

Keep walking, keep trying, keep growing.

That's true determination—the journey that never gives up, because it walks with faith.

TRY THIS OUT!

DON'T QUIT YET CHALLENGE

1. **CHOOSE:** Pick one task you usually feel like giving up on—homework, practise, reading, drawing, or any skill you find difficult.
2. **COMMIT:** Promise yourself: 'I will try this three more times before I quit.' No rushing. No complaining. Just sincere effort.
3. **COMPLETE**: After your third attempt, pause and notice: Did it become easier? Do you feel stronger or more confident?

You don't need to lift mountains like Hanuman. But trying one more time can move mountains inside you. Effort builds strength. Persistence builds character.

10 Cleanliness: Purity Outside, Peace Inside

The Muddy Hands

The final bell rang, and the students of Bluebell School rushed out to play. Aarohi loved gardening, and today she was helping the school gardener plant new flower saplings. She dug eagerly into the soft, wet soil, patting down the mud around the roots. Her hands were soon brown and sticky, but she didn't mind—she loved the smell of fresh earth.

When she finished, her friends called, 'Come for snacks!' Aarohi ran straight to the canteen and reached for her sandwich, just as her teacher, Mrs Rao, walked by.

'Aarohi,' she said gently, 'did you wash your hands?'

Aarohi blinked. 'Oh... I was just about to.'

Mrs Rao smiled. 'The flowers grow beautifully when the warm soil surrounds the sapling. But if you bring the soil to your food, it will harm you instead of helping.'

Aarohi ran to wash her hands properly, scrubbing them until they were clean. As she ate, she thought, 'Clean hands make everything feel fresh!'

That night, she helped her mother tidy her study table, put her toys back neatly, and even swept the floor. Her mother smiled, 'Clean surroundings keep your mind calm.'

Aarohi grinned. 'And clean hands keep you healthy!'

That day, Aarohi learned that cleanliness is not just about looking neat—it's about thinking, feeling, and living purely.

Takeaways from the Tale

- Cleanliness begins with small habits like washing, organizing, and caring.
- A clean body keeps you healthy; a clean mind keeps you happy.
- Cleanliness is not just about appearance—it's about respect for yourself and others.
- Purity in action leads to peace in the heart.

What Is Cleanliness?

The Sanskrit word for cleanliness is *saucha*, one of the foundational principles of a disciplined and spiritual life. Cleanliness means purity of body, mind, surroundings, and soul.

In the Bhagavad Gita (13.8), Lord Krishna lists *saucha*—cleanliness—as one of the qualities of true knowledge. A clean person is not only neat in appearance but also pure in thoughts, speech, and conduct.

Cleanliness is more than soap and water—it's an attitude of purity. It means keeping everything—our bodies, our rooms, our relationships, and even our intentions—fresh, organized, and sincere.

Cleanliness outside is hygiene; cleanliness inside is holiness.

Why Cleanliness Matters

Cleanliness is next to godliness. Cleanliness is the foundation of health, discipline, and respect. When we keep ourselves and our surroundings clean, we respect our bodies, our homes, and the world that serves us.

1. **Protects Health:** Germs and dirt cause diseases. Simple habits like washing hands, bathing daily, brushing teeth, and keeping nails trimmed protect us from illness.
2. **Brings Discipline:** An organized space creates an organized mind. Keeping your desk or room tidy helps you focus better.
3. **Inspires Respect:** When you keep yourself neat, others feel comfortable around you. It shows you value yourself and the people near you.
4. **Reflects Inner Order:** A clean outer life reflects a calm inner life. Purity outside helps build purity inside.

Levels of Cleanliness

Cleanliness is like a four-layered lamp—each layer must shine for life to stay bright. When all four glow together, they illuminate both our outer world and inner being.

1. **Physical Cleanliness—Body and Surroundings**
   This is the outermost layer—caring for the body and the space around us. It includes bathing regularly, keeping hair and nails neat, wearing clean clothes, washing hands before meals, and keeping our study and play areas tidy.
   Clean surroundings bring clarity and joy. A clean room invites positive thoughts, while a messy one attracts laziness and confusion. Clean body, clear mind. Cleanliness is not about luxury—it is about respect for life. When we keep our surroundings pure, our thoughts begin to sparkle, too.

2. **Mental and Emotional Cleanliness—The Inner Shine**

   Just as dust clouds a mirror, negative thoughts and emotions cloud the heart and mind. Mental and emotional cleanliness means keeping our minds free from envy, anger, resentment, pride, and arrogance.

   When unkind thoughts linger, they pollute our peace far more than visible dirt ever could. Cleansing the mind begins with forgiveness, gratitude, and goodwill. Avoid gossip, think kindly, and choose calm over irritation.

   Our relationships reflect the state of our hearts. When we hold on to grudges or pride, the reflection grows dull. But when we forgive and apologize sincerely, the mirror shines again.

   Chanting God's names, reading uplifting books, keeping good company, and showing gratitude daily purify the heart and refresh the spirit.

   When the mind is clear, and the heart is light, we begin to see goodness in everyone—just as a clean mirror reflects light beautifully.

3. **Environmental Cleanliness—Caring for Our World**

   Beyond our homes lies the larger home we all share—the planet. Environmental cleanliness means keeping our surroundings, air, water, and land pure and healthy. Throw waste into bins, plant trees, save water, and avoid plastic—each of these is an act of devotion to the Earth.

   When we care for nature, nature cares for us. Clean air, pure water, and green spaces nurture both body and soul. Keeping our environment clean is not just a duty—it's a gesture of gratitude to God for the world we live in.

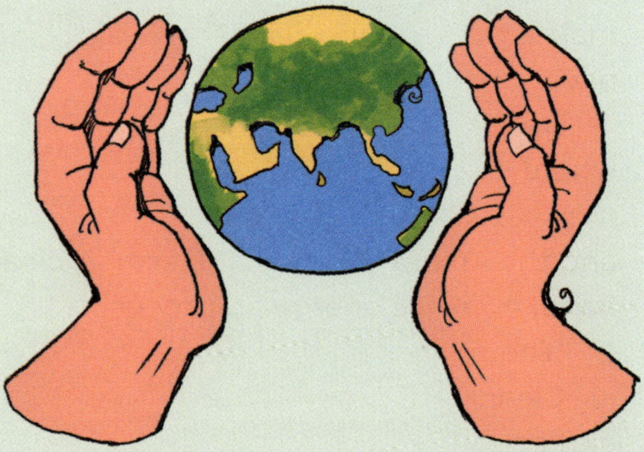

4. **Spiritual Cleanliness—The Heart and Soul**
   This is the deepest and most sacred layer of cleanliness. When our heart and mind are purified through spiritual practices, they become a spotless mirror that clearly reflects the Lord's presence. The Srimad-Bhagavatam teaches that hearing and chanting about Lord Krishna acts as a divine cleanser, washing away the dust of selfishness and ignorance. Many scriptures declare that chanting the holy name of the Lord is the easiest way to purify oneself in this age.
   A clean heart invites divine peace—just as a clear pond reflects the sky perfectly. Purity is not about being flawless; it is about being sincere, humble, and open to growth. When our hearts are pure, our actions naturally become pure, too—and that inner fragrance of purity spreads wherever we go.
   When the lamp of cleanliness shines in all its four layers, life glows with purity, peace, and divine grace.

Opposite of Cleanliness

Laziness and Carelessness

The opposite of cleanliness is not just dirt—it's carelessness. Laziness makes us postpone cleanliness. 'I'll clean later,' we say—but that later never comes.

Dust gathers where attention fades. Similarly, bad habits gather where discipline sleeps.

A lazy person's desk becomes messy, their thoughts become heavy, and their mind loses enthusiasm. A clean environment, on the other hand, awakens energy and focus.

'The dust on your desk may hide the brilliance of your mind.'

Cleanliness demands effort, but that effort returns as comfort, clarity, and confidence.

Cleanliness and Respect

When you keep yourself and your surroundings clean, you are silently saying: 'I respect myself. I respect others. I respect the world.'

Throwing garbage carelessly or writing on walls is not freedom—it's disrespect towards the earth that nourishes us. Even our textbooks, uniforms, and classrooms deserve respect through proper care.

Just as you wouldn't wear dirty clothes to meet a guest, we shouldn't keep our environment untidy when living in God's creation. Cleanliness is not decoration—it's devotion.

Misunderstood Cleanliness

Sometimes people become too focused on external purity and forget inner kindness. True cleanliness doesn't make us proud or distant—it makes us gentle and humble.

If we bathe ten times a day but speak harshly, we are not truly clean. Cleanliness must begin with the heart; water can wash dirt, but only love can wash hatred. So, don't look down on someone who is less tidy. Instead, help them. That's cleanliness of character.

Examples of Cleanliness from the Scriptures

Cleanliness in the Land of Joy

Far beyond the stars lies Vaikuntha, the wonderful abode of Lord Vishnu. Everything there is bright, peaceful, and full of joy. The trees are special—they bear flowers and fruits in every season! The palaces have marble floors that shine like mirrors, and gentle breezes carry the fragrance of lotuses everywhere.

The people in Vaikuntha love to serve the Lord. The ladies there are graceful and kind, wearing jingling bangles and holding lotuses. They happily sweep the marble floors, even though everything is already spotless! They do it with smiles, thinking, 'Let everything be pure and beautiful for our beloved Lord.'

In Vaikuntha, cleanliness is a way to show love. When we keep our homes clean, our hearts also feel peaceful and bright.

Clean surroundings and a clean heart make us happy and closer to God—just like the joyful people of Vaikuntha!

The Lord Who Loved to Clean

Every year in Puri, there is a grand festival called Ratha Yatra, when Lord Jagannath, Lord Baladeva, and Lady Subhadra ride on huge chariots through the streets, blessing everyone with their smiling faces. But before this festival, something very special happens—a day called Gundicha Marjana.

On this day, Lord Chaitanya Mahaprabhu (an incarnation of Krishna) performed a wonderful act. He gathered all His devotees and went to clean the Gundicha Temple, where Lord Jagannath would soon stay during the festival. Everyone carried brooms and water pots, singing joyfully as they walked.

When they reached the temple, Lord Chaitanya Himself began sweeping the floor! The Supreme Lord—who is worshipped by millions—was cleaning with His own hands! He swept every corner carefully, gathering dust and straw into piles. The devotees were amazed and inspired. Seeing their Lord working so lovingly, they, too, began cleaning with great enthusiasm.

After sweeping, the Lord brought water to wash the walls and floors. He even used His own clothes to wipe places that needed extra care. Whenever someone missed a spot, He gently showed them how to do it better—not scolding, but teaching them to serve with love and attention.

By the end of the day, the whole temple sparkled. It looked calm, bright, and ready to welcome Lord Jagannath. But the most beautiful thing was that everyone's hearts also felt clean and happy.

Mahaprabhu explained that cleaning the temple is like cleaning the heart. Just as we remove dust and dirt from a room, we must remove things like anger, pride, and jealousy from our hearts. Only then can the Lord live happily inside us.

That's why Gundicha Marjana is not just about cleaning—it's about love, humility, and purity. The Lord Himself showed us that the greatest service is to serve with a clean heart.

So next time you clean your room, your classroom, or the temple, remember Lord Chaitanya—the Lord who loved to clean, and who showed that every small act of service becomes great when done with love.

When we clean with our hands, we also clean our hearts. A clean place invites happiness—and a clean heart invites God.

How to Practise Cleanliness in Daily Life

At Home

- Take a bath every day and wear clean clothes.
- Keep your room tidy—fold clothes, arrange books, and make your bed daily.
- Help parents with cleaning common areas.
- Don't waste food or water—waste is impurity.

At School

- Keep your desk and bag organized.
- Throw waste in the dustbin, not on the floor.
- Maintain cleanliness in the washroom and playground.
- Keep your handwriting neat and your books well-maintained.

In the Community

- Avoid littering streets or parks.
- Participate in cleanliness drives.
- Use dustbins and segregate dry and wet waste.
- Appreciate those who clean—respect sweepers and helpers.

For the Soul

- Read scriptures daily to purify the mind.
- Chant or pray sincerely.
- Spend time in nature with gratitude.
- Keep good company and avoid bad habits.

People often spend time decorating the outside but neglect the inside. True beauty begins with inner purity. A clean room pleases the eyes; a clean mind pleases the soul.

Reflection Corner

- Is my body and room clean every day?
- Do I keep my surroundings tidy, or do I wait for others to do it?
- Are my thoughts pure, or do I let jealousy or anger stay too long?
- Do I respect those who clean, or do I ignore them?
- How can I clean my heart daily through prayer or service?

Lets Be Clean

Cleanliness is more than a habit—it's a way of honouring life. When your body, mind, and heart stay pure, you become peaceful, confident, and closer to God.

Cleanliness brings clarity. Dirt brings confusion. Purity attracts divinity; impurity drives it away.

Like Aarohi washing her muddy hands, we, too, must wash away the 'mud' of laziness, negativity, and pride.

Clean body, calm mind, pure heart—that is true cleanliness.

Let your hands serve cleanly, your heart love purely, and your life shine brightly. Because a clean life is a beautiful offering to God.

TRY THIS OUT!

Cleanliness brings peace—inside and outside.

1. **CLEAN:** Choose one small space—your desk, school bag, shelf, or room corner. Clean it fully and neatly.
2. **CLEAR:** Now pause and clear your mind and heart. Take three deep breaths, Let go of one negative thought or complaint, and think of one thing you are grateful for.
3. **CALM:** Sit quietly for one minute and notice how you feel. A clean space creates a calm mind.

Conclusion: The Brightest Virtue of All

Congratulations, dear kids! You've just learned about so many wonderful virtues—kindness, honesty, compassion, cleanliness, and many more. Each is like a beautiful flower that makes life sweet and fragrant. But do you know what helps all these flowers bloom? It's devotion to God—the love and service we offer from our hearts.

The scriptures say that when someone has true devotion to God, all good qualities naturally shine within them—just like stars glowing in the night sky. But if someone forgets God and becomes selfish or proud, even if they seem clever or talented, their good qualities slowly fade.

Think of it this way: if a room is dark, you don't have to chase away the darkness—you turn on the light! The moment the light appears, the darkness disappears on its own. In the same way, when we turn on the light of devotion in our hearts—by praying, chanting, remembering God, and doing good for others—the darkness of anger, greed, and envy goes away all by itself.

Devotion makes every virtue shine brighter. It teaches us to love everyone, serve happily, and see God in all living beings. When our hearts are filled with devotion, being kind, truthful, and humble becomes easy and natural—just like breathing.

So as you grow up and practise these virtues, always keep the light of devotion glowing within you. Then your life will not only be good—it will be truly divine.

Turn on the light of devotion to Lord Krishna in your heart, and all good qualities will shine bright!

Acknowledgements

Words fall short in expressing my gratitude to Srila Prabhupada, the founder-*acharya* of the International Society for Krishna Consciousness, who gifted the world the *Bhagavad Gita As It Is* with his lucid explanations. Through the lens of his illuminating purports, I have learned to perceive the depth and compassion of the Gita's teachings.

I am forever indebted to my beloved guru, His Holiness Radhanath Swami, Founder of Govardhan Ecovillage and an international bestselling author, for enlightening me about the ideal mood for scriptural study and for constantly uplifting me with his kind blessings. I have learnt profound truths not only from his enlightening discourses but also from observing his exemplary humility and dealings. My heartfelt gratitude extends to Gauranga Prabhu and many other revered devotees and friends who have inspired and guided me in countless ways on my spiritual journey.

I am deeply thankful to Tanay Shah and Parth Shah for their enthusiastic input and patient editing of the manuscript. Their honest and selfless efforts helped shape this book into its present form.

I express my sincere appreciation to Ashley Kumar for meticulously editing the manuscript and to Prerna Mathur for her dedicated coordination throughout the publication process. My heartfelt thanks also go to Charbak Dipta, whose captivating illustrations make this book engaging and enjoyable for children. I am equally grateful to the entire team at Scholastic India, including Sonal Grover and Gaurav Mattas, for their professional collaboration in bringing this work to readers worldwide.

Finally, I offer my warmest thanks to all the wonderful children who participated in my various online and onsite classes and courses. Their innocent yet intelligent questions helped me understand their hearts and needs more deeply. I also congratulate their parents and teachers, who have guided them with such care and values. It is my joy and privilege to offer this book, *Kind Hearts!*, as a humble gift to them all.

About the Author

Gauranga Darshan Das, a disciple of His Holiness Radhanath Swami, is a distinguished educator and bestselling author of over fifty-four books. He holds a Master's degree in Systems Science and Automation from the Indian Institute of Science (IISc), Bangalore. He has received several honors, including the 'Visionary Spiritual Leader Award', the 'Spiritual Scientist Award', and the 'Global Excellence Award', in recognition of his outstanding contributions to education and spiritual outreach.

After a brief corporate career as a researcher at TCS Innovation Labs and Force Motors, and after publishing over ten technical papers, he embraced monkhood in 2009. In his current role as the dean of Bhaktivedanta Vidyapitha at ISKCON Govardhan Ecovillage (GEV) near Mumbai, he conducts spiritual education programmes for audiences of varying ages worldwide. He is a prolific speaker and teacher, known for presenting timeless wisdom in a contemporary format. He has spoken at various forums, including TEDx, ISRO, DRDO, Intel, TechMahindra, Hindustan Times, and Sales Force, among others. He has lectured for over 9,000 hours and conducted over sixty online courses (available at www.vidyapitha.in).

He has penned several study guides, storybooks, self-enrichment works, and children's books, and also runs a monthly ezine called Bhagavata Pradipika. His dedication to disseminating spiritual wisdom has made him a respected figure in spiritual, educational, and corporate circles.

Know more about him on **www.gaurangadarshan.com**.

More by the Author